THE
GAP YEAR
GUIDEBOOK
1999/2000

PUBLISHED BY PERIDOT PRESS

Guidebooks and Directories
THE GAP YEAR GUIDEBOOK
THE BRILLIANT SCIENTIST'S GUIDEBOOK
THE GOLDEN OLDIE'S GUIDEBOOK
THE VISITING SPEAKERS DIRECTORY
THE INTERNET GUIDEBOOK

Memoirs and Biography
THE MILLERS' TALE
SERVICE TO OTHERS

Copyright Peridot Press Ltd
Seventh edition
Published August 1998

Printed in Great Britain by St Edmundsbury Press
First edition published August 1992

ISBN 0 9527572 2 2

Peridot Press Ltd
2 Blenheim Crescent
London W11 1NN
Tel: 0171-221 7404
Fax: 0171-792 0833
Web: *http://www.peridot.co.uk*

THE
GAP YEAR
GUIDEBOOK
1999/2000

Editor and Publisher •	Rosamund McDougall
Research Coordinator •	Juliet Mayhew
Advertising/Research •	David Allan
Research •	Marcus Gipps Hermione Love
Databases •	Dominique Lambert
Cover & Cartoons •	Rose Pomeroy

Peridot Press

Acknowledgements

With many thanks to all the organisations, voluntary workers and personnel managers who helped us with this seventh edition; to the gap-year students who told their stories to our researchers; and to parents, whose experienced advice is always welcome. And thanks, as always, to my husband Roddy, who doesn't get much food between April and July.

Rosamund McDougall

Peridot Press

THE GAP YEAR GUIDEBOOK is an independent guide without affiliation to any other organisation. Peridot Press receives neither support from the taxpayer nor charitable donations. It is dependent entirely on its readers and advertisers for revenue. Every effort is made to check information at source and feedback is welcome. Organisations are listed in this book at the discretion of the editor and the editor's decision is final.

Preface

There is an opportunity in Britain for 18-year-olds that not all students in other countries enjoy. Instead of just drawing a deep breath between leaving school and going to university, they can take a year off to do other things. It has become known as the 'gap year' or 'year out'.

The gap year in fact lasts nearly 15 months, from the June day when A-Levels are over to autumn the following year when students start fresh at university. It is a precious year, a time that can never be repeated. It is a chance to find out the difference between studying and earning a living, a time to make a picaresque journey round the world and perhaps to help other people. Things can go wrong. But at 18, if all goes well, it can be exciting beyond belief.

Much of the updating of this book is carried out by the hard-working gap-year students we employ each year. It is to one of these that this edition is dedicated. Nadia Rajan, who worked for us in 1996, died suddenly last September of meningitis while reading for a degree in medicine at Emmanuel College, Cambridge. Her talents were extraordinary, as was her capacity for friendship. Nadia was a bright star extinguished too soon.

Rosamund McDougall, July 1998

A YEAR OFF

By 16 May 1998, according to UCAS figures, 395,789 candidates had applied for university and other higher education courses starting in autumn 1998 — down 2.4 per cent from 405,590 the previous year. The number of under-21s applying, however, had risen by 1.1% to 286,397. With the final total number of applications expected to rise to 447,000 and some 320,000 places available, disappointed applicants will have to decide whether to reapply for a 1999 place. A year off?

For the lucky ones, a year off is a matter of choice, for others not. Some students decide they want to defer university entrance because there are things they would like to use the time to do. By mid-May 1998, 25,789 of all the 395,789 applicants who had submitted UCAS (Universities and Colleges Admissions Service) forms in 1997/8 had chosen deliberately to apply for deferred entry to one or more of their chosen courses — to 1999.

Some students have to take time off because their A-Level grades are not good enough to win a university place the first time round. Whatever the reason, the result is a gap year.

Contents

JUDE'S JERUSALEM

"It is a city of light," he said to himself. "The tree of knowledge grows there," he added a few steps further on. "It is a place that teachers of men spring from and go to. It is what you may call a castle, manned by scholarship and religion."

The city is Christminster, modelled on Oxford, and the dreamer is Thomas Hardy's Jude the Obscure, who is driven there by obsession and whose studies end in tragedy. Today one in ten* of the yearly intake of Oxford undergraduates plan a year off before they start.

(*Of 3,219 students who won places after applying in autumn 1997, 318 had deferred entry to October 1998. And 384 of the students who were to begin studies in October 1997 had not applied until after taking A-Levels.)

---

15 MONTHS OFF, ACTUALLY

Lower Sixth

AUTUMN	SPRING	SUMMER

Upper Sixth

AUTUMN	SPRING	SUMMER	GAP YEAR

GAP YEAR   GAP YEAR   GAP YEAR   GAP YEAR   GAP YEAR

University

AUTUMN	SPRING	SUMMER

A gap year for you?

1

The ordering of this book has been carefully thought out. A quick read through the introductory paragraph to each chapter now may save time.

Have you taken A-Levels?

If you found when you got your results (in August 1998) that you failed or got a lower grade than you expected in one or more subjects, you may not have the university place you wanted. If you did not take up your insurance place, or find a place through the clearing system or by negotiation, you may want to retake A-Levels and reapply for entrance to university in 1999.

•Gap year

Will you take A-Levels in summer 1999?

You are fairly confident that you will get a place at university. But by the end of the year you will be desperate to get away from books, uniforms, rules, teachers, brothers, sisters, parents... to do something completely different. You are young for your school year, independent, adventurous, and enterprising enough to find work. Why not apply for a university place for 2000?

•Gap year

Yes or no? Think about a gap year now

Will it work out? Not necessarily. There is no guarantee against making a mess of the time you spend between school and university. Some students end it bored after fruitlessly searching for work and kicking their heels at home. Some parents feel their childrens' absence abroad more deeply than they expect to, and vice versa. Some 18-year-olds die on their travels — several have drowned in tragic accidents. Some inevitably get into trouble: drug addiction, assault and serious accidents at worst, Delhi Belly and theft as a matter of course. But most of those who take a year off have a wonderful time and come to little harm.

The aim of this guidebook is to:

•**Spell out basic common sense.** Parents have got wiser to over-priced office skills training, for example, but some still overpay.

•**Give some idea of the choices available.** A whole gap-year 'industry' now offers opportunities for students who want to take a year off. We can't vouch for all of them, but we list as many as we can. The overseas voluntary work projects section, for example, covers most organisations based in the UK.

•**Help with timing.** Opportunities are missed and mistakes made because gap-year students have not thought out the order in which they can do things. We hope the suggestions made are useful for parents who have not been through this process before.

THE GAP YEAR GUIDEBOOK does not:

•Help you choose your university degree course. You will have made that choice already, although you may change your mind.

THE END OF FREE UNIVERSITY EDUCATION
The £1,000 annual university tuition fee due to be introduced in autumn 1998, combined with the phased abolition of the maintenance grant, barely affected applications for university entrance in 1998 by the under 21s. Being at university, however, is going to cost a lot more.

GAP YEAR — FOR AND AGAINST
FOR: *"A lot of people who show up here [reading chemistry] really ought not to be here at all or ought to be here a bit later... When I become dictator I shall make sure no-one goes straight from school to university." Professor Joe Connors, Pro-Vice Chancellor, University of Kent at Canterbury, 1994*

AGAINST: *Anyone with serious doubts about how a year off is going to be paid for. According to a survey published by NatWest Bank in May 1998, "most students who have an overdraft on graduation [1994-7] owe between £500 and £2,000." And that's before the introduction of tuition fees and the abolition of the maintenance grant. Nearly a third, however, leave university with their current account in the black. Sixthformers may think more carefully about taking a gap year if it adds to their burden of debt.*

The ticking clock

The student who wants to take a gap year needs to start planning as soon as his or her final A-Level year starts. Why? Because it is in the autumn term of the final sixth form year that university entrance application forms are filled in. Minds can be changed later, but many sixth-formers who want a year off decide at this stage to apply for a deferred entry place at university. In other words, for a degree course that starts two years ahead. This chapter unravels the whole procedure (see also UCAS Website at www.ucas.ac.uk) and explains how gap-year students can deal with UCAS forms. Thanks to UCAS for checking the procedures listed. Turn straight to CHAPTER 8 afterwards if you would like to go abroad.

A-Level results

Breakfast, Thursday 20 August 1998. Or 19 August 1999. This morning the alarm clock is set to go off early, because it is the day A-Level results are released across the country. Anxious school-leavers head back to school to find out how they have done.

Within 48 hours results will be posted on school noticeboards and an envelope will drop through the letterbox. It will be pulled open and the contents torn from it. A-Level result confirmations have arrived, and on one or two small, crucial pieces of paper appear the names of an examining board, a candidate, a school and a cryptic list of subjects with grades. For the student who has just left school, these flimsy sheets mark the end of two hard years of work.

If the grades are good enough, a letter comes soon from the university which was named as a 'firm (first) choice' confirming

UNIVERSITY ENTRANCE

UNIVERSITIES AND COLLEGES

Officially, a university is a higher education institution that awards its own degrees, has a wide mix of faculties, carries out academic research and (with very few exceptions) takes a minimum of about 4,000 students. Since the 1990s explosion in university education, however, the official criteria have not always been met.

At mid-1998 there were 90 universities as defined by the CVCP (Committee of Vice-Chancellors & Principals) if you count Oxford, Cambridge, London and Wales as one each, not as collections of individual university colleges. If you count the constituent colleges of the federal universities of London and Wales, you get 115. One new university, Lincolnshire and Humberside, has joined the list.

Radical change has taken place over the 1990s. In 1992 there were only 45 universities and nothing much had changed since the 'red brick' and 'white tile' universities of the 1960s were built. A university offered academic study, while a polytechnic gave vocational training. But in 1992 polytechnics were allowed to become universities if they met the four criteria given above, and almost all of them have converted.

UK universities are listed at the end of this chapter.

Former polytechnics are not to be confused with the 'technical colleges' of the 1960s or the training colleges which expanded in the 1970s to become Colleges of Further Education (where you start at 16). Some began as Colleges of Higher Education (where you start at 18).

For those with Internet connections, the CVCP has a list of universities and other useful information at Website: www.cvcp.ac.uk

the offer of a place. The student who planned a gap year can accept, put textbooks away and walk into the sun. If the grades are not good enough to win the coveted 'firm choice' place, there may be confirmation of an 'insurance (second choice) place'. If the grades are worse still, there's a chance of finding another place through the clearing system. In 1997, 54,401 students (16.2 per cent of the 336,338 going into higher education) found places in clearing. But if the flop is certain and ambitions high, a student will have to think again. Retakes ahead?

UNIVERSITY ENTRANCE

UCAS PROCEDURES

The Universities & Colleges Admissions Service (UCAS) is the system that handles applications to all UK universities (except the Open University). Even entrance to Oxford and Cambridge is now handled by UCAS, although applications to these two universities have to be in earlier than for others because they interview many more candidates.

ART & DESIGN

In 1997 most colleges of art and design (about 60 former members of the ADAR admissions system) joined the UCAS system. So if you want to apply for a fine art degree place at, say, Central St Martin's, you can now incorporate it into your applications for university places, using a UCAS entry form.

OXFORD AND CAMBRIDGE ROW WITH THE FLOW

Since 1997 entry, getting into Oxford no longer involves sitting the university's separate entrance exam. The old 'two-E offer' (where if you were accepted, the brilliance of your subsequent A-Level results barely mattered) has disappeared. Application is now through UCAS, either pre-A-Level or post-A-Level. But in addition to submitting a UCAS form naming Oxford as one of your choices, you must also submit an Oxford application form, common to all colleges. The closing date for applications, however, remains 15 October, not 15 December as for other universities, and Oxford University continues to set some separate written tests. To win a place to read Maths, for example, you will have a written test at your interview.

Cambridge University has also joined this system. Applications are made in the first instance through UCAS, and then you need to fill in a separate blue Preliminary Application Form (PAF) to one of the colleges. Cambridge still sets STEP exams (only for some subjects, mainly science) as well as A-Levels as a means of selection, and interviews every suitable candidate. The closing date for applications also remains 15 October.

UNIVERSITY ENTRANCE

At this point we hope it is useful to run through the university entrance procedure from scratch. A controversial new two-phase admissions system has been suggested, but according to UCAS there are not likely to be any more significant changes to procedures before the new millenium. So wise guys can skip a few pages.

Start from scratch

If you have just taken A-Levels, you should know the application routine by heart. If you are starting your final A-Level year, you will not. And for some parents the acronyms connected with university entrance procedure can bring on an attack of the vapours. So definitions first.

UCAS

UCAS (the Universities and Colleges Admissions Service) is the computerised clearing system based in Cheltenham which handles applications to universities as well as to most other higher education institutions in Britain. We start the cycle with the sixth-former who is due to take A-Levels in 1999 and wants to take a gap year before starting to study for a degree in 2000.

Application time

The autumn term is when final-year sixth-formers begin to apply for university and college places through the UCAS system. Where is Greenfields University of Central England? Is there a video in the library that shows the award-winning labs at Muckbrass? Soon the talk is about nothing else but UCAS forms. The forms are distributed and parents fret. Sixth-formers choose up to six of the several thousand degree courses on offer to make up their final list of choices. They practise the dazzling essays about themselves that will go on the third page. Weeks later the form-filling is over and the applications are posted.

Dates for those taking A-Levels in 1999

Information about how to apply for university places appears in the *UCAS Handbook* which is published every June and covers university entrance the following year. Free from UCAS. Tel: 01242-223 707. Some key dates (for 1999 entry) are given here:

• University open days organised from **summer 1998**.

• UCAS application forms available in the **summer term 1998**.

• Application forms which include either Oxford or Cambridge choices should be returned to UCAS by **15 October 1998**.

• Application forms for all universities (except Route B applicants for art and design courses: see *UCAS Handbook*) should be returned to UCAS between **1 September 1998** and **15 December 1998**.

• Applicants get an acknowledgement card from UCAS as soon as the form is received. This does not mean the form has been processed — this happens later when you are sent an acknowledgement letter stating your choices and application number. If there seems to be a mistake, call UCAS immediately, quoting your application number.

• Applicants receive decisions (via UCAS) from universities (interview, unconditional offer, conditional offer or rejection) after **October 1998**.

• Accept your best two offers as soon as you receive all your university decisions from UCAS.

• UCAS has two deadlines for late applications. 'Late applications' are those received between **16 December 1998** and **16 May 1999**. Those received even later — between **17 May 1999** and **30 June 1999**, are 'summer applications'. UCAS will process forms received after **30 June 1999** through the clearing scheme.

• (*UCAS Handbook* for 2000 entry available **June 1999**. This is the essential guide to all application procedures.)

• A-Level results will be published on Thursday **19 August 1999**.

• Note that UCAS advises that applicants should confirm their

UCAS HELPLINES

For anyone with queries about the application process	Tel: 01242-227 788
For applicants who are hard of hearing	Minicom: 01242-544 942
Internet Website	*http://www.ucas.ac.uk*

UNIVERSITY ENTRANCE

THE END OF FREE UNIVERSITY EDUCATION

As this book went to press in July 1998 the controversial *Teaching and Higher Education Bill* was about to be made law by the House of Commons after being rejected three times by House of Lords. The new Act finalises the introduction of £1,000 a year means-tested university tuition fees (from 1998/9 entry) and the abolition of the maintenance grant, to be phased out from 1999/2000 entry. The key point at issue in the House of Lords was that English, Welsh and Northern Irish students would have to pay the fee for the final year of a four-year degree at Scottish universities while Scottish and EU students would not. The government has agreed to put this question under a review of fee arrangements to report by 1 April 2000.

The radical changes in university funding which take effect from 1998/9 entry arise from the Dearing Committee's *Inquiry into Higher Education* published in July 1997, followed by the *Teaching and Higher Education Bill* published in November 1997. The aim of the reforms is to replenish university funding which declined, according to the Committee of Vice-Chancellors and Principals (CVCP), by 38 per cent between 1989/90 and 1996/7. The changes take place against a background of rapid increase in the number of university students: "Today one in three young people go on to higher education compared to one in six in 1989/90," according to the CVCP, and that target was raised to 35 per cent in the extra education spending pledges announced in July 1998.

The government has stated that "no student or parent will have to make a higher up-front contribution than under the current (past) arrangement". University-backed organisations such as the CVCP and UCAS have also presented the changes in a positive light.

We believe, however, that the facts have not always been impartially laid out. Even if students pass the means-tested family income tests which can exempt them from paying the £1,000 a year fee, they will suffer the loss of their maintenance grants. **The maintenance loans which are to replace grants are NOT the same as grants. Grants do NOT have to be repaid. Loans DO have to be repaid (when a graduate's income reaches £10,000).** Full details of the tuition fee and grant arrangements are available on the Internet at *www.cvcp.ac.uk* and *www.open.gov.uk/dfee/students/p97.htm* or call 0800-731 9133 (free) for information. There is also a free booklet from the DfEE: Financial Support for Students: A guide to grants, loans and fees in Higher Education 1998/9.

KEY POINTS: TUITION FEES, GRANTS & LOANS
See also page 33

- Students will have to pay an annual means-tested £1,000 tuition fee for each year of full-time undergraduate education at university.
- Means test levels have been set so that students with a gross family income of below £23,000 will not have to pay the tuition fee. With a family income of £23,000-£35,000 the student will have to pay from £45 to £1,000, and at more than £35,000 the full fee will have to be paid. Universities will be responsible for collecting the fees.
- From 1999/2000 no maintenance grants will be available. These will be replaced by maintenance loans.
- All students will be eligible for assessment for 100% maintenance loans, which will be related to parental income.These will not have to be repaid until a graduate's annual income reaches £10,000.
- A special hardship loan of £250 will be available for certain students in financial difficulties.
- Those starting courses in 1998 can apply for a grant towards living costs for the first year of study only, at about half the 1997/8 rate.
- Students who apply for a deferred entry place to start at university in autumn 2000 after taking a gap year will be treated on the same basis as any other student starting in autumn 2000.
- Tuition fees will not be charged to any student who entered university in 1997/8 or who took a gap year in 1997/8 and started in 1998/9. Maintenance grants will continue to be paid to these students under the old arrangements.

acceptance of an offer of a university place as quickly as possible.

•For those who have missed their grades or have not received offers earlier in the year, or who declined all offers made to them, or apply after **30 June 1999**, Clearing Entry Forms (CEFs) will be sent out to students by UCAS after their results are released.

•The list of unfilled degree places will be available on the UCAS Internet Website at *http://www.ucas.ac.uk* as soon as results are released, with up-to-the-minute updates, and will be published and updated on CEEFAX and in *The Independent* and the *Mirror* from **mid-August 1999**.

•Clearing closes at the end of **September 1999**.

UNIVERSITY ENTRANCE

DEGREES FOR ALL

Government, industry and education policymakers failed to predict the hell-for-leather growth of the university system in the 1990s. Now there are more than a million students studying for first-time degrees in the UK (more than double the number in 1989/90) and one in three young people go on to higher education. Today's Labour government wants the numbers to climb even higher: for 35 per cent of school and college leavers to enjoy higher education, with the creation of eight new universities, 80,000 new places at universities, and 420,000 in further education colleges.

Why? Surveys show that it is easier for graduates to get good jobs, but also that they are having to take jobs that do not need to be done by someone with a degree. The secure careers graduates used to expect (and which they will now need more than ever, to repay student debt) are also more difficult to find. Last year we suggested that demand for a university education might have peaked. For the moment, it has.

Dates for those taking A-Levels in 2000

These are expected to follow the same pattern as the 1999 dates already given.

UCAS forms

We are not going to tell you how to fill a UCAS form in (except the gap-year bits). But here are some key points.

•Perhaps the biggest changes which have taken place during the last few years are the reduction in the number of places a student can apply for and the number of offers of places a student can hold on to. Last year also saw the introduction of a new 'two-track' entry method if you are applying for places on art or design courses.

•You can apply for only six different courses at any UCAS institution. If you are using the 'two-track' application procedure for art and design courses you can use up to four of your choices in Route B. See your *UCAS Handbook* for full details.

UNIVERSITY ENTRANCE

ELECTRONIC APPLICATION

For 1998 entry electronic application was made available for all schools, colleges and careers offices. The forms are filled in by students using custom-made Windows software supplied by UCAS and confidential reports on each candidate are added by the school administrators. Forms are then sent to UCAS on disk or via E-mail together with the application fee and a signed declaration from the student. UCAS says that although the information required is the same as on the paper application forms it is much easier to complete, as it checks the data entered throughout its completion. Common mistakes such as incorrect course codes are therefore quickly discovered. About 7,000 applications were received electronically in 1998 and UCAS expects this figure to rise.

•You can hold on to only two of the offers you get: one 'firm (first) choice' and one 'insurance (second choice) place'. So you may have to be more cautious about the courses you pitch for: if you hold a conditional offer for law degree places, say, at two top universities, and you don't get the very demanding grades needed, there are no longer two other offers to fall back on.

•Universities, however, are grappling with shorter periods in which to make (financial) decisions about the number of places they can offer on courses. To avoid overshooting the number of students they know they can get funding for, they may set entrance grades higher than necessary, leaving greater scope for negotiation afterwards. Make sure your school is in the know.

•Those who sit A-Level retakes in January and get the grades needed for a chosen place will not have to wait until August for that place to be confirmed. Examining boards will feed the result directly into UCAS so you will know your place has been clinched. A technicality, but comforting for gap-year students who want to go away. And don't forget that if you have a firm choice conditional offer and you make the grades asked for, the university can't back out. It has an obligation to admit you.

APPLICATION FORM FOR ENTRY IN **1999**	Attach your application fee and completed acknowledgement card here with a paperclip ⬅	**UCAS** 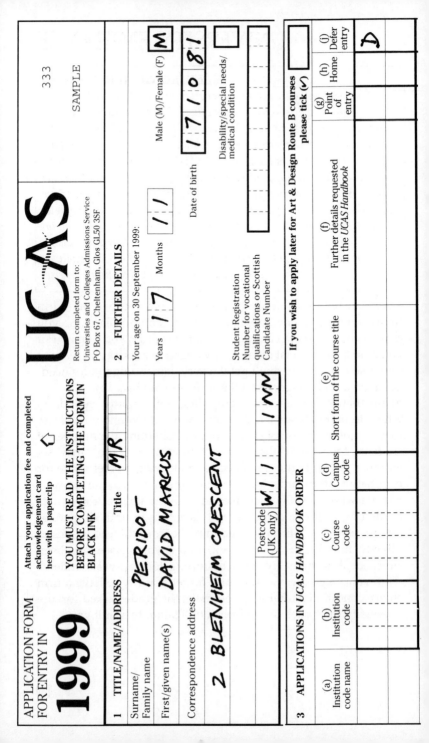	333
	YOU MUST READ THE INSTRUCTIONS BEFORE COMPLETING THE FORM IN BLACK INK	Return completed form to: Universities and Colleges Admissions Service PO Box 67, Cheltenham, Glos GL50 3SF	SAMPLE

1 TITLE/NAME/ADDRESS   Title **MR**

Surname/Family name   PERIDOT

First/given name(s)   DAVID MARCUS

Correspondence address

2 BLENHEIM CRESCENT

Postcode (UK only) **W11 1NM**

2 FURTHER DETAILS

Your age on 30 September 1999:

Years **17**   Months **11**

Male (M)/Female (F) **M**

Date of birth **17 / 08 / 81**

Disability/special needs/medical condition ☐

Student Registration Number for vocational qualifications or Scottish Candidate Number

3 APPLICATIONS IN *UCAS HANDBOOK* ORDER

If you wish to apply later for Art & Design Route B courses please tick (✓) ☐

(a) Institution code name	(b) Institution code	(c) Course code	(d) Campus code	(e) Short form of the course title	(f) Further details requested in the *UCAS Handbook*	(g) Point of entry	(h) Home	(j) Defer entry
								D

Gap year: deferred entry, rescheduled entry or late application?

There are three ways to handle university entrance if you want a gap year. Perhaps the safest is to apply for deferred entry.

1 Deferred entry

•Check first with the appropriate department of the university you want to go to that they are happy to take in students after a gap year. If it's a popular course, preference may go to the current year applications.

•On the front of the UCAS form there is a specific 'Defer entry' column in the key 'Applications' section. Write '**D**' in the '**Defer entry**' box for all (or some) of the courses you apply for, having checked that they will still be available a year later. Talk to your teachers first and follow instructions enclosed with the form.

•You will have to justify your reasons for taking a gap year in the 'Personal Statement' (section 10). Explain briefly and clearly in this section why you want to take a gap year. You need to convince the university that a year off will make you a better applicant, so give an outline of what you plan to do and why.

•You will send off your completed form to UCAS, like any other

---

OXFORD: QUEEN'S

The 1999 prospectus for Queen's College, Oxford, speaks for itself:
DEFERRED ENTRY

"In some circumstances there may be benefits to be derived from spending a year away from the educational system before coming up to university, whether to travel or work abroad or to gain practical experience in some subject-related field. If you want to defer entry, you can indicate this on your application form, and as long as you have an adequate reason for wishing to defer, this will in no way count against your chances of acceptance. Except in medicine: here the competition for places is so intense at all colleges that you need to be particularly impressive for the tutor to allocate in advance one of the three or four places available each year."

UNIVERSITY ENTRANCE

ENGINEERING CAREERS FOUNDATION YEAR

WHO? You are taking a year out before undertaking an engineering-related degree course at university.

WHERE? In the UK and other European countries.

WHAT? Part 1: 3 months basic engineering training in the UK.
Part 2: 4 weeks language tuition in Chambery, France.
Part 3: 13 weeks industrial placement in Europe.

COSTS? Grants provided by The Smallpeice Trust and the EU.

WHEN? Application forms must be returned by the end of October prior to your gap year.

INFO? The Smallpeice Trust, Industry Education Liaison Dept, 27 Newbold Terrace East, Leamington Spa CV32 4ES
Tel: (01926) 331 600/1   Fax: (01926) 331 603
Internet: *http://www.smallpeice.co.uk*
E-mail: *gen@smallpeice.co.uk*

---

student applying for entry without taking a gap year. Those who do so well before the 15 December deadline, however, may be among the first to start receiving replies (via UCAS). You will get a call for selection interview(s), a rejection or a conditional offer (conditional on getting specific A-Level grades).

•From the **15 December 1998** deadline to **30 June 1999** UCAS will forward late applications to universities 'for consideration at their discretion'. After that applications will be dealt with in clearing.

•NOTE: Some academics are not happy with deferred entry because it means it might be nearly two years before you reach higher education. During that time a course may have changed, or you may have changed. So your application may be looked on unfavourably without you knowing why. Departments at most universities are in favour of a gap year but they are not all in favour of deferred entry. If they interview you in November 1998 for a place in October 2000 it will be 23 months before they see you again. Check it out with the university department first.

2 Rescheduled entry

•Apply for a place for the coming university year, not the one after. If, after A-Level results, you have won a place at the university of your choice, you can negotiate directly with that university as an individual about deferring your entry for another year. When you have got your A-Levels, go back to the university and say you would like to take a gap year. If they say yes, you will receive a 'changed entry date confirmation letter', and you must send the attached form to UCAS within seven days to accept the place. If they say no, you have the option to take your insurance place or else you have to start the application all over again.

•*NOTE: Some admissions tutors say that to give up a place on a popular course is risky, because the university will not be happy after you have messed them about. Others say that if a course has over-recruited, your deferral will be welcome. Tread carefully.*

3 Post A-Level application

•If you take A-Levels in June 1999 without having filled in a UCAS form first, you can put in your application for a 2000 place in the next application cycle — between September and (ideally) 15 December 1999. Big brains who get outstanding results will probably get a place on the degree course they crave. If you like taking big risks you can do it even later, up to 30 June of the year you want to get in.

•*NOTE: For those with confidence only as popular courses won't have vacancies after 15 December. Ask admissions tutors if it will make a difference.*

UNIVERSITY ENTRANCE

Faculty check: all subjects

If you want to take a gap year, remember (before you apply) to contact the appropriate department or faculty at the university you would like to go to, and find out if they approve of a gap year or not. Prepare a good case for it before you phone. It is advisable to do this even if you are an absolutely outstanding candidate, because on some courses (such as maths) a year off is considered a definite disadvantage. This is usually the case where a degree course is very long or requires a large amount of remembered technical knowledge at the start.

Clearing

Although applications and places are being cleared and matched constantly by UCAS, the word 'clearing' usually refers to the process of juggling spare places in late August and September after A-Level results. Universities usually make more offers than they have places, so one person withdrawing from a course does not always create a spare place. Here are the basic steps:

•A-Level results are published on a Thursday in mid-August. Anyone whose grades are not good enough to clinch either the 'firm choice' offer or the 'insurance place' offer he/she is holding has to go into the clearing system to find another place.

•If you don't meet the conditions for your offer and the universities (or colleges) decide not to offer you a place, you will be able to use the clearing entry form (CEF) which UCAS will automatically send to you with an instruction leaflet which tells you how to find out about vacancies. Negotiations can start as soon as you have your results.

• As soon as results are released a list of all unfilled vacancies will appear on the UCAS Website at *http://www.ucas.ac.uk* (which also has hotlinks to higher education institutions' Websites), and within a week in *The Independent* and the *Mirror* (updated daily), as well as being on CEEFAX (updated daily in mid-afternoon) and available on the ECCTIS 2000 database. Advice will be given through other media (in the past this has included BBC Radio and TV), and some universities now put relevant information on their Internet Web pages (see Web address list at the end of this chapter).

• Clearing is described as a 'passport' system. The CEF is your passport. When you have identified a course you are interested in and qualified to get into, contact the admissions staff at the university or college and make your case. If the institution is interested it will ask for your CEF, and when it receives the CEF it must decide whether to make you an offer. If it does not make an offer it must return the CEF so that you can begin the process again with another institution.

• After A-Level results, the smart move in many cases is to phone university departments as quickly as possible to chase spare places. (Officially you should wait until you get your CEF form.) If you know what course you want, have been for an interview which seemed to go well and you are, say, only one grade short of those stipulated, quick direct contact could do the trick. From the university's point of view, you could have excellent qualities that more than make up for getting, say, B,C,C instead of B,B,C. You may, however, find the phone lines jammed (have you tried E-mail or faxes?) and have to rely solely on sending in the Clearing Entry Forms (CEF). If you make an informal approach, quote your clearing number and see if the tutor is interested. If so, you can follow up with the CEF itself for formal consideration. You will either be offered a place or your CEF will be returned.

• UCAS issues CEFs with a clearing number and leaves students to send off the form directly to each university in turn.

UNIVERSITY ENTRANCE

•Students have to do some of the paper-shuffling. But UCAS defends the passport system: "The involvement of UCAS in handling all the paperwork would reduce applicant flexibility and introduce potential administrative delays into the system at a time when speed is of the essence." We are not going to go into the details here but UCAS recommends that applicants shouldn't send off their CEF forms unless absolutely certain about the course they are applying for, as further applications can't be made until the university returns the form. If universities don't keep the CEFs in their in-trays too long, clearing should be quick. Applicants are encouraged by UCAS to provide an E-mail address if they have one as this could speed up communication with universities. But students going through the process in August and September may need to stay at home longer to see it through.

Special subjects: Music

Take care with music, because the Royal Academy of Music (RAM: apply direct) does not defer entry and the Royal College of Music (RCM: apply direct) only does it in some cases and on condition it can demand a confirmatory audition if required. (RCM also takes about a dozen students on a gap-year programme. This is a one year course designed to fill a gap year for

MUSIC BOX

"Quite a lot of the students who come to us take a year off and in most cases it's highly recommended. In the case of singers, we do take singers under 19 but the older they are the better. We do expect students to spend the year getting solid practice...if you are travelling round Siberia you can't take a piano on your back."
David Harpham, Admissions Tutor, Royal College of Music
"We don't object. But we don't defer entry so candidates would have to reaudition the following year."
Admissions Office, Royal Academy of Music

those who already have a place at a good university or who are still uncertain about what they want to do, but the standard is as high as for normal entry for a BMus, so this is for serious musicians-to-be, not dilettantes.) If you are determined to take a year off, reapply to RAM by early October 1999 or to RCM by 1 October 1999 for 2000 entry. Both RAM and RCM audition in December. RCM will let you know the results before Christmas and RAM by January.

American universities

To get into a university (sometimes called a college) in the United States you need to start planning at least a year ahead. Degree courses usually stretch over four years and the syllabus is much more varied than in the UK. Students can mix different 'elective' subjects with the subject they plan to concentrate on.

According to the US Institute of International Education there are over 4,600 British undergraduates (including exchange and gap-year students) scattered in some 500 of more than 3,500 institutions that award degrees in the US. But an American degree comes expensive and it is rare to get a scholarship for gap-year study. Tuition fees are likely to range from $5,000-$24,000 in 1998/9, with living costs for nine months coming to $8,000-$14,000: a total of $13,000-$38,000.

If you want to take a full four-year degree at a US university or college, you will need to start planning at least a year before

UNIVERSITY ENTRANCE

entry. If you are taking A-Levels in June 1999 and would like to start a US degree in 2000, get in touch with The Fulbright Commission's Educational Advisory Service (EAS) in London by summer 1999. You will then need to write to US universities, applying for the fall (autumn) term starting at the end of August or beginning of September 2000 (application forms available from the university in August 1999). Each September The Fulbright Commission holds a 'College Day' for prospective undergraduates: in 1997 more than 100 US universities were represented.

As well as A-Levels (best grades for Ivy League universities like Harvard and Yale or west-coast powerhouses like UCLA) you will almost certainly have to sit a three-and-a-half-hour, mostly multiple-choice standardised test known as a SAT I (Scholastic Assessment Test) and possibly extra subject tests (SAT II), usually one year ahead of entry. SATs are staged in Britain five times a year and you can get a test application bulletin and sample questions from The Fulbright Commission EAS, by sending a large SAE with 70p postage.

If you would prefer just to spend a gap year studying at a US university as a 'special' or 'non-degree' student, you need to contact the institution directly a year before you hope to begin studying, making clear in your letter that you are applying to spend a gap year in the US as a non-matriculating student before beginning a degree in the UK. Bear in mind that there are likely to be more gap-year possibilities in small liberal arts colleges than state universities or colleges.

• NOTE: For advice and information on US universities send a large (A4) s.a.e. with 39p postage to The Fulbright Commission's Educational Advisory Service (EAS), 62 Doughty Street, London WC1N 2LS, requesting a copy of the Beginner's Guide to Undergraduate Study in the USA (also available on Website: www.fulbright.co.uk). Tel: 0171-404 6994 E-mail: education@fulbright.co.uk. Open most Mondays: 13.30-19.30; and Tue-Fri: 10.30-16.00.

UNIVERSITY ENTRANCE

> **GETTING IT RIGHT FIRST TIME**
> *Some universities don't let you get away with boosting your A-Level grades by retaking modules or complete exams. "We expect slightly higher requirements if you don't get good enough grades at the first sitting," says Glasgow University. For its 1999 Classics degree course, you need B,B,C if these grades are all achieved at a first sitting. If you take two sittings to improve your marks, you need to get higher grades: B,B,B.*
> *Check this out with the university you want to go to.*

Permutations

Here are examples for students sitting A-Levels in the summer. The degree courses and entry standards are based on ones offered for 1999.

Elizabeth X's notice tells her she has a B grade for French, a C for German and a B in English. She knows she has met the B,B,C minimum set by the University of Durham for a four-year degree in Japanese with a second language (French) starting in 1999. If she wants to change her mind and accept her insurance place course — Modern Languages (French and German) at Bristol — she will have to reapply because the grades demanded (A,B,B/B,B,B) are higher. If she gets an offer from her firm (first) choice she has to accept. Elizabeth makes up her mind and wants to get on. She accepts the place at Durham.

•Grades OK •Accept firm choice university place •No gap year

Alison X wants to read Mathematics on its own or as part of a joint degree. She listed six universities on her original application, going for a choice of 1999 places at six UCAS institutions: the universities of Birmingham, Bradford, Brunel, Huddersfield, Keele and Kingston. Her school predicts she will get A,A,B and they all offer her a place. She turns down four places, accepts her firm (first) choice and accepts her second choice as an 'insurance place'. But her final two module grades are lower than expected — not good enough for her firm choice place. Alison would like

29

UNIVERSITY ENTRANCE

to retake the Maths modules in January 2000 (having made a fresh UCAS application for an autumn 2000 place), work until Easter 2000 and backpack round Latin America until starting her degree at her original firm (first) choice university. But her Maths teacher advises against it because she believes a year off can make borderline Maths students too rusty. So Alison accepts her insurance offer for 1999.

•Grades disappointing •Accept best offer •No gap year

When Michael X fills in his UCAS form in September 1999 he puts down Ancient History at King's College London (B,B,C) as his firm (first) choice. His second choice (insurance choice) is an Archaeology and Greek course at A.N. Other University (B,C,D) followed by four more courses that mix his favourite subject — Greek history and culture — with others. Michael X's prayers to Zeus the night before his History A-Level are not answered. He feels ill the next day and fails the exam completely. But the course at King's is the only one he really wants to do, so it's not worth trying to negotiate with another university. With a B for Classical Civilisation and a B for Art History he decides to retake History and reapply to King's again in autumn 2000 for a 2001 place.

•Gap year with retakes •Reapply via UCAS •Choose where to retake

Fred X is only 17 when he sits his A-Level exams in June 1999. His first choice is a four-year course in Chemistry at Imperial College, London, and he is confident he can get better grades than the B,B,B demanded. (He starts planning his gap year in the Lower 6, applies for a deferred entry place and also has a place to go on a scientific expedition in March 2000.) With his A,B,B grades in the bag (including a B in Chemistry), Fred now concentrates on raising money for his overseas expedition.

•Accept 2000 place •Plan how to earn some money

Sybilla X is also 17 when she sits her A-Levels in June 1999, and has also applied for deferred entry. After dining, dancing and debutanting her way through the Upper 6, she effortlessly scores

UNIVERSITY ENTRANCE

MEDICINAL ALCOHOL

"A common misconception is that taking a year out before medical school is not a good thing. However, when I was faced with the prospect of at least another six years in education before qualifying there really seemed to be no choice. As a medic when you qualify it is almost impossible to take time off as you may well miss one-off career chances and it is also difficult to take time out between years. If I had not taken up my gap when I did the opportunity would have been missed completely. I also found that with a year's more life experience I was able to approach both the academic and social side of university life with a more mature attitude. The heavy nights in the bar are easier to take in your stride after a year in the 'real world' and this drinking experience saved me a lot of embarrassment not spared to the younger and more impressionable 'first years' who had come straight from school. Alcohol poisoning in your first week does not look good to your tutors.

Lots of people think that it must be difficult to get back into your work after a year without routine. I don't think it was much harder than it would have been after three months' holiday, but after a year off I was itching to get back into work.

The only downside to it is that you will already be fairly old when you qualify and the year off delays this further. But it doesn't really make much difference if you are 26 or 27 when you finish. Most medical schools encourage a year out now because of the length of the course, and some even insist on it."

Ben Pearch, St Thomas's Hospital, 1998

five A-Level A grades and pockets her conditional place to read PPE (Philosophy, Politics and Economics) at Christ Church, Oxford. Blessed with fluent Spanish as well (life isn't fair, is it?) Sybilla is also set to go to Mexico to work in an orphanage in Spring 2000.

•Accept 2000 place   •Plan rest of gap year

Mark X leaves his Scottish school near Loch Granite in a cloud of rebellion, half way through the spring term of Lower 6 in 1999.

UNIVERSITY ENTRANCE

DEGREE/DipHE APPLICATIONS FOR 1998 ENTRY

At 16 May 1998 (selected subjects excl. HNDs) Source: UCAS, June 1998. Figures are for total applications, including overseas and mature students. The total number of applicants (incl. HNDs) at this stage was 395,789 (405,789)

Subject	1998	(1997)
Pre-Clinl Medicine	57,657	(59,016)
Nursing	19,833	(19,550)
Social Work	12,100	(13,164)
Computer Sci	70,093	(61,405)
Pharmacy	17,107	(16,878)
Biology	30,663	(32,711)
Biochemistry	12,409	(12,509)
Chemistry	21,155	(21,771)
Physics	17,838	(18,344)
Geography	33,383	(33,019)
Environment sci/other phys.sci.	11,384	(13,024)
Mathematics	22,322	(22,293)
Fine arts	17,953	(13,006)
Civil engineering	16,761	(18,213)
Mech. engin'g	28,090	(28,287)
Electronic engin'g	17,237	(18,187
Engineering/tech	14,189	(17,592)
Architecture	15,023	(16,102)
Building	10,925	(11,102)
Economics	31,438	(31,194)
Sociology	27,102	(30,471)
Psychology	65,191	(69,125)

Subject	1998	(1997)
Politics	16,430	(16,401)
Law	80,559	(81,782)
Social studies	25,143	(27,437)
Business/Mgment	127,156	(125,677)
Accountancy	32,239	(33,175)
Marketing	15,004	(12,769)
Instit management	18,663	(21,148)
Communication	10,180	(10,440)
Media studies	13,189	(14,233)
English	50,971	(54,543)
Language combs	26,493	(28,928)
Pre-clin dentistry	10,348	(11,939)
History	34,701	(35,906)
Design studies	57,214	(38,381)
Tourism	10,814	(10,767)
Music	19,433	(19,397)
Drama	34,874	(33,201)
Cinematics	15,239	(12,798)
Humanities	12,877	(14,522)
Sports science	30,497	(28,783)
Total:	1,181,907	(1,184,851)
All Subjects:	1,885,432	(1,920,669)

After a few stormy weeks, he picks up his studies (A-Level Biology, Chemistry and Physics) at a London sixth-form college and later puts in a UCAS application for a 2001 degree place. In August 2000 he learns that he has scored B,C,C, with a B in Biology. On to read Oceanography with Marine Biology at the University of Southampton. Time to sail round the world now and become a shipping millionaire later.

•Accept 2001 place •Start thinking about a gap year now

UNIVERSITY ENTRANCE

ETERNAL OPTIMISM

The number of under-21-year-olds applying for higher education starting in 1998/9 through UCAS was 286,397, up 1.1% from the 283,219 who applied for 1997/8. Optimism or a rush to get the last year of maintenance grants?

FROM A-LEVELS TO BACCALAUREATE?

Debate about reforming A-Levels has been going on for years, and many are against changing this 'gold standard' of education. Talk of broadening the A-Level syllabus so that students will take, say, a five-subject 'baccalaureate' instead of the traditional specialised and academic three A-Levels is unlikely to fuel change before September 2000. Many students, however, under increased pressure to gain a place at university, combine three A-Levels with one or more AS-Levels in order to broaden their horizons and their chances.

... AND WIDER CHOICE?

The number of courses you can apply for on a UCAS form was reduced from eight to six from 1996 entry onwards: the choice has now been halved in a decade. Does this limit scope for students? UCAS insists that it hasn't made much difference: when eight choices were allowed for 1995 entry an average of only 6.6 were actually specified. They also claim that this system makes it easier for institutions to consider applications.

Getting your grant

As everyone knows by now, students will have to pay a £1,000 a year fee for their higher education (see box on TUITION FEES on page 17). Maintenance grants are being reduced by about half for the year 1998/9 and there will be no grant from 1999/2000 onwards. Grants will be replaced by loans. Because of the complexity of these new arrangements, we suggest you call the Student Loans Company (Tel: 0800 405 010) about student loans, and refer to Internet Websites giving information on both grants and loans for the year 1998/9. A good starting point is the guide at: *http://www.open.gov.uk/dfee/students/p97.htm*

UNIVERSITY ENTRANCE

GRANTS AND LOANS

GRANT	1996/7	1997/8	1998/9	1999/2000
Full grant London	£2,105	£2,160	See	None
Elsewhere	£1,710	£1,755	p.33	None
LOAN (EXCEPT FINAL YEAR)				
Living in London	£2,035	£2,085	See	See
Living elsewhere	£1,645	£1,685	p.33	below
Living in parental home	£1,260	£1,290		
FINAL YEAR LOAN				
Living in London	£1,485	£1,520	See	See
Living elsewhere	£1,200	£1,230	p.33	below
Living in parental home	£920	£945		

Spare degree places

You didn't get the grades for the place you wanted. You would like to secure another place on a different course without retaking A-Levels. You know where your subject is on offer but you've lost the UCAS Handbook (UCAS is at P.O. Box 67, Cheltenham, Glos GL50 1SF, General Enquiries Tel: 01242-222 444, Applicant Enquiries Tel: 01242-227 788). Starting here is the 1998 list of UK universities with their main phone numbers and Internet Web addresses. Ask for the admissions staff, special or the appropriate department if you have specific rather than general questions.

•Remember always to quote your UCAS application number (printed on UCAS correspondence with you) or your clearing number (on your CEF form).

Your UCAS number:

Your clearing number:

Universities in the UK

There were 90 universities at mid-July 1998 — if you count the universities of London,Wales, Oxford and Cambridge as one each. Telephone numbers marked 'S' are main switchboard numbers. Ask for the Admissions Officer if you have questions about entry. We have added to our list each university's World Wide Web home page address (URL) on the Internet. You are more likely to find up-to-date information on these Websites than last year — but not all these addresses have been tested and you may have difficulty getting through. There is also a UCAS Website at http://www.ucas.ac.uk Don't forget to key in http:// before each address below. We have also added the Clearing helplines when these have been available — these are marked 'C'. Some were not ready when we went to press; other universities do not participate in the clearing system, such as Cambridge and Oxford.

University of Aberdeen	S: 01224-272 000/C: 01224-273 504
	www.abdn.ac.uk
University of Abertay Dundee	S: 01382-308 000/C: 01382-308 080
	www.tay.ac.uk
Anglia Polytechnic University	*www.anglia.ac.uk*
East Rd, Cambridge	S: 01223-363 271
Victoria Rd South, Chelmsford	S: 01245-493 131
Sawyers Hall Lane, Brentwood	S: 01277-264 504
Aston University	S: 0121-359 3611/C: 0121-359 6313
	www.aston.ac.uk
University of Bath	S: 01225-826 826/C: 01225-323 180
	www.bath.ac.uk
University of Birmingham	S/C: 0121-414 3344
	www.bham.ac.uk
Bournemouth University	S/C: 01202-524 111
	www.bournemouth.ac.uk
University of Bradford	S: 01274-733 466/C: 01274-235 400
	www.brad.ac.uk
University of Brighton	S/C: 01273-600 900
	www.bton.ac.uk
University of Bristol	S: 0117-928 9000
	www.bris.ac.uk
University of the West of England, Bristol	S: 0117-965 6261/C: 0117-976 3801
	www.uwe.ac.uk

UNIVERSITY ENTRANCE

Brunel University, West London	S: 01895-274 000/C: 01895-203 192/3/4
	www.brunel.ac.uk
University of Buckingham	S: 01280-814 080/C: 01280-820 299
	www.buckingham.ac.uk
University of Cambridge	S: 01223-337 733
	www.cam.ac.uk
Cambridge Business School	S/C: 01223-363 159
University of Central England in Birmingham	S/C: 0121-331 5000
	www.uce.ac.uk
University of Central Lancashire	S/C: 01772-201 201
	www.uclan.ac.uk
University College, Chester	S: 01244-375 444/C: 01244-392 780
	www.chester.ac.uk
City University	S: 0171-477 8000/C:0171-477 8028
	www.city.ac.uk
Coventry University	S/C: 01203-631 313
	www.coventry.ac.uk
Cranfield University	S/C: 01234-750 111
	www.cranfield.ac.uk
Royal Military College of Science	S/C: 01793-782 551
	www.rmcs.cranfield.ac.uk
Silsoe College	S/C: 01525-863 000
	www.silsoe.cranfield.ac.uk
De Montfort University, Leicester	S: 01162-551 551/C: 0645-45 46 47
	www.dmu.ac.uk
De Montfort University, Milton Keynes	S/C: 01908-695 511
	www.mk.dmu.ac.uk
University of Derby	S: 01332-622 222/C: 01332-621 300
	www.derby.ac.uk/
University of Dundee	S: 01382-223 181/C: 01382-344 160
	www.dundee.ac.uk
University of Durham	S: 0191-374 2000/C: 0191-374 2932
	www.dur.ac.uk/
University of East Anglia	S: 01603-456 161/C: 01603-592 216
	www.uea.ac.uk
University College Suffolk	S: 01473-255 885/C: 01473-296 606
	www.suffolk.ac.uk
University of East London	S: 0181-590 7722/C:0181-849 3443
	www.uel.ac.uk

UNIVERSITY ENTRANCE

University of Edinburgh	S: 0131-650 1000
	www.ed.ac.uk
University of Essex	S: 01206-873 333/C: 01206-873 666
	www.essex.ac.uk
European Business School, London	S/C: 0171-487 7507
	www.regent.ac.uk
·University of Exeter	S/C: 01392-263 263
	www.ex.ac.uk/
University of Glamorgan	S: 01443-480 480
	www.glam.ac.uk
University of Glasgow	S: 0141-339 885/C: 0141-330 6068
	www.gla.ac.uk/
Glasgow Caledonian University	S: 0141-331 3000/C: 0141-331 3138
	www.gcal.ac.uk
The University of Greenwich	S: 0181-331 8000
	www.gre.ac.uk
Heriot-Watt University	S: 0131-449 5111
	www.hw.ac.uk
University of Hertfordshire	S: 01707-284 000/C: 01710-284 848
	www.herts.ac.uk
University of Huddersfield	S: 01484-422 288/C: 01484-472 777
	www.hud.ac.uk
University of Hull	S: 01482-346 311/C: 01482-466 100
	www.hull.ac.uk/
Keele University	S: 01782-621 111/C: 01782-584 005
	www.keele.ac.uk
University of Kent at Canterbury	S: 01227-764 000/C:01227-827 272
	www.ukc.ac.uk
Kingston University	S: 0181-547 2000/C: 1081-547 7575
	www.kingston.ac.uk
Lancaster University	S: 01524-65201
	www.lancs.ac.uk
University of Leeds	S: 0113-243 1751/C: 0113-233 3999
	www.leeds.ac.uk
Leeds, Trinity and All Saints University College	S: 0113-283 7100/C: 0113-283 7123
University College of Ripon and York St John	S: 01904-656 771/C: 01904 616 980
Leeds Metropolitan University	S: 0113-283 2600/C: 0113-283 3113
	www.lmu.ac.uk/
University of Leicester	S: 0116-252 2522/C: 0113-252 5281
	www.le.ac.uk

UNIVERSITY ENTRANCE

University of Lincolnshire and Humberside	S: 01482-440 550
	www.humber.ac.uk
University of Liverpool	S: 0151-794 2000
	www.liv.ac.uk
Liverpool Hope University College	S: 0151-291 3000/C: 0151-291 3899
	www.livhope.ac.uk
Liverpool Institute for Performing Arts	S: 0151-330 3000/C: 0151 330 3131
	www.lipa.ac.uk
Liverpool John Moores University	S: 0151-231 2121/C: 0151-231 5090/5091
	www.livjm.ac.uk
St Helens College	S/C: 01744-733 766
University of London (contact colleges directly)	S: 0171-636 8000
	www.lon.ac.uk
British Institute in Paris (University of London)	S: 00 331-4411 7383/84
Courtauld Institute of Art	S: 0171-872 0220
Goldsmith's College	S: 0171-919 7171/C: 0171-919 7500
	www.goldsmiths.ac.uk
Heythrop College	S/C: 0171-795 6600
	www.heythrop.ac.uk
Imperial College of Science,Technology and Medicine	S: 0171-589 5111
	www.ic.ac.uk
Imperial School of Medicine at St Mary's	S: 0171-723 1252/C: 0171-594 8056
	www.sm.ic.ac.uk
Jews' College	S/C: 0181-203 6427
King's College London	S/C: 0171-836 5454
	www.kcl.ac.uk
King's College School of Medicine and Dentistry	S: 0171-737 4000
London Hospital Medical College	S: 0171-377 7000/C: 0171-475 5511
London School of Economics and Political Science	S: 0171-405 7686
	www.lse.ac.uk
Queen Mary and Westfield College	S: 0171-975 5555/C: 0171-975 5511
	www.qmw.ac.uk
St Bartholomew's and The Royal School of Medicine and Dentistry	S: 0171-982 6000/C: 0171-975 5511
	www.mds.qmw.ac.uk
Royal Academy of Music	S: 0171-873 7373
Royal Free Hospital School of Medicine	S: 0171-794 0500/C: 0171-830 2686
Royal Holloway College, University of London	S/C: 01784-434 455
	www.rhbnc.ac.uk
Royal Veterinary College	S: 0171-468 5000

UNIVERSITY ENTRANCE

School of Oriental and African Studies	S: 0171-637 2388
	www.soas.ac.uk
School of Pharmacy	S: 0171-753 5800/C: 0171-753 5831
School of Slavonic and East European Studies	C only: 0171-862 8519
	www.ssees.ac.uk
St George's Hospital Medical School	S: 0181-672 9944
Trinity College of Music	S: 0171-935 5773
United Medical and Dental Schools	S: 0171-928 9292/C: 0171-922 8013
of Guy's and St Thomas's Hospitals	*www.umds.ac.uk*
University College London	S: 0171-387 7050/C: 0171-380 7365
	www.ucl.ac.uk
Wye College, University of London	S/C:01233-812 401
	www.wye.ac.uk
London Guildhall University	S: 0171-320 1000/C: 0171-320 1111
	www.lgu.ac.uk
Loughborough University	S: 01509-263 171/C: 01509-222 298/9
	www.lboro.ac.uk/
University of Luton	S: 01582-734 111/C: 01582-405 251/2/3
	www.luton.ac.uk
University of Manchester	S: 0161-275 2000/C: 0161-275 2077
	www.man.ac.uk
Manchester Business School	S: 0161-275 6333
	www.mbs.ac.uk
Institute of Science and Technology (UMIST)	S/C: 0161-236 3311
	www.umist.ac.uk
University College Warrington	S: 01925-814 343/C: 01925-494 381/2/3/4/5
	www.warr.ac.uk
Manchester Metropolitan University	S: 0161-247 2000/C: 0161-247 2966
	www.mmu.ac.uk
Middlesex University	S: 0181-362 5000/C: 0181-362 6565
	www.mdx.ac.uk
Napier University	S: 0131-444 2266
	www.napier.ac.uk/
University of Newcastle	S: 0191-222 6000/C: 0345-887 722
	www.ncl.ac.uk
University of North London	S: 0171-607 2789/C: 0171-753 3355
	www.unl.ac.uk/
University of Northumbria at Newcastle	S: 0191-232 6002/C: 0191-227 4777
	www.unn.ac.uk/

UNIVERSITY ENTRANCE

University of Nottingham	S: 0115-951 5151/C: 0115-951 6565
	www.nottingham.ac.uk
Nottingham Trent University	S: 0115-941 8418/C: 0115-948 6402
	www.ntu.ac.uk
Open University	S: 01908-274 066
	www.open.ac.uk/
University of Oxford	S: 01865-270 207
	www.ox.ac.uk
Oxford Brookes University	S: 01865-741 111/C: 01865-483 040
	www.brookes.ac.uk
University of Paisley	S: 0141-848 3000/C: 0800-027 1000
	www.paisley.ac.uk/
University of Plymouth	S: 01752-600 600/C: 01752-233 400
	www.plymouth.ac.uk
University of Portsmouth	S/C: 01705-876 543
	www.port.ac.uk
Queen's University of Belfast	S: 01232-245 133/C: 01232-335 -81
	www.qub.ac.uk
University of Reading	S/C: 01189-875 123
	www.reading.ac.uk
Robert Gordon University	S: 01224-262 000/C: 01224-262 105
	www.rgu.ac.uk
University of Salford	S: 0161-745 5000/C: 0161-295 5555
	www.salford.ac.uk
University of Sheffield	S: 0114-222 2000
	www.shef.ac.uk
Sheffield Hallam University	S: 0114-225 5555
	www.shu.ac.uk
South Bank University	S: 0171-928 8989/C: 0171-8158158
	www.sbu.ac.uk
University of Southampton	S: 01703-595 000/C: 01703-595 959
	www.soton.ac.uk
University of St Andrews	S: 01334-476 161/C: 01334-462 150
	www.st-and.ac.uk
University of St Martin, Lancaster and Cumbria	S: 01524-384 384/C: 0800-389 2424
	www.ucsm.ac.uk
University College of St Mark and St John	S: 01752-636 700/C: 01752-636 848
	www.marjon.ac.uk
Staffordshire University	S: 01782-294 000/C: 01782-292 752
	www.staffs.ac.uk

UNIVERSITY ENTRANCE

University of Stirling	S: 01786-473 171
	www.stir.ac.uk
University of Strathclyde	0141-553 4170/1/2/3
	www.strath.ac.uk
University of Sunderland	S: 0191-515 3000
	www.sunderland.ac.uk/
University of Surrey	S: 01483-300 800/C: 0800-980 3200
	www.surrey.ac.uk/
University of Sussex	S: 01273-606 755/C: 01273-678 416
	www.sussex.ac.uk/
University of Teesside	S/C: 01642-218 121
	www.tees.ac.uk
Thames Valley University	S/C: 0181-579 5000
	www.tvu.ac.uk
University of Ulster	S: 01265-44141
	www.ulst.ac.uk
University of Wales (contact colleges directly)	01222-382 656
University of Wales, Aberystwyth	S: 01970-623 111/C: 01970-621 998
University of Wales, Bangor	S: 01248-351 151/C: 0800-328 0352
	www.bangor.ac.uk
University of Wales College of Cardiff	S: 01222-874 000/C: 01222-874 412
	www.cf.ac.uk/
University of Wales College of Medicine	S: 01222-747 747
University of Wales, Lampeter	S/C: 01570-422 351
	www.lampeter.ac.uk
University College of Swansea	S: 01792-205 678/C: 01792-295 097
	www.swansea.ac.uk/
University of Wales Institute, Cardiff	S: 01222-551 111/C: 01222-506 050
	www.uwic.ac.uk
University of Warwick	S: 01203-523 523/C: 01203-533 544
	www.warwick.ac.uk
University of Westminster	S/C: 0171-911 5000
	www.wmin.ac.uk
University of Wolverhampton	S: 01902-321 000/C: 01902-323 232
	www.wlv.ac.uk
University of York	S: 01904-430 000/C: 01904-433 020
	www.york.ac.uk

UNIVERSITY ENTRANCE

Useful information

UK Course Discover is a CD-ROM information service produced by ECCTIS 2000 covering more than 100,000 'course opportunities' in higher and further education. Users can search by course subject, location, method of study and institution. Can be accessed from most schools, libraries and careers services or by annual subscription for £275. Tel: 01242-252 627.

The Big University and College Entrance Guide is the offical guide published by UCAS which gives course details and expected entry requirements for the following year of entry. It comes with a CD-ROM, *Study Link UK 1998.* Available in careers libraries, bookshops, schools and public libraries from June each year. Distributed by Sheed & Ward, £19.95. Tel: 0171-702 9799.

The Times Good University Guide is a useful annual guide published by Times Books. The 1998 version is edited by John O'Leary, £9.99.

Telegraph Books publishes *Making the Most of Being a Student,* part of their *Life Planner* series. Written by Judy Bastyra and Charles Bradley, it gives details of how to survive your first year at university, and is priced at £8.99. Tel: 0171-538 5000.

THE CALEY GAP SCHOLARSHIP

The Royal Caledonian Educational Trust has launched a series of scholarships to help students fund gap-year projects, available to the children of Scottish servicemen and women. The value of these grants is up to £1,000, and the applicants must show, in writing, the value of their project for the community on which it is based, why they want to do it, and how they will raise the necessary money. Contact John Horsfield at the Royal Caledonian Educational Trust, 80a High Street, Bushey, Herts WD2 3DE. Tel/Fax: 0181-421 8845

A-Levels again?

Paying for a university education concentrates the mind: sixthformers now know how important it is to get good enough grades for the right university place first time round. If you don't, you may have to start looking quickly for the best place to retake them, and some universities will ask for higher grades if you have taken a module or exam more than once. With tutorial colleges competing intensely for business, however, there is scope to shop around, and with modular A-Levels you can be more flexible about timing. Planning is important because exams sittings vary according to both subject and examining board.

"Mrs Noreen Tauber, B.A. (Aberdeen), went on to bore me some more about dates and things. Then, with a frowsy sigh, she offered to take me on a tour of the school, probably with nothing more ambitious in mind than to show me it wasn't a workhouse or blacking factory after all. We walked up a corridor, admired two identical classrooms, and walked back down over it again, over wobbling parquet, past farting radiators..."

THE RACHEL PAPERS, Martin Amis, 1973

Charles Highway — the oversexed, clever, spot-squeezing teenage hero of Martin Amis's The Rachel Papers — lusts his way through tutorial college. On one side of Bayswater Road, Highway crams for entrance to Oxford while his target Rachel Noyes swots for A-Levels the other. It's all petulance, passion and Bambi thighs.

Parents' expectations of tutorial or sixth-form colleges, of course, tend to be more prosaic: a crammer is simply an alternative place to take A-Levels first time round, or the only place to

43

A-LEVEL RETAKES

take them second time round. For the gap-year student, a key issue is the possibility of having to retake an A-Level after leaving school. It may happen because grades won are too low to meet a conditional offer, or because illness interfered with exams.

The number of students in tutorial colleges which teach for A-Level resits is reported to be increasing (although the rising trend for overseas students to sit A-Levels for UK university entrance may soon be reversed). UK students have firmly cottoned on to the fact that it is important to get in to a good university if you want to get ahead, not just any of the plethora of universities which now exist. Should you switch from school to a sixth-form or tutorial college before A-Levels, half-way through, or after?

Before you flop or after you flunk?

•Don't leave your present school on a whim. If you did well in GCSE and the A-Level teaching is good, why move? The grass is not always greener on the other side, whether you move from day school to a cloistered boarding school or from the country to

SIXTH FORM AND A-LEVEL MOVES

Over the 1990s decision-making about how to take A-Levels and where to go afterwards has dramatically changed.

• *One key change has been the introduction of regular school and college A-Level league tables. Whatever their defects, and however unpopular with teachers, these tables have helped parents to judge the relative success or failure of schools, and they have also introduced healthy competitiveness into some over-complacent institutions. Parents are now better equipped to decide where their children should study for crucial A-Level exams. (Don't hesitate to ask a school or college for a full explanation of its A-Level results and the improvement of its students' grades.)*

• *The expansion in universities is widely believed to have led to declining entry standards in the 1990s and recently to a polarisation between good and bad universities. "You can still get into one law degree course with two Es," said one observer in summer 1998.*

• *The perceived decline in A-Level standards is being tackled by the Qualifications and Curriculum Authority, a new government regulatory body.*

• *The number of A-Level examining boards is being reduced. "A-Level examining boards have amalgamated with GCSE and GNVQ awarding bodies to form three unitary awarding bodies," says Jeremy Tafler of Edexcel. "Edexcel includes London Examinations, the Assessment and Qualifications Alliance (AQA) includes AEB and NEAB and OCR includes the Oxford and Cambridge examining boards."*

• *Meanwhile, A-Level syllabuses are decreasing in number and becoming more interchangeable. "Tuition fees are accentuating the difference between sitting retakes and taking a full-year upper sixth at tutorial college," says Andy Long of Abbey Tutorial College in London. "About five years ago 70 per cent of our students were doing retakes. Now it's more like 50 per cent. I think there is a levelling up of standards again. The exam boards are more standardised. This means that although we only teach Edexcel exams our teachers can adjust more easily to teaching another board."*

A-LEVEL RETAKES

SPACED MODULES

The way modular A-Levels work is like this. Most boards set four modules for modular Maths, but you could face six. Say you take six modules of a modular Maths A-Level during your final sixth form year in 1998. The syllabus covers: a core of Pure Maths (modules 1,2,3); and a choice of three more from Mechanics (1-6) and Statistics (1-6). You get good marks for four of the six modules, but you completely flunk the fifth and sixth. You do not 'cash in' (declare) the points you score for these modules, but retake them instead. This time you score well and your whole Maths A-Level grade goes up. You reapply for a university place in 1999, citing only your final, higher grades on the UCAS form. Some universities, however, will ask you to tell them about all your exam results, including earlier attempts.

a London sixth-form college. It won't be less of a strain on your parents' pockets to spend two years covering your A-Level syllabus at a crammer: tuition fees for three A-Levels at a London tutorial college are likely to be more than £11,000 a year.

•However, if A-Level teaching is poor or you are in a state of near-rebellion — so bored and repressed that you can think of nothing but getting out of school, your parents will probably consider a sixth-form college or tutorial college. Be warned: after authoritarian rule, the distractions may prove too tempting.

•If an A-Level subject is not going to be well taught (sadly, maths and science subjects in some girls' schools are not), extra coaching is a good idea. (Perhaps you want to do unusual A-Levels that are not taught at some schools — Arabic, law, psychology?) You can move any time after GCSE into a tutorial college, but some sixth-form colleges are less flexible.

•If you are worried about failing or not making the grade in a particular subject, you can throw away your reservations about extra revision and fit coaching into the Christmas or Easter holidays in your final year. You may find it makes a vital difference: what is important is the A-Level grade you get the first time you sit the exam. If it works it will leave your whole gap year free.

A-LEVEL RETAKES

•For gap-year students it is also important to pass (linear) A-Levels first-time around, because subjects are not always available to be retaken in January or February — leaving the rest of the year free. (See tables later on in this chapter.) If it is not possible to switch from a subject started with one exam board to another board (for example, a language with set texts), students may have to resit A-Levels a whole year after the original exams. Bad news for the student who can't remember what he learnt at school when he comes back from a holiday abroad. But modular A-Levels, now firmly entrenched, are good news for gap-year students: you can retake the modules you did badly in while you are still at school instead of having to retake in your year off.

Permutations

•Andrew X needs grades A,B,B for the autumn 1999 place he wants at All Saints University. In June 1999 he gets an A and a B in two subjects, but only a D for Maths. Andrew wants to resit Maths (Associated Examining Board) and try All Saints again for 2000. He can be clear of A-Levels well before Easter 2000, because AEB usually sets a January retake.

A-LEVEL RETAKES

A-LEVEL EXAMINATION BOARDS

KEY: L Linear   LC Linear with coursework   M Modular. We do not have space to list AS Levels. Please check this timetable in all cases with the relevant exam board, as plans can change. Note: Candidates can take A-Level examinations for the first time or as retakes in both winter and spring. N/a: not available.

AEB

(Now part of AQA, the Assessment and Qualifications Alliance).The Associated Examining Board, Stag Hill House, Guildford, Surrey GU2 5XJ Tel: 01483-506506

Nov 1998 *None*   **Jan 1999** *Applied Maths ((L)(M), Biology (M), Business Studies (M), Chemistry (M), Economics (L), English (L), English Literature (L)(LC) , Human Biology (M), Mathematics (L)(M), Maths and Further Maths (L)(M), Mechanics (M), Physics (M), Psychology (M), Pure Maths (L)(M), Sociology (L)(M), Statistics (LC)(M)*   **May/June 1999** *All subjects*   **Nov 2000** *None*   **Jan 2000** *N/a*   **May/June 2000** *N/a.*

CCEA

Northern Ireland Council for the Curriculum, Examinations and Assessment, Clarendon Dock, 29 Clarendon Rd, Belfast BT1 3BG Tel: 01232-261 200

Nov 1998 *None* **Jan 1999** *None*   **Feb 1999** *Biology (M), Chemistry (M), Computing (M), English Literature (M), Geography (M), Maths (M), Physics (L)(M), May/June 1999 Accounting (L), Art & Design (L), Art & Design Historical Studies (L), Biology (L)(M), Business Studies (L), Chemistry (L)(M), Classical History and Civilisation (L), Computing (L)(M), Design and Technology (L), Economics (L), English Literature (L)(M), Geography (L)(M), Geology (L), Government & Politics (L),History (L), Home Economics (L), Latin (L), Maths (L)(M), Modern Languages (L), Music (L), Physics (L)(M), Religious Studies (L), Sociology (L)*   **Nov 1999** *None*   **Jan 2000** *None* **Feb 2000** *Same as Feb 1999* **May/June 2000** *All subjects.*

EDEXCEL

(Incorporating London Exams & BTEC), Stewart House, 32 Russell Square, London WC1B 5DN Tel: 0171-393 4444

Nov 1998 *None*   **Jan 1999** *Accounting (L), Biology (M), Chemistry (L)(M), Chemistry Nuffield (M), Economics (L), English (M), French (M), German (M), Geography (M), Goverment & Politics (M), Human Biology (M), Law (L), Maths (M), Physics (M), Spanish (M)*   **May/June 1999** *All subjects*   **Jan 2000** *Same as Jan 1999*   **May/June 2000** *All subjects..*

A-LEVEL RETAKES

NEAB

Northern Examinations and Assessment Board, Devas Street, Manchester M15 6EX Tel: 0161-953 1180

Nov 1998 None *Feb/Mar 1999* Biology (M), Business Studies (M), Chemistry (M), Electronics (M), Environmental Science (M), Geography (M), Geology (L/M), Government & Politics (M), Maths & Further Maths (M), Physics (M), Psychology (M), Sociology (L/M). *May/June 1999* All these subjects plus: Accounting (L), Archaeology (L), Art & Design (L), Biology (L:Assessment) (Nuffield), Business Studies (L:Ass), Chemistry (L:Ass), Classical Civilisation (L), Classical Greek (L), Computing (L/M:Ass), Dance (L), Design & Tech (L), Design & Tech: Tech Sys (L),Economics (L), English Lang (L), English Lit (L), English Lang & Lit (L), Environmental Science (L:Ass), French (L), Further Maths (M), Further Maths (L) Pure; App, Mech), General Studies (L/M:Ass), Geography (L/M:Ass), Geology (L:Ass), German (L), History (L:A,B,C,YZ), Home Economics (L), Human Biology (M), Information Tech (L/M:Ass), Italian (L), Latin (L), Law (L/M:Ass), Maths (M), Maths (L:Met,App,Mech,Stat), Media Studies (L), Music (L), Panjabi (L), Philosophy (L/M:Ass), Physics (L:Ass), Psychology (L:Ass), Relgiious Studies (L:A-K), Russian (L), Science (M), Social & Environmental Biology (M), Sociology (L/M:Ass), Spanish (L), Statistics (L:Ass), Statistics (M). *Feb-Mar 2000* N/a *May/June 2000* All subjects

OCR (Oxford, Cambridge & RSA Examinations)

1 Regent Street, Cambridge CB1 2GG Tel: 01223-552 552 Fax: 01223-552 553 Web: www.ocr.org.uk

From 1 October 1998 all syllabuses formerly run by OCEAC, which includes all former UODLE, OCSEB and UCLES A-Levels (except international A-Levels) will be run by the new unitary awarding body OCR. In the following list former University of Cambridge Local Examinations Syndicate (UCLES) syllabuses are indicated by 'C'; former UODLE (University of Oxford Delegacy of Local Examinations) syllabuses by 'O'; and former Oxford and Cambridge Schools Examination Board (OCSEB) syllabuses by 'OC'. Final exam dates only are given: please contact OCR for full information about resit timetable.

June 1999: Accounting (L/C), Ancient History (L/C/OC), Art (L/OC), Art & Design (L/OC)(M/C), Art with Art History (L/O), Biology (L/OC), Biology Structured Science Scheme (L/OC), Business Studies (M/O), Chemistry Structured Science Scheme (L/OC), Classical Civilisation (L/C), Design & Technology (L/C/OC), Economics (M/OC/O), Economics, Government & Politics (L/OC), English Language & Literature (L/O), English Literature (M/O), French (M/OC), French for Business (L/O), French for Professional Use (L/OC), Geography (M/C/O), Geometrical & Mechanical Drawing (L/C), German (M/OC), German for Business (L/O), German for Professional Use (M/OC), Government & Politics (M/OC), History of Art (L/OC/O), Home Economics (L/C),

A-LEVEL RETAKES

Law: Law for Business) (M/O), Maths (L/OC), Maths Foundation (L/OC), Maths (M/O), Maths Nuffield (M/O), Further Maths (L/OC), Further Maths (M/O), Further Maths Nuffield (M/O), Pure Maths (M/O), Music (L/OC/O), Physics Structured Science Scheme (M/OC), Religious Studies (L/O), Science Single Award (M/O), Science Double Award Structured Science Scheme (M/C), Science Single Award Structured Science Scheme (M/OC), Science Double Award (M/O), Social Biology (L/C), Spanish (M/OC), Spanish for Business (L/O), Spanish for Professional Use (M/OC).

June 2000 N/a
June 2001 *Accounting (M/O), Ancient History (JACT)(L/C/OC), Archaeology (L/C), Art & Design (L/C), Art & Design 3D Studies (L/C), Art & Design Graphics (L/C), Art & Design Historical & Critical (L/C), Art & Design Photography (L/C), Art & Design Textiles (L/C), Biology (L/C),Biology (M/C), Business Studies (L/M/C), Business Studies & Economics (M/C), Chemistry (L/M/C)(M/C), Chemistry Salters (M/OC), Christian Theology (M/C), Classical Civilisation (JACT) (M/OC), Classical Greek (L/C/OC), Computing (M/O), Design & Technology Communication (L/C), Design & Technology Design (L/C), Design & Technology: Technology (L/C/OC), Dutch (L/C), Economics (L/C), Economics (M/C), Electronics (M/OC), English (L/C), English Language (L/C), English Language & Literature (M/OC), English Literature (L/C), English Literature (M/C), French (L/C), French (M/O), General Studies (L/0). General Studies with Coursework (C/OC) G.S. without Coursework (C), Geography (L/C), Geography (M/A), Geology (Structured Science Scheme) (M/OC), German (L/C), German (M/C), Government & Politics (M/O), History (L/C), History (M/O/OC), History Cambridge History Project (L/C), Home Economics (L/O), Italian (M/O), Latin (L/C/OC), Law (L/O), Maths (L/C), Maths (M/C), Further Maths (L/C), Further Maths (M/C), Pure Maths (M/C), MEI Further Maths Additional (M/OC), MEI Further Maths (M/OC), MEI Maths (M/OC), MEI Mechanics (M/OC), MEI Pure Maths (M/OC), MEI Statistics (M/OC), Media Studies (L/C), Media Studies (M/C), Music (L/C), Performing Arts (M/C), Physical Education (L/C), Physics (L/C), Physics (M/C/O), Physics Nuffield (M/OC), Portuguese (L/C), Psychology (M/OC), Religious Studies (L/C/OC), Russian (M/OC), Science Dual Award (M/C), Science Single Award (M/C), Social Biology (M/C), Social Biology (M/C), Sociology (L/Interboard), Spanish (L/C), Spanish (M/O), Textiles (L/C).*

WJEC
Welsh Joint Education Committee, 245 Western Avenue, Cardiff CF5 2YX Tel: 01222-265000
Nov 1998 *None* ***Jan 1999*** *Biology (M), Business Studies (M), Chemistry (M), Computing (M), Electronics (M), English (M), Geography (M), Maths (M), Physics (M).* ***May/June 1999*** *All subjects.* ***Nov 1999*** *N/a* ***Jan 2000*** *N/a* ***May/June 2000*** *All subjects.*

A-LEVEL RETAKES

•Julia X needs B,B,C for a 1999 place at the University of White Heat (UWH) to read Biotechnological Sciences. She parties her way through the sixth form and gets two Bs in Maths and Biology (linear) and good grades in all except one module of Chemistry (modular). But because Edexcel will set retake exams in a several subjects in January 2000, Julia X can re-sit the module of Chemistry, enjoy the rest of her gap year and go to UWH in autumn 2000.

•*A-Level resits are staged in November or January as well as June. Check with your exam board (see table on following pages, for guidance only).*

Retake timing: linear and modular

It has become easier to raise your A-Level grades. In the early 1990s, A-Levels were almost all linear exams which tested you on two years' acquired knowledge in a single sitting. If you did not do well, you had to revise the whole syllabus again and sit a retake at a time which suited the exam board but prevented you doing anything else for months on end.

Confident schools and students are happy with linear A-Levels. But now modular A-Levels are well-entrenched, and you can go into a gap year with, perhaps, just one-quarter (one module) of an A-Level to retake and the other three-quarters (three

A-LEVEL RETAKES

modules) already passed with good grades that count towards your overall result. Better still, you can get an indication from the results of your early modules of how you are going to perform overall — and work harder. And if you know that the two (of four) A-Level modules you have passed will automatically give you an AS-Level, this may in some cases be all you need. Less worry, more flexibility: the AEB, for example, may set exams for a whole linear Sociology A-Level in January 1999 as well as each of the modules in the modular Sociology A-Level.(As already stated, make sure your chosen university course doesn't set higher entry grades for exams taken at a second sitting.)

Tutorial colleges like to keep students working on A-Levels for a full year. That keeps the college full and tutors paid. But many also agree that the best thing is to get resits over before work already done is forgotten. So the best timing, if you are academically confident and want to enjoy your gap year, is to go to a 'crammer' in September and resit the whole exam or the relevant modules in November, January or February.

A-LEVEL RETAKES

Choosing a crammer

Standards vary. As already mentioned, you can check with BAC, CIFE or the Independent Schools Association (ISA, Tel: 01799-523 619) — or you can ask the college to produce independently compiled performance tables. The best references are usually from former students, but there are other equally important checks to make:

•**Basics first.** You need to find out if a college teaches the subject that you have been doing at school? Does it teach that syllabus (e.g. AEB/Maths) for retakes, and if so, when? If so, does it do so in classes or only by finding a specialist tutor?

•**Impartial advice?** Some colleges may try to persuade you to start an A-Level again by taking a different subject. But that may suit their intake figures better than your plans — why attempt a different subject or syllabus unless you have to? Now that syllabuses are becoming more interchangeable between boards, make them justify their advice.

•**Who will teach you?** This is probably more important than whether there are six or eight people in a class (if the number gets into double figures, it certainly isn't a tutorial). If you are taking coaching or a resit, make sure an individual tutor is completely familiar with the syllabus you have been doing. If you do not know anyone who has been taught by history tutor Percival Smith at Palladian Tutors, say, you can usually arrange a single individual lesson first to see how you get on.

•**Compare conditions** — have a look. Common sense dictates that it helps to be near public transport and shops yet have quiet rooms for study inside.

•**Compare standards.** Only recently has real light been shed on the relative academic performance of schools and colleges — for years parents had to rely on assessment by grapevine. On 3 September 1997 the *Daily Telegraph* revealed that average A-Level retake grade improvements at 26 private colleges varied from -2.00 (Bosworth Tutorial College, Northampton) to +1.79 (Modes Study Centre, Oxford) and the percentage of first-time A-Level A/B grades they produced ranged from none to 83.1 per

53

A-LEVEL RETAKES

cent of their entries. If a crammer can match the highest school standards it is doing well.

•**Coaching costs.** These are usually charged by the hour and you don't know how long you need. Compare hourly rates and what you get for it — how many hours of group teaching each week and how many one-to-one tutorials? The figures opposite give a rough idea.

•**Reputation or accreditation?** The best of reputations need checking out and parents and ex-students are the best source.

•**Summary:** see for yourself, ask questions, get ex-students' references. Ask to see complete A-Level results (actual grades and grade improvements) for recent students.

Accreditation and certification

Those who do not have inside information can check when a college has been inspected by the Department for Education and Employment (DFEE) or an independent body. Certification takes four forms:

First there is inspection by the DFEE. Second, there is membership of CIFE (the Conference for Independent Further Education, a trade association that says it aims to keep standards high). Third, there is BAC (the British Accreditation Council for Independent Further and Higher Education), a small body that inspects colleges before giving them a seal of approval (see list at

---

EASTER A-LEVEL REVISION COSTS

All prices are at July 1998 and are inclusive of VAT.

Bosworth Tutorial College, Northampton

Standard rate= £25/hour (individual tuition).

Six days tuition, 3 subjects = £350/week; 1-2 subjects, 2 days tuition per subject = £130/week per subject (group work).

Cambridge Arts and Sciences, Cambridge

Standard rate = £28/hr (individual tuition). Residential and non-residential easter revision courses are also available, priced at £450/week and £360/week respectively.

Davies, Laing & Dick, London

Standard rate = £38/hr (individual tuition).

Full day, 40 hr week = £415/week (group work).

---

the end of this chapter). Fourth, there is the Independent Schools Association (ISA).

Languages

If you have only language A-Levels to retake, there are several options:

•Take an extra course or stay in the country of the relevant language and return to revise for a summer resit, choosing the same exam board (courses abroad, however, are not usually geared to A-Level texts).

•If your A-Level is not offered in modules, check with tutorial colleges how much of your syllabus (the set literature texts are crucial) overlaps with that of other exam boards. This may give you the chance to switch exam boards and do a quick retake in November or January.

•Cram for as long as necessary at a specialist language college.

FAILURE WHERE IS THY STING?

"We've had one person here who has been retaking Maths A-Level for 10 years." London college tutor

HERE

"Maths A-Level has definitely been getting easier."
Another London college tutor

A-LEVEL RETAKES

Some British tutorial colleges and language course organisers have links with teaching centres in France (for example, Challenge Educational Services arranges A-Level revision in Boredaux) so it is worth checking this out before signing on.

•See also CHAPTER 5: LANGUAGES.

Oxford and Cambridge entrance

As Oxford and Cambridge universities have now given up set-ting their own separate entrance exams (except additional tests) and joined the UCAS admissions system, it is your A-Level grades that will matter now. You are supposed to be clever to get into either these or the other top academic UK universities, so you should only need to retake A-Levels if you have had an acci-dent, illness or other mishap or if you were too young when you tried to get good grades at the first attempt.

Some Cambridge colleges ask you to take STEPs (Sixth Term Examination Papers) as well as A-Levels. You can't retake them but some tutorial colleges can coach you for them. STEPs are set in the summer (after A-Levels), and are used to supplement aca-demic interviews (which take place the previous December or January).•See also CHAPTER 2: UNIVERSITY ENTRANCE

American SATs

There are tutors who coach for SATs (Scholastic Assessment Tests), the multiple-choice exam needed for entry to US univer-sities, and there are crammers that give coaching. Contact The Fulbright Commission's Educational Advisory Service in London. •See CHAPTER 2: UNIVERSITY ENTRANCE

Colleges accredited by BAC

The following 47 independent sixth-form and tutorial colleges (June 1998) which offer A-Level tuition (one-year, two-year, complete retakes, modular retakes or coaching) are recognised by the British Accreditation Council (Tel: 0171-487 4643). This is not an exclusive list: the Independent Schools Association (Tel: 01799-523619) also accredits a few colleges and they can have a good reputation without accreditation by either. An asterisk denotes membership of CIFE (the Council for Independent Further Education).

College	Telephone
Abacus College (Oxford)	01865-240 111
The Abbey Colleges (Malvern)	01684-892 300
Abbey Tutorial College (Birmingham)*	0121-236 7474
Abbey Tutorial College (London)*	0171-229 5928
Albany College (Hendon, London)*	0181-202 5965
Ashbourne Independent Sixth Form College* (London W8)	0171-937 3858
Bales College (London W10)*	0181-960 5899
Basil Paterson College (Edinburgh)	0131-556 7695
Bellerby's College (Hove)*	01273-723 911
Bosworth Tutorial College (Northampton)*	01604-239 995
Brooke House College* (Market Harborough)	01858-462 452
Cambridge Arts and Sciences	01223-314 431
Cambridge Seminars (Cambridge)	01223-313 464
Cambridge Tutors College (Croydon)*	0181-688 5284
Centre for International Education (Oxford)	01865-202 238
Cherwell College (Oxford)*	01865-242 670
Collingham (London SW5)*	0171-244 7414
Collingham College (Oxford)*	01865-728 280
Concord College (Shrewsbury)*	01694-731 631
David Game College (London W11)	0171-221 6665
Davies Laing & Dick (London W2)*	0171-727 2797
Davies's College (London WC1)*	0171-430 1622
Dean College (London N7)	0171-281 4461
d'Overbroeck's (Oxford)	01865-310 000
Duff-Miller Sixth Form College (London SW7)*	0171-225 0577
Educare College (Manchester M19)	0161-442 0858

A-LEVEL RETAKES

Exeter Tutorial College (Exeter)*	01392-78101
Harrogate Tutorial College (Harrogate)*	01423-501 041
Irwin College (Leicester)*	01162-552 648
Lansdowne Independent Sixth Form College* (London W8)	0171-616-4400
Mander Portman Woodward (Birmingham)*	0121-454 9637
Mander Portman Woodward (Bristol)*	01179 255 688
Mander Portman Woodward (Cambridge)*	01223-350 158
Mander Portman Woodward (London SW7)*	0171-584 8555
Modes Study Centre (Oxford)*	01865-245 172/249 349
New College (Cardiff)	01222-463 355
Oxford Tutorial College (Oxford)*	01865-793 333
Padworth College (Nr. Reading)*	01734-832 644
Queen's Secretarial and Business College (London SW7)	0171-589 8583
Rochester Tutors Independent College (Rochester)*	01634-828 115
St Andrew's (Cambridge)	01223-60040
St Clare's (Oxford)*	01865-52031
St James's College (London SW5)	0171-373 3852
St Joseph's Hall (Oxford)	01865-711 829
Stafford House International Sixth Form and Tutorial College (Canterbury)	01227-453 237
Surrey College (Guildford)*	01483-65887
Tuition Centre, The (London NW11)*	0181-201 8020

4

Essentials

If you have your A-Levels sorted out (and perhaps a place on an overseas vol-untary work project) the next thing to go for is work to pay for the rest of your year off. You can look for vacation work like shelf-stacking in supermarkets (see CHAPTER 7: WORK UK) or get enough training to find better-paid office work. The skills most 1990s offices need are based on computers, so here is some advice on training and a list of colleges that run short courses in basic computer and office skills.

Skills for work

What business skills do you really need to learn between school and university? The short answer is — just enough to get you work. In fact, you may not need training at all. If you work as a barman, waiter or shop assistant you will get trained on the job.

But if you want to earn enough to travel widely, in the shortest possible time, there is nothing to beat competence on a comput-er keyboard. Work can be dull, but London 'temp' agencies pay £5-£9 an hour to students who are numerate, literate, efficient and can type information into computers accurately and fast. And if you're so far ahead with information technology that you can use HyperText Mark-up Language to create World Wide Web pages, you could earn twice as much.

OFFICE SKILLS

Laugh no longer, those who used to laugh at the idea that bosses might have to learn how to use a computer keyboard. Just walk through an inter-city train and see who's busy with a laptop. Now everyone needs to be able to process information for themselves, because the people who don't need a personal secretary will get jobs first. Being able to type fast on a computer keyboard can also be useful at university if you want to submit a well-presented essay or thesis.

Take college prospectuses with a pinch of salt, however, when you are looking at courses in business administration or office skills. You don't have to bend over a keyboard for nine months before looking for a job. Nor do you have to pay four-figure sums to learn — you can do day or evening courses at a local college of further education for less than £300 and practise your word-processing at home. A few public libraries also have computer training and practice areas.

Most people agree that to earn money before you go to university and in the holidays afterwards, it is enough to learn basic

OFFICE SKILLS

office skills in one 12-week term or less. If you can fit in a short course before the end of the autumn, you will have qualifications when you look for work before Christmas. Many colleges now offer these courses, often dividing them into modules so that you can pick and choose what you want to learn.

•Local area networks of computers are the norm in most offices, along with flexible telephone communications and fax machines. So challenge the argument that it is better to learn keyboarding on a typewriter because you can progress to a computer keyboard later: typewriters are nearly extinct. And it is fast becoming as important to know how to send E-mail (electronic mail) and access Internet data as it became in the 1980s to send a fax. So it is worth finding out just how up-to-date a college's technical knowledge is.

•If you have not mastered computer keyboards and software already, they should be high on the list. Before looking at courses, make sure your parents know how far you got with information technology (IT) at school. IT is now part of the national curriculum, and you may have done the RSA Computer Literacy and Information Technology (CLAIT) exam at school between the ages of 12 and 15. This means you know the basic workings of three out of some fourteen areas of computer operations; for example, the three most popular which are word-processing, database use and spreadsheet use. If you progressed from there to take the RSA Integrated Business Technology Stage II exam (which means you can perform set WP, database, spreadsheet,

OFFICE SKILLS

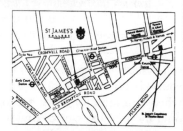

OFFICE SKILLS

INTENSIVE SHORT COURSES: MORE OR LESS?

Queen's Business & Secretarial College, London & Cambridge

£2,310*, 12 weeks x 25 hours, intensive business skills, one-term certificate course. WP to 40wpm, Teeline shorthand to 80wpm, SS, DTP, administration & communication skills.

Stroud College of Further Education

£235 (no VAT), 12 weeks x 15 hours, intensive office skills course, RSA I and II, WP, DTP (*Quark*) Teeline shorthand to 50wpm, etc. Exam fees extra

Pitman Training Centres

Diploma in Secretarial Skills: £1,908 (incl VAT), 8 weeks x 30 hours, intensive skills course, WP (*Word for Windows*), *Windows 95, Excel, Powerpoint, Access*, DTP, options to do Net training, Lotus WordPro, Teeline shorthand to 50 wpm. Writing for business + seminars.

WP: *Word processing.*	DB: *databases.*
SS: *spreadsheets.*	TT: *Touch-typing.*
DTP: *Desk top publishing.*	

*Price before NVQ Tax Relief (23% deduction). Figures at July 1998

---

graphics and integration tasks in a set number of hours) you may need only to add touch-typing speeds to make you are good enough to get work through an employment agency. Make sure you are not paying for the same training twice.

• As far as gap-year work is concerned, you certainly do not need to learn 120 words-a-minute shorthand. If you want to be a secretary, then go ahead.

• Concentrate on useful computer skills first: touch-typing (touch-keyboarding) to produce word-processing documents quickly and accurately; and operating photocopiers, using laser printers and fax machines. Minimum speeds for keyboarding need not be as high as colleges insist, but if you do not get up to 40 words a minute (without looking) you are probably wasting your time. With practice you can improve this to the 50 wpm or more that employment agencies demand. Mastering computer databases, spreadsheets and desk-top publishing programmes will get you higher rates of pay — and more chance of getting a job.

OFFICE SKILLS

•Other courses — from public relations and marketing to grooming — are usually taken only for fun or if you eventually want to work in a specialised field. Many are useful but expensive and not enough to provide a qualification that will get you a job.

Choosing a course

Almost every large town in Britain has colleges offering to teach school-leavers 'essential skills'. But for the reasons given above, we list at the end of this section only ones which run full-time office skills courses of 12 weeks or less or part-time courses for up to 18 weeks. They all cover core computer skills.

Some of these colleges run language courses (not necessarily for A-Level retakes) and two- or three-term secretarial courses as well. You may have decided already where you want to go, perhaps because friends have recommended a particular course. If you have not made a choice, you can phone for prospectuses or download information from Websites, checking key details

OFFICE SKILLS

WHICH WORD-PROCESSING PACKAGE?

"I would estimate that about 70 per cent of our clients request temps able to use Microsoft's Word for Windows — the other 30 per cent requiring WordPerfect and other packages," says Peter Toner, managing director of Fasttrack, the Professional Association of Secretaries and Support Personnel. "In addition, temps versed in Word earn between 40 per cent and 50 per cent more than others as it tends to be used in a higher level commercial environment. The next most popular is the spreadsheet Microsoft Excel and I would recommend learning PowerPoint as well. With businesses moving away from the use of overhead projectors, the ability to create impressive presentations and graphics using PowerPoint is becoming more sought after by employers."
Peter Toner, managing director, Fasttrack, 1997

---

about fees, hours and equipment before you go, and arrange a visit. The biggest and best-known are not necessarily the best value or the most fun to go to. Find out first.

Fees

There is tax relief for vocational training, designed to encourage school-leavers to train for an NVQ (National Vocational

---

DAYDREAMING

"I spent one month on a secretarial course at Scope in Slough. I was plonked in front of a computer for two hours a day with a tape — no formal teaching — and I could already type a bit so that helped. I came out with a certificate which was helpful to wave at people when applying for jobs with agencies. The training itself is easy. You could teach yourself. I was lucky enough to work at the same place for the entire five months at the same company [before going on a teaching assignment in Africa], where I was treated really well. I was paid £5 an hour which isn't bad for a first job, just entering data into a computer. It was absolutely mind-numbing but I survived by dreaming about the trip. I knew I was working for a reason and that gave it all a bit of coherence."
Polly Someone, New Hall, Cambridge University, 1997

OFFICE SKILLS

Qualification) or SVQ (Scottish Vocational Qualification). This means that you should be able to get a 23 per cent reduction on some course tuition fees: very short courses may not qualify, but longer vocational training courses do.

•Under the NVQ scheme the government pays a college, or 'course provider' 23 per cent of the fees quoted and the student pays 77 per cent. The college should give you a form to fill in (VTR 1) and the course provider claims the relief.

•Check that VAT and all extras are included in the figure given to you. Your parents may be happy to pay extra for a good reputation and pleasant surroundings, but how much?

•Work out how many hours a week of teaching you are getting for your money. The table on page 63 quotes fees mainly for London courses, but these can be used as a benchmark. Some so-called 'full-time' courses run for very short hours. And don't forget to check in what circumstances you can change a booking or get a refund.

Qualifications

Do you end up with skills that can be refreshed later somewhere else? Do you get certified standards (e.g. carrying out a database task in a certain time) that have been properly tested? Do you take a recognised exam (e.g. RSA or London Chamber of Commerce). Note: keep copies of any certificates you do get and take them abroad when you travel if you plan to look for work.

Teaching

Teaching hours vary from course to course. Students need a lot of practice time, and complex equipment means that even practice sessions now need some supervision — but you are paying for teaching as well as tapes. If you are left in front of a PC and told to follow the instruction manual, what are you going to do if you get locked into an unknown sequence and no-one is there to show you how to get out?

•Find out first how much time experienced teachers will spend with you; and second, how much supervised or unsupervised time you can have to practise.

66

OFFICE SKILLS

OXFORD, CAMBRIDGE & RSA EXAMINATIONS (OCR)

RSA CLAIT (Computer Literacy & Information Technology) Stage I CLAIT includes: word processing, spreadsheets, databases, accounting and graphical representation of data, computer-aided design, desktop publishing and on-line communications.

RSA Integrated Business Technology Stage II is a step ahead of CLAIT, including WP, database, spreadsheets, graphics and integration.

RSA Integrated Business Technology Stage III: the emphasis is on interrogating/manipulating existing data. The candidate needs good WP or DTP skills to produce a publication and an automated presentation.

RSA Text Processing Diploma includes word processing and medical WP, audio-transcription, medical transcription, mailmerge and shorthand.

RSA Administrative and Secretarial Procedures Diploma: developed specifically for secretarial students, the diploma incorporates Stages I and II of text processing, and allows students to specialise in those aspects of secretarial and administrative work which are most relevant to their needs or interests.

Information Technology NVQs ('implement' strand) Level 2 & 3: These Information Technology NVQs awarded by RSA are based on standards developed by the Information Technology Industry Training Organisation. The two qualifications are:

Install Information Technology Products NVQ Level 2

Implement Information Technology Solution NVQ Level 3

These two NVQs are aimed at candidates who install computer systems: both hardware and software.

Information Technology NVQs ('create' strand) Level 2, 3 and 4: The NVQs available under this banner are as follows:

-Software Creation NVQ Level 2: aimed at a candidate who works as a programmer, database programmer or software engineer.

-Information Systems Acquisition NVQ Level 3: aimed at candidates who are involved in evaluating and selecting an Information Technology solution.

-Information Systems Design and Programming NVQ Level 3: covers software creation but will also involve the candidate in the initial design of the briefs and the provision of support documentation.

-Information Systems Analysis NVQs Level 2 & 3: aimed at candidates who help organisations and individuals seeking to achieve quality performance in the field of administration.

For more details of any of the above qualifications, please contact OCR's helpdesk at Tel: 01203-470 033.

OFFICE SKILLS

Equipment

Make sure you know what equipment you will be using on the course. Is the word-processing application (software) on the personal computer, for example, *Word* or *WordPerfect for Windows*, and if so, is it a fairly recent upgrade? Colleges may, however try to charge through the nose for the most recent applications, while learning the basics of an earlier version will teach you everything you need to know. Don't be seduced too much by famous names. There are now a lot of other packages which perform just as well in a similar way. If a college is able to use cheaper but well-tested software, it can keep down its fees. On the whole, once you have mastered one it is easy to transfer your

68

DESIGNER ANORAKS

Rates for computer skills vary according to which software applications you can use. If you are good but not experienced, try the pages of 'Guardian Online' (with The Guardian newspaper on Thursdays). Those with more than a year's experience can do even better. "If you know how to make up a presentation in PowerPoint or Persuasion on a Mac or a PC with Windows you could earn £10-13 an hour, and people who can operate Quark XPress are getting £12.50 or more an hour," says Cara Ostryn of Mac Temps in London. "HTML skills are worth £15-20 an hour," adds the Internet division's Steve Hudson, "but you do need to be able to deal with designers who are in a flap and telling you to move things over by two pixels pretty quickly." Some freelances earn more than £20 an hour for creating interactive Web pages using Photoshop and Director.

---

knowledge to another. Finally, if you have done some IT (information technology) at school, what new things will you be learning?

Jobs

Does the college keep records of where its leavers work afterwards? How many people who finished the last course got a

---

WHICH QUALIFICATIONS?

"RSA qualifications are still the best known and best respected by employers — RSA Stage III in typing is an assurance that you have reached over 45 words a minute. NVQs are still less well established, so it is worth explaining what particular skills you have gained from any NVQ you take. More important than any paper qualification is that your typing speed and accuracy are strong enough to take you through the tests which agencies will ask you to undertake. Practice is vital in building up your speeds but don't despair. If you don't reach the magic 45 words per minute in the test, there may be other options available which will help you build up your speeds while you are working."
James Reed, Chief Executive, Reed Employment Services

OFFICE SKILLS

job? Does the college have links with employment agencies? Ask these questions before you choose — and, if you want to be obsessively thorough, why not call the named agencies or employers as well? They may remember your initiative later if you go to see them.

MONEY MANAGEMENT

"I took a loan of £2,000 from my parents to go to Africa, but after I did voluntary work I needed more money to travel, so I used my father's credit card and owed about £3,000 by the time I came back to work. Most other people did a secretarial course but things happened so quickly... After about two days I got a waitressing job which was hard work and didn't pay well, so I left after three weeks. Then in April I got a job at the GAP shop in Watford and will finish in late August. I think I'll pay off the whole debt."
Emily Imeson, Business Studies, Nottingham Trent University, 1997

Colleges

To help gap-year readers across the country, we provide this list of colleges which run intensive office skills courses, listing ones in almost every part of Britain. This list is only an indicator of what is available, not a guarantee of quality. We welcome information from (and reports about) any training centres which offer short courses in office skills as we have defined them. Research shows that for office work employers ideally need the following computer qualifications from you — but initiative and intelligence count for as much as certificates: Typing: 45 wpm + competence with wordprocessing using recent applications and with database and spreadsheet packages.

*Key **L: Large** 100+ full-time students   **M: Medium** 50-100   **S: Small** 0-50*
* **I: Intensive** course   **Md: Modular** course.*

The colleges marked 'I' offer an intensive course, usually 12 weeks or less. Those marked 'Md' specialise in modules which can be arranged so that an individual can cover the course specifications in less than 18 weeks.

London	Telephone
Cavendish College (L) (I)	0171-580 6043
209-212 Tottenham Court Rd, London W1P 3AF	*www.cavendish.ac.uk*
The City College (L) (Md)	0171-253 1133
University House, 55 East Road, London N1 6AH	*www.citycollege.ac.uk*
Ealing Tertiary College (L) (I) (Md)	0181-231 6000
Acton Centre, Mill Hill Road	*www.ealingcoll.ac.uk*
London W3 8UX	
London College of Business & Computing (L) (I)	0181-880 9015
Anna House, 214-218 High Road, London N15 4NP	
Lucie Clayton College (M) (I) (Md)	0171-581 0024
4 Cornwall Gardens, London SW7 4AJ	
Office Skills Centre (S) (Md)	0171-404 3636
Dragon Court, 27-29 Macklin St, London WC2B 5LX	
Pitman Training Centre (L) (I) (Md)	0800-220 454
154 Southampton Row, London WC1B 5AX	
Queen's Business & Secretarial College (L) (I)	0171-589 8583
24 Queensberry Place, London SW7 2DS	
Southgate College (L) (Md)	0181-886 6521
High Street, Southgate	*www.mdx.ac.uk/www/southgate*
London N14 6BS	

OFFICE SKILLS

South Thames College (L) (Md)   0181-918 7222
Wandsworth High Street, London SW18 2PP

•*Intensive PA/Sec/Admin skills course: an 18 week course for those wishing to aquire Sec/Admin skills quickly. Syllabus covers word processing, audio processing, IT, reception, book-keeping and business communications: all leading to nationally/internationally recognised RSA qualifications. Timetable runs over 2.5 days per week. Free tuition for UK and EU students.*

St James's College (M) (I)   0171-373 3852
4 Wetherby Gardens, London SW5 0JN

Avon
City of Bristol College (L) (I) (Md)   0117-904 5000
Brunel Centre, Ashley Down, Bristol BS7 9BU   *www.cityofbristol.ac.uk*

Berkshire
East Berkshire College (L) (I) (Md)   01753-793 000
Station Road, Langley, Berkshire SL6 4EZ   *www.eastberks.ac.uk*

Birmingham
East Birmingham College (L) (Md)   0121-743 4471
Garrets Green Lane, Birmingham B33 6TS   *www.ebham.ac.uk*

Cambridgeshire
Cambridge Regional College (L) (I) (Md)   01223-418 200
Kings Hedges Road, Cambridge, Cambs CB4 2QT

Huntingdonshire Regional College (L) (I)   01480-52346
California Road, Huntingdon, Cambs PE18 7BL

Peterborough Regional College (L) (Md)   01733-767 366
Park Crescent, Peterborough, Cambs PE1 4DZ

OFFICE SKILLS

Cheshire

Newton Secretarial School, Chester (S) (I)   01244-681 814
12 P&Q Chesterbank Business Park, River Lane
Saltney, Chester, Cheshire

West Cheshire College (L) (Md)   01244-677 677
Handbridge Centre   *www.dspace.dial.pipex.com/town/parade/hq56*
Eaton Road, Chester, Cheshire CH4 7ER

Cornwall

Cornwall College (L) (I) (Md)   01209-712 911
Trevenson Road, Pool, Redruth, Cornwall TR15 3RD

•*Wide ranging skills courses available, using Word, including: touch-typing; text and word processing; audio; IT skills; shorthand. Skills programmes that are individually designed to meet everyone's needs.*

Penwith College (L) (Md)   01736-362 604
St Clare Street, Penzance, Cornwall TR18 2SA

Cumbria

West Cumbria College (L) (Md)   01900-64331
Park Lane, Workington, Cumbria CA14 2RW

Derbyshire

Derby Tertiary College-Wilmorton (L) (Md)   01332-757 571
Harrow Street, Wilmorton, Derby   *www.wilmorton.co.uk*
Derbyshire DE24 8UG

Devon

East Devon College (L) (I) (Md)   01884-235 200
Bolham Road, Tiverton, Devon EX16 6SH   *www.eastdevon.ac.uk*

Durham

Darlington College of Technology (L) (I) (Md)   01325-503 191
Cleveland Avenue, Darlington, Durham DL3 7BB

East Sussex

Hove College of Business & Travel Studies (M) (I)   01273-731 352
Medina House, 41 Medina Villas
Hove, East Sussex BN3 2RP

•*Hove College specialises in intensive training programmes for graduates and mature students who need to gain commercial skills. Specialist options are available for those interest in Personnel, the Media and European Business.*

OFFICE SKILLS

Essex

Chelmsford College (L) (I) (Md)　　　　　　01245-265 611
Moulsham Street, Chelmsford, Essex EM2 0JQ

Harlow College (L) (I)　　　　　　　　　　01279-868 000
College Square, The High, Harlow, Essex CM20 7LT

Havering College of Further and Higher Education　01708-455 011
(L) (Md)
Ardleigh Green Road, Hornchurch, Essex RM11 2LL

Glamorgan

Bridgend College (L) (Md)　　　　　　　　01656-766 588
Cowbridge Road, Bridgend,　　　　　　*www.bridgend.ac.uk*
Mid-Glamorgan CF48 1AR

Merthyr Tydfil F.E. College (L) (Md)　　　01685-726 020
Ynysfach, Merthyr Tydfil,　　　　　　　*www.merthyr.ac.uk*
Mid-Glamorgan CF48 1AR

Gloucestershire

Gloucestershire College of Arts & Technology (L) (I)　01242-532106
Fairview Annexe, Fairview Road　　　　*www.gloscat.demon.co.uk*
Cheltenham, Glos GL52 2EN

•*GLOSCAT, Cheltenham, offers an intensive one-year RSA 'Higher Diploma in Administrative Procedures' course, plus IT skills to Stage III, with Shorthand and Audio. Ring 01242-532106 for information.*

Greater Manchester

City College Manchester (L) (I) (Md)　　　0161-957 1790
Barlow Moor Road, West Didsbury　　*www.manchester-city-coll.ac.uk*
Manchester M20 2PQ

Hopwood Hall College (L) (Md)　　　　　0161-643 7560
Rochedale Road, Middleton, Gtr Manchester M24 6XH

Greenock

James Watt College (L) (Md)　　　　　　01475-724 433
Finnart Street, Greenock, Scotland PA16 8HF　*www.jameswatt.ac.uk*

Gwynedd

Coleg Menai (L) (I) (Md)　　　　　　　　01248-370 125
Ffriddoedd Road, Bangor, Gwynedd LL51 2TP

Hampshire

Cricklade College (L) (Md)　　　　　　　01264-363 311
Charlton Road, Andover, Hants SP10 1EJ　　*www.cricklade.ac.uk*

OFFICE SKILLS

Highbury College (L) (Md)   01705-383 131
Dovercourt Road, Cosham, Portsmouth, Hants PO6 2SA

Hertfordshire
Hertford Regional College (L) (Md)   01992-466 451
Broxbourne Centre, Turnford, Herts EN10 6AE   *www.hertreg.ac.uk*

St Albans Office Training (S) (I)   01727-860 195
20 London Road, St Albans, Herts AL1 1NG

Kent
Bexley College (L) (Md)   01322-404 190
Tower Road, Belvedere, Kent DA17 6JA

•*Courses commence September and February and cover skills requried for text processing, word processing, database and spreadsheet examinations.*

Canterbury College (L) (I) (Md)   01227-811 111
New Dover Road, Canterbury, Kent CT1 3AJ   *www.cant-col.ac.uk*

Mid Kent College (L) (I) (Md)   01634-402 020
Horsted Centre, Maidstone Road, Chatham, Kent ME5 9UQ

Lancashire
Lancaster & Morecambe College (L) (I) (Md)   01524-66215
Morecambe Road, Lancaster   *www.ednet.lancs.ac.uk*
Lancashire LA1 2TY

Leicestershire
Leicester South Fields College (L) (Md)   0116-224 2200
Aylestone Campus, Aylestone Road   *www.lsfc.ac.uk*
Leicester LE2 7LW

Lincolnshire
Boston College (L) (Md)   01205-365 701
Skirbeck Road, Boston, Lincs PE21 6JF   *www.boston.ac.uk*

Grantham College (L) (Md)   01476-400 200
Stonebridge Rd, Grantham   *www.cityscape.co.uk/users/cb08/index/html*
Lincs NG31 9AP

North Lincs College (L) (I) (Md)   01522-876 000
Monks Road, Lincoln, Lincs LN2 5HQ   *www.nlincs-coll.ac.uk*

Liverpool
Liverpool Community College (L) (I)   0151-252 1515
Old Swan Centre, Broadgreen Road, Liverpool L13 5SQ

•*Intensive Skills course in word processing, information processing and DTP which will help you to present assignments whilst at university. It will also*

OFFICE SKILLS

make you more 'marketable' when looking for employment. Courses are free to students doing more than 13 hours per week.

Middlesex

Greenhill College (L) (Md)   0181-869 8689
Lowlands Road, Harrow, Middlesex HA1 3AQ   *www.greenhill.ac.uk*

Richmond Adult College (L) (I) (Md)   0181-891 5907
Clifden Road Centre, Twickenham, Middlesex TW1 4LT

Weald College (L) (Md)   0181-420 8888
Brookshill, Harrow Weald, Middlesex HA3 0EA   *www.weald.ac.uk*

Northampton College (L) (I) (Md)   01604-734 567
Booth Lane, Northampton   *www.northampton-college.org.uk*
Northamptonshire NN3 3RF

Norfolk

Norfolk College (L) (I) (Md)   01553-761 144
Tennyson Avenue, King's Lynn, Norfolk PE30 2QW
•*Why not come to Norfolk College? We have an excellent Business Centre providing high quality training in all aspects of administration.*

Oxfordshire

Oxford and County Business College (S) (I)   01865-310 100
34 St Giles, Oxford, Oxon OX1 3LH   *www.oxfordandcounty.demon.co.uk*

Oxford Business College (M) (I) (Md)   01865-791 908
15 King Edward Street, Oxford,   *www.oxfordbusinesscoll.co.uk*
Oxon OX1 4HT

St Aldates College (L) (I) (Md)   01865-240 963
Rose Place, Oxford,Oxon OX1 1SB

West Oxfordshire College (L) (I) (Md)   01993-703 464
Holloway Rd, Witney, Oxon OX8 7EE *www.osfe.ac.uk/witney/home/htm*

Pembrokeshire

Pembrokeshire College (L) (I) (Md)   01437-765 247
Haverfordwest, Pembrokeshire SA61 1SZ

Shropshire

North Shropshire College (L) (Md)   01691-653 067
College Road, Oswestry, Shropshire SY11 2SA

Somerset

Bridgewater College (L) (I) (Md)   01278-455 464
Bath Road, Bridgewater *www.rmplc.co.uk/edweb/sites/fosterd/index.html*
Somerset TA6 4VS

OFFICE SKILLS

Staffordshire

Burton College (L) (I) (Md)   01283-545 401
Lichfield Street, Burton upon Trent, Staffs DE14 3BL

•*Burton College can help you acquire skills in Business Applications of Information Technology: Spreadsheets, Graphics, Databases and Word Processing on an intensive or modular basis. We also offer full time, one year courses for Senior Administrators/Secretaries. Excellent exam results and accommodation.*

Cannock Chase Technical College (L) (Md)   01543-462 200
The Green, Cannock, Staffs WS11 1UE

Newcastle under Lyme College (L) (I)   01782-715 111
Liverpool Road, Newcastle-u-Lyme, Staffs ST5 2DF

Staffordshire College (L) (Md)   01785-223 800
Earls Street, Stafford, Staffs ST16 2QR

Stirlingshire

Falkirk College (L) (I) (Md)   01324-403 000
Grangemouth Road, Falkirk, Stirlingshire FK2 9AD

Suffolk

Otley College (L) (I) (Md)   01473-785 543
Otley, Ipswich, Suffolk IP6 9EY   *www.otley.ac.uk*

Lowestoft College (L) (Md)   01502-583 521
St Peter's Street, Lowestoft, Suffolk NR32 2NB

Surrey

Carshalton College (L) (I) (Md)   0181-770 6800
Nightingale Road, Carshalton Surrey SM5 2EJ

Croydon College (L) (I) (Md)   0181-686 5700
Fairfield, Croydon, Surrey CR9 1DX

East Surrey College (L) (I) (Md)   01737-772 611
Gatton Point, Claremont Road, Redhill, Surrey GU1 3UL

Merton College (L) (Md)   0181-640 3001
Morden Park, London Road, Morden, Surrey SM4 5QX

Tyne & Wear

City of Sunderland College (L) (Md)   0191-511 6000
Success Road, Philadelphia, Houghton-le-Spring
Tyne & Wear DH4 4TL

Newcastle College (L) (I)   0191-200 4000
Rye Hill Campus, Scotswood Road   *www.ncl-coll.ac.uk*
Newcastle upon Tyne NE4

OFFICE SKILLS

Warwickshire
Warickshire College (L) (I)   01926-318 000
Warwick New Road, Leamington Spa   *www.rmplc.co.uk/warkscol*
Warwickshire CU32 5JE

West Midlands
Sutton Coldfield College   0121-355 5671
Lichfield Road, Sutton Coldfield   *www.sutcol.ac.uk*
West Midlands B74 2NW

West Sussex
Crawley College (L) (I)   01293-442 400
College Road, Crawley,   *www.rmplc.co.uk/eduweb/sites/crawcol*
West Sussex RH10 1NR

Wiltshire
Trowbridge College (L) (Md)   01225-766 241
College Road, Trowbridge, Wilts BA14 0ES

Worcestershire
Worcester College of Technology (L) (Md)   01709-725 555
Deansway, Worcester WR1 2JF

Yorkshire
Barnsley College (L) (I)   01226-730 191
Church Street, Barnsley, South YorkS S70 2AX   *www.barnsley.ac.uk*

•*European Executive Secretary — One year programme includes training in European Secretarial Skills. Work placement offered at home / abroad.*

Dearne Valley College (L) (I) (Md)   01709-513 333
Manvers Park, Wath-upon-Dearne, Rotherham
South Yorkshire S63 7EW

Doncaster College (L) (Md)   01302-553 553
Waterdale, Doncaster, South Yorks DN1 3EX

Hull College (L) (Md)   01482-329 943
Queen's Gardens, Hull, East Yorks HU1 3DG

Park Lane College (L) (Md)   0113-216 2000
Park Lane, Leeds, Yorks LS3 1AA

Selby College (L) (I) (Md)   01757-211000
Abbott's Road, Selby, N. Yorks Y08 8AT

Civilisation

5

Britain now has a concrete umbilical cord that ties it to continental Europe. Many believe that neither to speak continental European languages nor understand our European background is to live in an intellectual wasteland. Here we list language courses both at home and overseas, plus cultural events in England and overseas cultural courses which don't involve learning languages. CHAPTER 6: OTHER EXTRAS gives information on other courses you might like to fit in — useful, hedonistic or otherwise. If you need to work first, you can turn straight to CHAPTER 7: WORK UK.

Essential extras

You may be committing yourself to a four-year course if you are going to university to read for a language degree. If you are doing, say, European studies, French, German or Italian, one year of your course will probably be spent at a foreign university or on a teaching attachment. Exposure to the language before you start at university will make the first year easier, even if you do not take formal tuition. For those with only a basic knowledge of another language, the ability to make better use of it is just as important. The gap year is an ideal time to do it.

LANGUAGES

If you applied to do a language degree but did not make the A-Level grade demanded, an autumn course before a spring retake may be possible. Or you could go on a course later and gamble on a successful resit in June.

Useful for your degree and your career

Languages add to other subjects. It is hard to find a history of art degree, for example, that does not cover the Italian renaissance. Steeping your art history in Italian or your Italian in art makes the experience richer. Almost any language course in a university city in Europe will immerse you in local culture, history, geography, religion, customs and current affairs — as well as good food and wine.

No language at A-Level?

You have forgotten most of the French you learned for GCSE. You can ask for a *bière*, but that is about as far as it goes. So what? English is irrevocably established as the language of international business, finance, technology and even of diplomacy: conversations between Thais and Poles are usually held in English. But speaking the local language does open extra doors: it is a cliché because it is true. Speaking another language is an advantage if you find yourself abroad, be it for work or play, and European languages don't just tie you to Europe. Spanish opens the way to South America, and French is still useful in many parts of Africa.

Learn in the UK?

Many European countries have their own language-teaching institutes (like the *Institut Français*) in cities outside their own borders. London-based ones do not necessarily teach French, German, Italian or Spanish A-Level syllabuses, however, so to cover A-Level texts you may need to stick to the better-known tutorial colleges. Check first. You can also study a wide range of languages at universities throughout Britain — many offer part-time or vacation courses. Ask at you local town hall's education office — or if you live in London, check the *Floodlight* or *Oncourse* magazines.

LANGUAGES

Or a course abroad?

You can try the foreign universities that are best known as international summer school centres or, for braver linguists, the less well-known. The first move is often to call the education or cultural section of the relevant foreign embassy in London and ask for information — but don't expect a rapid response. For those who would prefer to dip their toes in gently, there is the popular network of British Institutes abroad (see following pages).

LANGUAGES

There are also consultants who provide advice, such as Peter Bingley of the Cambridge Advisory Service. CAS represents permanent language schools in France, Germany, Italy, Spain, Switzerland, Mexico, and Ecuador, and a summer school programme in Japan (April to October). Peter Bingley can advise you on your choice and organise the placement for you (he earns a commission from the school). There are courses aimed at foreigners, lasting from two weeks to nine months. The prices for, say, a two-week course in Nerja, Spain (20 lessons a week) is about £530, including half board. A four-week course in Madrid (24 lessons a week) costs about £850, including half board; and a month in Paris (25 lessons a week) is roughly £1,350 including tuition and half board. Other courses form C.A.S. include four weeks in Berlin: you can stay with a family in a self-catering flat where you have access to the kitchen and get 20 hours a week tutition at the language school for £995. Or Italy, where £923 gets you 20 lessons a week for four weeks in Siena. See advertisement on page 96.

Cambridge Advisory Service	Tel: 01223-264089
Rectory Lane, Kingston, Cambridge CB3 7NL	Fax: 01223-264089

You can also try CESA Languages Abroad, a family company which acts as an agent for language schools and individuals. It has selected schools in many countries in Europe and beyond (Japan for example), and can offer advice on the most appropriate one for you and organise your placement. The three-month course seems popular with gap-year students developing their language skills, although CESA also runs four-week crash courses. A two-week course in Nice (20 lessons of 45 minutes each week) should cost around £660 for tuition and half board. See advertisement on page 80.

CESA Languages Abroad	Tel: 01872-225 300
Western House, Malpas,	Fax: 01872-225 400
Truro, Cornwall TR1 1SQ	E-mail: *languages@cesa.demon.co.uk*

LANGUAGES

European Community programmes

Information on European Community action programmes for education and training is available from the Commission of the European Communities.

Commission of the European Communities   Tel: 0171-973 1992
Jean Monnet House, 8 Storey's Gate
London SW1P 3AT

Live with a foreign family

One way of learning another language is staying with a foreign family as an au pair or tutor (giving, say, English or music lessons to children) and going to part-time classes locally. (See CHAPTER 8: OVERSEAS PAID WORK, for more details on au pair work.)

Plenty of agencies are happy to organise this for you. One of them, En Famille Overseas, can arrange for you to stay with a family in France, Germany, Italy or Spain as a paying guest. You can attend a suitable language course nearby, or have private coaching from your hostess. Costs are around £200-270 a week for board and lodging. Tuition costs are extra (around £13 an hour is typical). Various types of stay are available including summer courses and Easter courses. En Famille usually needs about a month's notice to fix it up.

Eurolingua Institute offers several different types of course. One option is an individual 'homestay', available in France, Italy, Germany, Spain (and the Canary Islands), Russia and the Ukraine, South America, Sweden, Norway, Hungary, Austria, Holland, Israel, Taiwan and Japan. This involves staying in the home of a school or university tutor for one to four weeks. During this time you receive one-on-one lessons with your tutor at home, doing a course designed specifically for you, for 15-20 hours a week. It is possible to arrange such stays at short notice: sometimes as little as a week if you are prepared to be flexible about your exact destination, and a month is normally enough to get you where you want. These courses are available throughout the year, and sample costs are £1,195 for a two-week course, 15 hours a week tutoring, or £2,635 for a four-week course with 20 hours a week tutoring. Prices include full board and some excursions, but not your travel costs to get there.

Join a group course

Another choice offered by Eurolingua Institute is a group course. These are usually available in the same countries as the individual courses, but you learn in a group of international students, all in the same boat as you, at a language school. (There's a test to determine your level when you arrive.) Courses last up to 12 weeks, but are often shorter. The minimum length is two weeks, and it costs £150 a week, with discounts after five weeks.

One-on-one lessons are also available. You pay for your travel. Eurolingua arranges stays with local families (there's a flat fee of £45 for this) and you then pay your family directly; usually about £15 a day for half board (slightly different in Spain as the main meal is taken at midday). Courses begin every week (every month for absolute beginners' courses), so very little notice is needed. The courses run all year except over Christmas and there are special excursion-based programmes in the summer.

Find a work placement

The third option is a work placement. Through Eurolingua these are only on offer in Germany (mainly Berlin), but plans are under way to begin a programme in France. For a £300 fee, Eurolingua will organise a work placement with a German company, and types of work include marketing, computing and social work. The pay's not much to write home about and varies by company. Placements typically last 8-12 weeks. There is a selection interview by your prospective employer and proficiency in German helps. All candidates have to attend German courses for at least four weeks when they begin working, and possibly for longer, depending on progress. Again, you pay for your own accommodation and travel, although Eurolingua can help you to find suitable accommodation.

Interspeak organises work placements in France (as well as

LANGUAGES

Germany, Italy and Spain) for varying lengths of time. The shorter placements come as a package, £299 for one week, or £499 for two, including half board and lodging with a host family, but not travel. For longer placements (up to six months) there is a flat fee of £250 for arranging the placement. Interspeak will also arrange a family for you to stay with, at a cost of £130 a week, although you can make your own arrangements if you prefer. The variety of placement jobs is wide, from camp assistants and vets to work with Internet companies and a company which organises music events (including the Spice Girls' European Tour — sorry, too late). The pay is usually little or nothing, but people working on commission sometimes make a tidy profit. Around a month's notice is needed; less in some cases such as Nice, a very popular destination. In Nice Interspeak also runs a language class (£459 per week, 15 hours' class plus five hours language lab work, full board and lodging) which can be done on its own or before a placement.

En Famille Overseas   Tel: 01903-883 266
Old Stables, 60b Maltravers Street,   Fax: 01903-883 582
Arundel, West Sussex BN18 9BG

Eurolingua Institute   Tel/Fax: (00 33 4) 67 15 04 73
Havre St Pierre, 265 Allée du Nouveau Monde
34000 Montpellier, France   Web: *www.eurolingua.com*

Eurolingua House, 61 Bollin Drive   Tel/Fax: 0161-972 0225
Altrincham WA14 5QW

Interspeak   Tel: 01555-894 219
The Coach House, Blackwood   Fax: 01555-894-954
Lanark ML11 0JG   Web: *www.interspeak.mcmail.com*

•*Turn to* CHAPTER 7: WORK UK *and* CHAPTER 8: OVERSEAS VACATION WORK *for details of au pair work, and also for details of TEFL (Teaching English as a Foreign Language) courses.*

French

There is a busy French community in London, a large French Lycée, and more than one teaching institute run by French nationals. So French is one language with a life of its own in Britain. Thousands of students pass through the *Institut Français* each year (the official French government centre of language and culture in London). Courses are mainly in the evening and for working people, but that need not put you off. The *Institut* will happily send you their excellent free leaflet detailing lots of courses. Examples: art and literature, cinema and society, French for business, the news in French. Fifteen to a class. Sadly you will have missed the *Special World Cup 98* course and the one for hopeful lovers, *Parlez-lui d'amour*, was broken off long ago. (Surely not undersubscribed?) At Easter it runs a one-week crash course which costs £185 (you get a £15 discount for applying 14 days before the start of your course).

Another well-known centre in London is the *Alliance Française*, a non-profit-making organisation funded by a trust. There is a network of *Alliances* in more than 130 countries, but the British-based one does not deal with applications to others. However, you can look at the *Alliance Française* Website which has info on *Alliances* everywhere. Of the courses run by the London *Alliance* a popular one with younger people is the four-week intensive course which begins each month, with 60 hours of tuition in the month (three hours a day, Monday to Friday) at £300 (1998). The classrooms are bright and the European students are friendly. According to the manager of the *Alliance Française de Londres* many students, having completed these courses, go on to France to work in a chalet or as an au pair.

Then there are the places to learn French in France. A booklet with comprehensive information on all language courses in France is available from the embassy: *Cours de Français Langue Etrangère* (in French). It is all-embracing (from beginners through to intermediate and advanced) and very useful. As with all embassies, it will not arrange things for you: it just has the information.

LANGUAGES

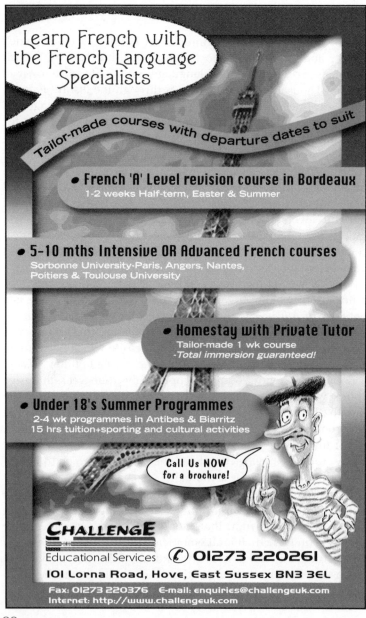

LANGUAGES

The British Institute in Paris is popular with English-speaking students. It does not run a specific gap-year course, but there are courses available covering grammar, translation, and French literature and civilisation which last 10 weeks, with between two and eight hours teaching per week. Course costs depend on the value of the pound, but start at around £170 for the two-hours-a week course, going up to £680 for the eight-hour course.

In the next category are local private language schools. CERAN runs intensive residential language programmes at various places in France, Belgium (also covering German, Japanese and Dutch), Spain, Japan (Osaka, in summer) and the US. There is a *baccalauréat* class (ages 17 and 18) suitable for gap-year students (classes are aimed at those preparing for A-levels or university). All its schools are mixed ages (usually minimum 19), and courses generally last two weeks, although you can just do one. Tuition is quite intense (66 hours of 'total immersion' per week) including about eight teaching periods a day and other activities conducted in the target language. The cost is around £800 per week, including full board and accomodation at the CERAN centre. Courses begin every week and run throughout the year, except for the course in France which only runs in the summer.

Challenge Educational Services organises language courses in collaboration with several French universities, as well as a private German language school in Berlin. A full academic year, semester or summer course is offered at the universities of the Sorbonne, Angers, Nantes, Poitiers, and Toulouse. Prices range from £855 for a three-week summer university programme at the University of Poitiers (18 hours a week) to £4,495 for a full academic year at the same university, including tuition and half board residential accommodation; staying with a family costs £6,560. One semester (1 October to 31 January) at the Sorbonne in Paris costs £4,890 (21.5 hours a week maximum) and summer courses there run for about four weeks at £1,415. Similar prices for Germany.

Finally, for those who like French but not the French *(c'est vraiment possible?)* a possibility is *Vis-A-Vis,* who offer language courses in Montreal as well as various places in France and Belgium. Prices for Montreal start at £284 for a two-week course,

LANGUAGES

LANGUAGES

20 hours a week, tuition only, extra for accommodation; various options available including family stays. Enrolment fee extra.

Alliance Française de Londres
1 Dorset Square, London NW1 6PU
Tel: 0171-723 6439
Fax: 0171-224 9512
Web: *www.paris.alliancefrancaise.fr*

British Institute in Paris
11, rue de Constantine, Paris 75007
Tel: (00 33 1) 44 11 73 83
Fax: (00 33 1) 45 50 31 55

CERAN Lingua International S.A.
Avenue du Chateau, 16
B-4900 SPA, Belgium
Tel: (00 32) 87.79.11.22
Fax: (00 32) 87.79.11.88
Web: *www.ceran.com*

Challenge Educational Services
101 Lorna Road, Hove,
East Sussex BN3 3EL
Tel: 01273-22 02 61
Fax: 01273-22 03 76
Web: *www.challengeuk.com*

French Embassy
Language Centre
14 Cromwell Road, London SW7 2EL
Tel: 0171-838 2055
Fax: 0171-838 2088

Grenoble University
Centre Universitaire d'Etudes Françaises
BP 25, 38040 Grenoble Cedex 9
Tel: (00 33 4) 76.82.43.27
Fax: (00 33 4) 76.82.43.70
Web: *www.u-grenoble3.fr/stendhal*

Institut Français
Language Centre
14 Cromwell Place, London SW7 2JR
Tel: 0171-581 2701
Fax: 0171-581-2910

LANGUAGES

DIPLOMA AT THE SORBONNE

"I learnt about the language course while I prepared for A-level from a girl at school who had done it during her year out. I wrote to the Sorbonne for a prospectus and application form during the September after leaving school. I then sent the application form back with a copy of my A-level results. The Sorbonne has no entry requirements other than that you have passed the equivalent of the International Baccalauréat (A-level) and you are over 18 by the time you take up the place.

The course I took was quite intense. It ran from the beginning of February to the end of May solidly — bar a two-week vacation at Easter. We had about 20 to 25 hours of teaching per week. The people on the course were quite mixed, with many English-speaking students. However, partly because the course demands that you speak French constantly and partly because one of my main tutors was very weird (demanding absolute silence unless individuals were asked to speak) I did not make many friends on the course itself. At first, this was a problem. There is not much of a student life in Paris, and it can get very lonely if you do not have friends to experience it with.

After two miserable and lonely weeks, I met an English couple staying in the same quarter as me. Life started to really pick up — it is amazing how willingly you exchange telephone numbers with strange people simply because they speak your language and share your culture.

Accommodation can be a real problem. I was lucky because I found a place to stay through a friend. The university does provide lists, but this is really only for the brave since most lodgings owners need to interview you before offering a place. In practice, this means spending several weeks in grimy hostels before you find a decent place. Although I got a good A grade at A-level, I found that the quality of my French took a gigantic leap forward. The cost of the course was around £700. This sounds a lot, but in comparison to school fees or extra language coaching of this quality in the UK it's a bargain."

Helen Cartwright, Durham University, 1995

LANGUAGES

Université de Savoie   Tel: (00 33) 79 75 84 14
Institut Savoisien d'Etudes Françaises pour Etrangers
3 Rue de Martyrs de la Déportation   Fax: (00 33) 79 75 84 16
74940 Annecy le Vieux   Web: *www.univ-savoie.fr/isefe/*

La Sorbonne   Tel: (00 33 1) 40 46 22 11
1 rue Victor Cousin, 75005 Paris

Vis-A-Vis   Tel: 0181-786-8021
2-4 Stoneleigh Park Rd   Fax: 0181-786-8086
Epsom KT19 0QT, Surrey   Web: *www.teclata.es/visavis*

German

The same principles apply, though the German Embassy and German Academic Exchange Service would prefer you didn't call them first (they deal mainly with undergraduates). You could start with the *Goethe Institut*, probably the best-known international German language school network. It is a non-profit organisation funded by the Federal Republic of Germany, and it offers a wide variety of courses as well as having a lending library and multimedia centre. Courses in London cater for all levels and include a three-week intensive Easter course. Typical prices are £175 for three and a half hours a week for a 15-week semester.

The *Institut* will also happily send you information on studying in Germany, including the booklets 'Learn German in Germany' and 'Sommerkurse in Deutschland'. The former details courses run by the *Goethe* network in Germany, including some specifically for young people which include sport and leisure activities. The latter (produced by The German Academic Exchange Service, also funded by the German government), lists summer courses at German universities in language, literature, regional studies and music, but is for university students, although you moght be able to get in if you're about to go to university.

For work experience and exchange programmes, contact the Central Placement Office of the German employment service (*Zentralstelle für Arbeitsvermittlung*).

LANGUAGES

The Anglo-Austrian Society (AAS) acts as an agent for German language schools in Austria (Vienna, Kitzbühel, Graz, Melk and Haindorf) and organises occasional language courses in Britain. The first option it recommends for gap-year students is a summer school at Vienna University for (July, August or September). This costs £744 for four weeks, which including flights and accommodation but not meals.

Another option is to to study at the language school in Vienna. This programme consists of either a four- or 12-week language course followed by a job placement. The AAS finds the job for you and accommodation will be found and paid for by the company employing you. However, you're unlikely to get paid unless your German is pretty hot. Costs are around £1,000 for the four-week language course or around £2,500 for the 12-week option. On top of this the AAS charges a £300 fee for arranging the placement. You need to have a good German to start the course (a good A-Level grade), and for those who are weaker the 12-week option is advised. Jobs include many in the tourist industry and ski resorts, hotel work and some office work.

German Embassy (ask for Cultural Department)
23 Belgrave Square, London SW1X APZ   Tel: 0171-824 1570

German Academic Exchange Service   Tel: 0171-235 1736
34 Belgrave Square, London SW1X 8QB   Fax: 0171-235 9602
                                             Web: *www.daad.de*

LANGUAGES

Goethe Institut   Tel: 0171-411 3451
50 Princes Gate, Exhibition Road   Fax: 0171-594 0210
London, SW7 2PH   Web: *www.goethe.de/gr/lon/enindex.htm*
(Also regional ofices in Manchester, Glasgow and York)

Anglo-Austrian Society   Tel: 0171-222 0366
46 Queen Anne's Gate, London SW1H 9AU   Fax: 0171-233 0293

Intuition Languages   Tel: 0171-409 2252
International House, 106 Piccadilly   Fax: 0171-491 8147
London W1V 9FL

Zentralstelle für Arbeitsvermittlung   Tel: 00 49 69 71111
Feuerbachstrasse 42-46
60325 Frankfurt-am-Main

Italian

There are well-tested choices for those who want to study in Florence, Venice or Rome, mixing Italian with other subjects. Returners recommend Perugia or Florence among universities, or international schools like the *Dante Alighieri*, for making real language progress.

The British Institute in Florence is good for those who prefer to be in mainly Anglo-Saxon company and learn extra subjects. Italian language courses of various lengths and standards are offered (including an Easter A-Level review course) as well as cultural courses including History of Art, Opera, Italian Cooking and more. Courses generally last one to four weeks and prices range from £80 to £475 for tuition. A-Level Italian and History of Art courses are also available; these last a whole year and cost £1,850 and £1,950 respectively. The Institute can also help arrange accommodation. (See advertisement opposite.)

Fans of both Art History Abroad and the John Hall Pre-University Course praise their breadth. As they are not strictly language courses, however, but cultural ones, we have moved them to CHAPTER 6: OTHER EXTRAS this year.

In Florence the *Dante Alighieri* school puts on language and cultural courses of varying lengths. A two-week intensive language course (25 lessons a week) costs Lire 750,000 (around £250) and a

LANGUAGES

more relaxed four-week cultural course Lire 290,000 (about £100, with four lessons a week, so there's plenty of time to go sightseeing). Other schools include the Lorenzo de' Medici and the Leonardo da Vinci.

For those who would like to do some research in London first, the Italian Cultural Institute has a bookshelf brimming over with free leaflets on courses in Italy (courses other than languages are also here: Italian cookery, musical culture and fashion design for example). Unless you're specific the Italian lady in charge won't send them to you. They also produce a booklet (in Italian) listing lots of language schools in Italy which they will happily send you.

LANGUAGES

British Institute of Florence
Piazza Strozzi 2, 50123 F irenze, Italy

Tel: (00 39 55) 28 40 31
Fax: (00 39 55) 28 70 71
Web: *www.fol.it/british*

CLI Dante Alighieri
Via dei Bardi 12, 50125, Firenze

Tel: (00 39 55) 234 29 34
Fax: (00 39 55) 234 27 66
Web: *www.hyperborea.com/dante-alighieri/*

Italian Cultural Institute
39 Belgrave Square
London SW1X 8NX

Tel: 0171-235 1461
Fax: 0171-235 4618
Web: *www.martex.co.uk/italculturuk*

Istituto di Lingua e Cultura Italiana Michelangelo Tel: (00 39 55)240 975
Via Ghibellina 88
50122 Firenze

Fax:(00 39 55) 240 997
E-mail: *michelangelo@dada.it*

Leonardo da Vinci
Via Bufalini 3, 50122, Firenze

Tel: (00 39 55) 29 44 20
Fax:(00 39 55) 29 48 20
Web: *www.trident.nettuno.it/Mall/leonardo*

Lorenzo de' Medici
Via Faenza 43, 50123 Firenze

Tel: (00 39 55) 28 73 60
Fax: (00 39 55) 239 89 20
Web: *www.dada.it/ldm*

Spanish

Intuition Languages offers courses in Spain and Ecuador. In Spain, this involves studying at an international language school, mainly with group teaching, for courses ranging from one or two weeks to full semesters. A sample price is £1,500 for 12 weeks (tuition, half board, accommodation but not travel). The Ecuador school is popular, especially with people who want to travel afterwards in South America, as you can learn Spanish there before going on somewhere more exciting or dangerous. Depending on your competence, you can get to a high enough level in about four weeks to be fairly confident travelling. At £215 per week for full board and accommodation with a family and 25 hours of individual language teaching, it's good value, although getting there will cost a fair bit.

Spanish as a foreign language is available at more than 30 city universities. The *Universidad Pontificia de Salamanca* is popular, as are those of Madrid and San Sebastian. The Spanish Embassy will send information on studying in Spain (mainly universities).

LANGUAGES

If you're interested in studying in Britain, a good starting point is the *Instituto Cervantes* which is based in London. This is a Spanish government-funded centre for educational studies and cultural events in London. It runs A-level and GCSE standard courses on Saturday mornings (£130 and £90 a term respectively). There was no Easter revision course in 1998, but there may be in the future. There are also general language courses at four levels and four- and six- week intensive courses at three levels. Typical prices; £170 for 10 hours a week on a six-week course, or £175 for four hours a week for a 10-week term.

EF International Language Schools offer courses in Spanish in Spain, Ecuador and Costa Rica. Various options are available, but the most common is a year-long course (September to May/June) for any level from beginner to post A-Level and beyond. On this course you'll stay in one place for the whole time, but another option is to do a 36-week course. This is split into six six-week chunks so that you can move about within the EF network, studying more than one language if you like. Shorter courses are also available (starting at two weeks.) It's not supposed to be like school; there's more of an emphasis on meeting native speakers as a way of learning the language. Prices range from £490 for two weeks in Quito, Ecuador (tuition and half-board included but not flights) to £7,900 for a whole year in Munich. Short notice arrangements are possible, but three months notice is better. Some work placements available in Nice.

LANGUAGES

Canning House Education Department's publication is more useful than the embassy's one. Canning House is a centre which provides information for UK residents only, about Latin America, Portugal and Spain. It publishes a comprehensive list of universities and language centres offering language courses in these countries containing prices and dates (£3). Canning House also publishes various information leaflets, such as guides to employment and opportunities for young people in Latin America, Portugal or Spain (three leaflets). These include organisations and useful contacts for teaching posts, summer jobs, international voluntary workcamps and au pair work in each country. You can use the centre's library, with books in English, Spanish and Portuguese, to research your trip. Should you be even more intersested in matters Spanish, becoming a member of Canning House (£30 a year) gets you involved in all sorts of London-based Hispanic/Latin events (such as film, poetry readings and talks).

LANGUAGES

GALA (an organisation in Surrey) acts as an agent for private schools in Barcelona, Logroño (between Madrid and Pamplona), Madrid, Nerja, San Sebastian, Seville and Valencia. Courses range from two weeks to nine months: lowest cost is around £360 for two weeks with half-board accommodation in Seville (£1,780 for three months) and highest is for courses in Madrid.

The *Don Quijote* schools organise language courses in Barcelona, Granada, Malaga (all 18+) and Salamanca (16+). The shortest course is two weeks (four hours a day, five days a week for £317, accommodation is extra — a variety is available). Long courses run for 12-36 weeks. A certificate of attendance is awarded at the end provided you have attended 90 per cent of the lessons. Activities and excursions are organised for free time.

Canning House
2 Belgrave Square, London SW1X 8BJ
Tel: 0171-235 2303
Fax: 0171-838-9258

Don Quijote
2/4 Stoneleigh Park Road
Stoneleigh, Epsom
Surrey KT19 0QT
Tel: 0181-786 8081
Fax: 0181 786 8086
Web: *www.teclata.es/donquijote*

EF International Language Schools
Kensington Cloisters, 5 Kensington Church St
London W8 4LD
Tel: 0171-878-3550
Fax: 0171-795-6625

GALA
Woodcote House, 8 Leigh Lane
Farnham, Surrey GU9 8HP
Tel/Fax: 01252-715 319

Intuition Languages
International House
106 Piccadilly London W1V 9FL
Tel: 0171-409-2252
Fax: 0171-491-8147

Instituto Cervantes
102 Eaton Square
London SW1W 9AN
Admin Tel: 0171-235 0353
Library Tel: 0171-235 0324
Enrolment Tel: 0171-245 0621

Spanish Embassy Education Dept
20 Peel Street, London W8 7PD
Tel: 0171-727 2462
Fax: 0171-229 4965

SWEET, SOUR AND CHEESY

"I went to Beijing to a language school to learn Chinese. I was completely thrown in the deep end because nobody spoke any English whatsoever — all the other students there were from overseas and mainly from Indonesia, Japan, Korea and Thailand. They all spoke their own languages to each other and it was difficult to meet them properly. I did make really good friends with the Italians because they were Western so we understood each other a bit better. In class, Chinese was spoken the entire time. This meant it was extremely difficult at first, but my Chinese skills improved very quickly. We had 24 hours of work a week and quite a lot of homework. Because the Chinese teaching was so intense I think the course attracted quite a few geeks. On the whole the interaction with the Chinese and everyone speaking Chinese in the school was extremely rewarding. It was a really big bonding experience. In my spare time at weekends I saw a couple of English friends who were in Beijing. It is such a gorgeous city with loads to see and we had a laugh in some really cheesy clubs."
Clare McDowell, Bristol University, 1998

Chinese

The Council on International Educational Exchange (CIEE) fixes up combined language and cultural courses at Fudan University in Shanghai for all levels or language study at Peking University for students with some knowledge of Mandarin (summer course lasting eight weeks for around $5,800 or a 15-week term beginning in August or February at a price to be announced). Courses also run at National Chengchi University in Taipei, Taiwan or Nanjing University, China, for those with more knowledge of Mandarin (15-week terms as above at around $10,000 or a whole year at around $17, 000). Eurolingua (see page 84) also organises language courses, in Taiwan.

EF International (see opposite) may soon run courses in China, and The School of Oriental and African studies (see section on **Japanese**) runs courses in London in Mandarin or Cantonese, ranging from a one-week course to a full-year diploma.

LANGUAGES

Council on International Educational Exchange
52 Poland Street
London W1V 4JQ

Tel: 0171-478 2000
Web: *www.ciee.org*

Japanese

If you contact the Japanese Embassy it will send you a long list of
Japanese language courses in Britain. The embassy also has a
website with info on studying in Japan. The Cambridge
Advisory Service may also be able to help (see beginning of this
chapter). The embassy also has a big library which contains
material on learning Japanese, Japanese newspapers and *The
Japan Times*, which has information on jobs in Japan. The Japan
Centre in Piccadilly has an excellent bookshop and is a good
starting point for gathering information about Japan. You could
also try the School of Oriental and African Studies which offers
year-long courses in London (£185 per 10-week term, two hours
a week tuition) or intensive summer courses (£800 for four
weeks) for beginners or those continuing their studies.

If you're interested in studying Japanese (or English) in Japan,
CERAN (see under **French** for address) runs courses there. Prices
start at around £900 a week, (full board, lodging, tuition) and go
up depending on how much individual tuition you want to
recieve. Alternatively CESA (see beginning of this chapter) also
arrange language courses in Japan, as does Eurolingua.

LANGUAGES

Japanese Embassy
101-104 Piccadilly, London W1V 9FN

Tel: 0171-465 6500
Fax:0171-491-9347
Web: *www.aiej.or.jp*

Japan Centre
212 Piccadilly, London W1V 9LD

Tel: 0171-439 8035
Fax: 0171-287 1082

School of Oriental and African Studies
SOAS Language Centre, SOAS
University of London, Thornhaugh St
Russell Square, London WC1H 0XG

Tel: 0171-323-6384
Fax: 0171-637-7355

Russian

The Russian Language Experience in London offers a flexible approach to language learning, with a range of courses available: 'standard', 'accelerated' and 'private'. The classes run in the evenings and a term's 'standard' course (one evening a week) costs from £250. You can also be sent to Russia as it has partnerships with the Moscow and St Petersburg state universities. A course of any length from two weeks to a year can be arranged. Summer course start from £435 (excluding accommodation). (See advertisement opposite.)

EF International runs a two-week course in conjunction with the Plekhanor Academy which costs £630 half board. No previous knowledge of the language is required for any of the courses offered. Eurolingua also arranges Russian language courses, in Belarus, Russia and the Ukraine.

The Russian Language Experience
53-56 Great Sutton St
London EC1V ODE

Tel: 0171-608 3794
Fax 0171-608 3792
E-mail: *russian_language@compuserv.com*

English

The English Speaking Union was set up to promote understanding between nations. There is a scholarship scheme for students who would like to spend their gap year studying in a US high school for two to three terms or a Canadian school for three terms. Apply well ahead: the closing date for a January 1999 start (two terms) is the end of September 1998 and for September 1999

LANGUAGES

LANGUAGES

(three terms) it is the end of January 1999. Apply to the Awards Manager at the ESU.

Challenge Educational Services (see opposite) also offers an academic year in the USA. Everyone studies American History plus six or seven other subjects for either one semester or a whole year. This scheme would be particularly suited to sporty people — in the past, a student on the programme has been offered a sports scholarship at an American university. You stay with a host family, and the cost is £2,695 for a five-month semester or £3,150 for the ten-month year. Apply at least six months ahead, and be aware that the programme is only open to those aged under 18 and six months at the start of the programme. Also internships with organisations like stockbrokers Merrill Lynch and the National Oceanic and Atmospheric Administration (marine research).

CIEE (see under **Chinese** for contact details) offers a programme called 'Summer Study in the USA', which involves you living on campus and studying at either UCLA or UC Berkeley (both in sunny California) for 3-10 weeks There's a very wide range of courses at all levels, from film studies to politics, and it costs £265 a week, including tuition, accommodation and meals, but not travel. CIEE also runs a 'Study and Work Experience Programme' at the American University, Washington DC. This is aimed at undergraduates or above, lasts for a summer, a semester or a year, and involves you doing a course such as Journalism, Justice or Museum Studies and the Arts, including unpaid work experience (an 'internship') at big organisations like the Smithsonian Institution, congressional offices and embassies or ABC TV News. It costs around £290 a week.

You could get a different perspective by going to the American School in Switzerland (TASIS). Switzerland, legendary home of 1950s finishing schools where a girls' prospects could be truly finished off by teaching her how to spend someone else's millions, is now home to some more egalitarian institutions. TASIS offers a 'post-graduate year' (referring to the American high-school graduates who are 18). The curriculum is like a liberal arts course, but the emphasis is on 'making Europe a classroom'.

LANGUAGES

Visits are made to some of the cultural centres of Europe such as Paris, Prague and Barcelona (and London) learning as you go. About a third of the students are American, with the remainder coming from 37 different countries. A good place to get in with the rich set, as a year's fees are a cool $26,900.

English-Speaking Union (ESU) Tel: 0171-493 3328
Dartmouth House Fax: 0171-495 6108
37 Charles St London W1X 8AB E-mail: *ESU@mailbox.ulcc.ac.uk*

TASIS Tel: 01932-565- 252
Coldharbour Lane, Thorpe, Surrey TW20 8TE Fax: 01932-564-644
and at: E-mail: *ukadmissions@tasis.com*
CH 6926, Montagnola-Lugano, Switzerland

Languages as you travel?

The unserious way, but a good method on long journeys if you have a walkman. The place to go for language learning is Grant & Cutler, who stock a large variety of books and tapes for many many different languages, at all sorts of prices. W H Smith stocks a few book-and-tape language sets starting from beginner's level (and lots of stand-alone books). Your local library will probably have a good selection of materials — just make sure you give the books back before you head off to Mongolia. BBC Education produces courses for European languages (the Travelpacks series: £9.99 for a cassette and book set), plus some more unusual ones, for example Indonesian and Japanese. Stanfords, the traveller's pit-stop, specialises in books but has a few sets of cassettes too.

Orders c/o **BBC Languages** PO BOX 120 Tel: 01937 541001
Wetherby, West Yorkshire LS23 7EU
Web: *www.bbc.co.uk/education/languages*
Grant & Cutler Tel: 0171-734 2012
55 Great Marlborough Street Fax: 0171-734 9272
London W1V 2AY Web: *www.grant-c.demon.co.uk*

Stanford's Map & Travel Tel: 0171-836 1321
12-14 Long Acre, Covent Garden,London WC2E 9LP

6

Thrills, spills and frills

You can speak two languages fluently and tell the difference between Bernini, Bellini and Berlusconi. (For those who flunked this test when we published our first edition in 1992, Berlusconi moved from media magnate to prime minister of Italy in 1994 and by 1996 was opposition leader and a media magnate again. Then he was offical leader of the Forza Italia party and now he's going to jail for two years for tax offences). You can show your father how to computerise his multi-million pound sausage conglomerate. What is there left to do? This chapter is for those with even more time and money to spare.

Driving

Essential if you can afford the lessons — when did you last find your friend and driver under the table after a party clutching a bottle? Some students learn to drive at school and have a full licence before taking A-Levels, which can be a convenient way to do it. If you have not passed your test yet, a gap year gives you plenty of time.

The test comes in two parts, theory and practice, and you need to pass the theory test (a 40-minute test where you have to get 30 out of 35 multiple-choice questions right: fee £15) before you apply for the practical test (fee £32.75). You can start learning

OTHER EXTRAS

practical driving before you take the theory part, but to do that you need a provisional driving licence. You have two years in which to pass the practical test once you have passed the theory part. For the provisional driving licence you need to get a D1 application form from a post office and the provisional licence fee is £21. (You also need to check that you are insured for damage to yourself, other cars or other people, and if you are practising in the family car, your parents will have to add cover for you.)

Don't think about getting a friend to take the practical test for you: you have to turn up with photo ID. (When you finally pass your test you may also need a photo for your full driving licence, because new 'photocard' licences are being gradually introduced). The bad news is that the tests are tough and every time you fail, driving school and government coffers get replenished. What's more, a new driving test will be introduced in 1999 The good news is that once you pass your practical test, you can exchange your provisional licence for a full licence free of charge.

Some checking out is a good idea if the driving school is not a well-known name. You can make sure that it is registered with the Driving Standards Agency and the instructor is qualified. (Fully qualified instructors have a green hexagonal badge on the

OTHER EXTRAS

windscreen, trainee ones a pink one.) The AA (Automobile Association) and BSM charges can be used as a benchmark if you are trying other schools (see previous page). Prices are lower outside central London. It is worth knowing that a UK driving licence is valid in all other EU member states, though you may need to take additional proof of identity.

BSM Kensington   Tel: 0171-602 6272
269 Kensington High Street W8 6NA

Automobile Assocation   Tel: 0800-60 70 80
The Driving School, Fanum House
Bristol, BS1 5LY

Driving Licence Information   Tel: 01792-77 21 51

Driving Standards Agency   Tel: 01602-47 42 22

Cooking

Cookery (standard, ethnic, exotic) is likely to be well-represented at day or evening classes at local colleges of further education — you can check them out at your local library. Usually the fees are low (in London the range is £10-£75) but you have to pay for ingredients.

For those with money to spare, there is the panache of private cookery schools. Le Cordon Bleu and Leith's School of Food and Wine, two of the best-known in London, offer courses lasting from a week to a three-term year. Leith's four-week *Foundation Course* (£1,540.50) starts in mid July, and runs five days a week. Of the courses useful for chalet-people-to-be, the three-month

OTHER EXTRAS

OTHER EXTRAS

Beginner's Certificate in Food and Wine is the most popular (£3,300, September to December); the *Basic Certificate in Practical Cookery* (£1,500, full-time from August) includes the professional exam qualification required by some ski companies; and the brief *Chalet Cook Course*, designed for ski chalets covers high altitude cooking. Leith's also runs evening classes for beginners (£395) and intermediate/advanced (£400).

Le Cordon Bleu is more of a professionals' training ground. Courses range from the 'IFC' (*Introduction to French Cuisine*) to specialised courses in *boulangerie*, and *patisserie à la carte*. The IFC will set you back £3,380 for the 10-week course (three days a week) with 30 demonstrations and 29 practicals. More suitable for rich young foodies is the intensive five-week *Basic Cuisine* course at £3,380 (six days a week from 7 September to 9 October 1998), and *The Essentials Course* which is geared to gap-year students and runs for four weeks full-time: £1,700.

Le Cordon Bleu
114 Marylebone Lane,
London W1M 6HH

Freephone: 0800 980 3503
Tel: 0171-935 7621
Web: *www.cordonbleu.net*

Leith's School of Food & Wine
21 St Alban's Grove, London W8 5BP

Tel: 0171-229 0177
Fax: 0171-937 5257
Web: *www.leiths.com*

Outside London

London is an expensive place to live if you have no base there, so it is useful to know that there is no shortage of cookery courses in the country. Taking a cooking course could also help you find a job abroad. Working as a cook in ski resorts, on yachts in the Caribbean or in villas in Tuscany or the South of France not only allows you to see the world, but pays you while you see it.

John Childs, managing director of Tante Marie in Woking, says he has a number of gap-year students taking courses only so that they can go on to do the ski season. Tante Marie's one-term course is the most relevant here — a 12-week certificate course which starts in September, January and May. The course costs £3,300 (£2,541 if you claim the 23 per cent vocational training tax-relief for which all UK residents are eligible).

OTHER EXTRAS

For those who can go west, The Grange in Somerset offers an intensive residential cookery course. A popular student course is *The Essential Cookery Course*, which runs for four weeks, starting eight times a year. The cost is £1,990 (1999), which includes accommodation in twin-bedded rooms. The Grange also has a four-day chalet course where students can cook typical chalet-style menus and learn about running a chalet (£490).

Finally, if you fancy a completely different environment to cook in, you could try a cookery course with 'Babette' in Montpellier, France — contact Eurolingua (see CHAPTER 5: LANGUAGES) for details.

OTHER EXTRAS

Tante Marie   Tel: 01483-726 957
Woodham House, Carlton Road,   Fax: 01483-724 173
Woking, Surrey GU21 4HF
                    Web: *www.uk/courses.co.uk/html/colleges/tante.htm*

The Grange   Tel/Fax: 01373-836 579
Whatley, Frome, Somerset BA11 3JU
                    Web: *www.hi-media.co.uk/grange-cookery/*

Culture

Attracted to art? Interested in Italy? Captivated by civilisation? If the answer to any of the above is yes, you may be interested in doing a cultural course in Italy. One way of doing this is through Art History Abroad. This company offers a variety of courses of different lengths. The idea is that you study great art and architecture first hand. You are taught on site in groups of eight (overall party size 24) by experts in their field. There are two gap-year courses. The longer (only during a gap year) is in spring (late Jan-mid March). There is an initial week in London followed by five weeks in Rome, Florence and Venice, with shorter stays in Bologna and Siena. The shorter course (which can be done either during or after A-levels) is for two weeks during the summer and covers Rome, Florence and Venice. Also, if you're studying Art History for A-level, there is an Easter revision course lasting 7-10 days, or you might be able to persuade your school to organise a group trip, as AHA arrange these too. Costs are £3,400 for Easter, £1,500 for the summer or £750-1050 for the Easter revision course. Half-term courses available in autumn/early summer.

Fans of the John Hall Pre-University Course, a cultural rather than a language course, praise its breadth: a seven-week course (plus two optional extra weeks) is based in Venice, and each January to March students bathe in lectures on Italian history, art, architecture and music, and practise life drawing and photography; Italian language lessons extra. Sadly no psychiatrist in the crew now. Dorothea in George Eliot's *Middlemarch* would have enjoyed it much more than her tour with Casaubon. But it is expensive at £4,365 for the time in Venice and an introductory

OTHER EXTRAS

week in London. Critics say the hotels chosen could be less scruffy and the outward train journey takes too long. Extra for extensions to Florence and Rome.

Skiing

You don't have to take a cooking course to get to the ski slopes, of course. There is bar work and casual work for non-cooks, and the chance to work as a ski guide for the more advanced. The British Association of Ski Instructors (BASI) can help you out if you are already an experienced skier. They run a course for potential instructors from February to April costing £3,600. The training includes a foundation course and shadowing ski instructors in Andorra. At the end there is an assessment and if you are successful, you gain an instructor's licence. The book that tells you everything you need to know on this subject is *Working in Ski Resorts: Europe & North America*, by Victoria Pybus, from Vacation Work Publications in Oxford (£8.95). See also CHAPTER 8: VACATION WORK.

BASI (British Association of Ski Instructors)　　Tel: 01479-861 717
Glenmore, Aviemore　　Fax: 01479-861 718
Invernesshire PH22 1QU　　Web: *www.basi.org.uk*

Tennis

If you think you can sell your sports skills, tennis coaching is one way to do it. The Lawn Tennis Association (LTA) runs coaching courses with three levels of qualification: basic, elementary and professional. To be a coach you need the elementary qualification. One job often leads to further offers. See CHAPTER 8: OVERSEAS VACATION WORK.

Lawn Tennis Association　　Tel: 0171-381 7000
(National Training and Coaching Dept)
The Queen's Club　　Fax: 0171-381 0033
West Kensington, London W14 9EG

OTHER EXTRAS

Mountaineering

For those hoping to reach dizzy heights the national mountain schools run courses for beginners.

National Mountaineering Centre (min. age 16) Tel: 01690-720 214
Plas-y-Brenin, Capel Curig Fax: 01690-720 394
Bettws-y-Coed, Gwynedd LL24 OET
(Rock-climbing: Five-day courses: £365, Weekend courses: £165)

British Mountaineering Council Tel: 0161-445 4747
177-179 Burton Road, West Didsbury Fax: 0161-445 4500
Manchester M20 2BB Web: *www.thebmc.co.uk*

Archaeology

Not quite fit enough to climb Everest? If you're more interested in historical remains, you can try to get on an archaeological dig. The best starting point is to get hold of a magazine called *British Archaeology*, which comes out ten times a year. Alternate editions contain *CBA Briefing*, a supplement with information about events and courses, as well as digs where volunteers are needed.

Council for British Archaeology Tel: 01904-671 417
Bowes Morrell House, 111 Walmgate Fax: 01904-671384
York YO1 2UA Web: *www.britarch.ac.uk/cba/*

DIZZY HEIGHTS

Some tips from mountaineering journalists:
"Your climbing wall is a good place to meet like-minded mountaineers." Rebecca Stephens, who became the first British woman to climb Mount Everest, 1993

"It's worth joining the British Mountaineering Council — it's very cheap and has reciprocal rights which means you can use Alpine huts in other countries. Always wear your climbing boots when you travel, because you can't replace those if they get lost; and check the small print in your insurance policy to make sure it covers helicopter rescue."
Jules Stewart (who climbs active volcanos like Cotopaxi) 1995

The Museum of London (Tel: 0171-600 3699) runs four archaeology courses from September to March, one evening a week (with a break at Christmas and Easter). The prices are £131 (£66 concessions) for the whole course. They also have study days; to find out whatgoing on, phone the Interpretation Unit. See also CHAPTER 8 OVERSEAS VOLUNTARY WORK.

Creative?

Taking a degree in Maths does not preclude you from acting Hamlet. If you have ability and some experience in the performing arts (at school but preferably outside as well), it is worth phoning drama or music colleges, theatre companies, orchestras and choruses to find out about courses or unpaid work.

RADA (the Royal Academy of Dramatic Art), for example, runs four-week and eight-week summer school classes at £1,700 and £2,650 respectively and a more affordable two-week design course costing £500. If you are happy to spend a year among the greasepaint sticks in Stratford, Stratford-upon-Avon College runs a course aimed at people who have done Theatre Studies for A-level; the drama equivalent of an art foundation course. Ten to 16 people take this year-long course for about £3,500

For singers, the BBC Symphony Chorus and other choruses audition regularly for places: there is not usually any pay for singing, but it is great fun and brings an occasional recording fee.

For painters and designers, courses range from evening classes at local colleges to a full one-year foundation course at art schools like Camberwell or Chelsea — and some 300 people each year go to summer schools at the Slade School of Fine Art (see advertisement overleaf). Some of them discover talent, some don't. The new Richmond School of Art offers a variety of summer courses, some of which involve going into Kew Gardens and drawing along the river.

For musicians, The London Music School is a contemporary music school that runs a one-year course and a summer course, teaching vocals, bass, guitar and drums. Bands like *Placebo* and *Morcheeba* metamorphosed here.

OTHER EXTRAS

The Slade Summer School

29 June - 4 September 1998
Short Courses in Fine Art

A Ten week intensive Foundation Course in Fine Art
plus .. Drawing, Painting, Sculpture, Printmaking and
Poetry courses, all taught be the regular Slade staff

Further details: Fiona Taylor-White
The Slade School of Fine Art
UCL Gower Street London WC1

Tel: 0171 380 7772 Fax: 0171 380 7801
E-Mail: slade.summer@ucl.ac.uk

The Slade Summer School

Blake College
162 New Cavendish St, London W1M 7FJ
Tel: 0171-636 0658
Fax: 0171-436 0049

Camberwell College of Arts
Peckham Road, London SE5 8UF
Tel: 0171-514 6300

Central Saint Martins
Southampton Row, London WC1
Tel: 0171-514 7015
Web: *www.csm-li.co.uk*

Chelsea College of Art and Design
Manresa Road, London SW3 6LS
Tel: 0171-514 7750
Fax: 0171-514 7777

London Music School
131 Wapping High St, London E1 9NQ
Tel: 0171-265-0284
Web: *www.tlms.co.uk*

Royal Academy of Dramatic Art
62 Gower Street, London WC1 6ED
Prospectus: 0171-436 1458
Tel: 0171-636 7076

Slade School of Fine Art (Summer School)
University College, Gower St,
London WC1E 6BT
Tel: 0171-380 7772
Fax: 0171-380 7801
Web: *www.ucl.ac.uk/slade/*

Stratford-upon-Avon College
Stratford-upon-Avon CV37 9QR
Tel: 01789-266245
Fax: 01789-267524

Wimbledon School of Art
Merton Hall Road, London SW19 3QA
Tel: 0181 540 0231
Fax: 0181-543 1750

Useful reading

Floodlight (Full-time) Annual directory of full-time courses in London which lists all courses and colleges; *Floodlight (Part-time)*; *Floodlight (Summertime)*; Also *Oncourse* magazine. Web: *www.uk courses.co.uk*

Paid and voluntary work in the UK

This chapter deals with work in the UK and is divided into three parts. First, we give general advice for those who want it (apologies to those who think it's all obvious, but readers abroad like to have it clearly explained). Those who know the ropes can move straight to the subsections on work opportunities. The first — BIG BUSINESS — gives gap-year work information from Britain's biggest companies. The second and third sections briefly tackle VOLUNTARY WORK and VACATION WORK in the UK.

Money

Times are getting tougher now that students will have to pay tuition fees to study for a degree. Unless your parents have lots of loot, they cannot be expected to pay for a year off as well as three to four years at university.

It's easy to make the mistake of thinking you will be able to pick up jobs as you travel to pay for your gap year. By mid-1998 the UK economy looked as if it was tipping into recession again after the boom of the mid-1990s, but the situation in Asia was worse. That's one of many reasons why many gap-year students

WORK UK

GRADUATE EMPLOYMENT PROSPECTS IMPROVE

Roly Cockman, chief executive of the Association of Graduate Recruiters, says that 280 of its 500 members indicated in a survey that they wanted to recruit 18 per cent more graduates (17,058 jobs) in 1997 than in 1996 — at a higher median starting salary of £16,000.

Of the students who graduate each year, he adds, only 40 per cent look for work straight away. The rest are mature students or twenty-somethings who want to travel or do other things before they commit themselves to a career. With 87 applications for each vacancy in 1996, ditherers probably lost out.

prefer to apply for places on organised voluntary work schemes overseas. (See CHAPTER 8 OVERSEAS VOLUNTARY WORK). Another way to fund your gap-year travel is to look for an employer that will place you on its gap-year work scheme and pay you enough for travel afterwards (see BIG BUSINESS section).

One way to plan a gap year is to set a target to finance something you want to do — like earning £2,000 in different jobs soon after leaving school to pay for a place on an overseas project and a few months' travel. A further target could be to earn £1,000 at the end of a gap year towards university expenses. It's useful to remember when working out a timetable that some casual work is seasonal: there are more jobs in stores at Christmas, for example, and on farms in the summer. Unless you know that you have a place abroad on a sponsored project or a concrete job offer overseas, however, it is a good idea to concentrate on earning as much money as you can first in the UK.

But those determined to work abroad can usually find it. You can plan ahead, using overseas contacts, so that a job is waiting for you when you arrive (check first with the relevant embassy to find out if a working visa is required). Or you can just get travelling and gamble on finding work when you get there.

School careers advisers are usually happy to advise and will have a mine of information to hand. There should be relevant books at school, at local public libraries and at more than 100

SCREWING IT UP

"Through an employment agency I got a job in a factory that made speakers. The first day was a nightmare. I was putting screws into speaker brackets and the work was mindnumbingly boring. I had to try to switch off completely and basically became a zombie. I was really bad at it (especially compared with the workers who had been there for 26 years) and cocked several up, but being an optimist I thought that the next day would be better. By the second day my imagination had run out of things to do. I had the seemingly point-less task of putting speaker coils on the conveyor belt. It turned out nobody had told me I was also supposed to be checking the coils as I put them on the conveyor belt. Loads of faulty ones had gone through the whole system, causing a batch reject. Fifteen hundred speaker coils had to be thrown away."

Simon Croker (in his second gap year, doing retakes), 1998

---

local authority careers offices — these act as centres for advice and training as well as employment agencies. Useful books include: *The Directory of Jobs and Careers Abroad*, Jonathan Packer (£10), *The Directory of Work and Study in Developing Countries* (£8.99) by Toby Milner, *Summer Jobs Abroad* (£7.99) by David Woodworth, all published by Vacation Work; and *How to Get a Job Abroad* (£10.99) by Roger Jones, published by How to Books.

Contacts, CV and follow-up

Many jobs are filled by personal contact before being advertised: it is no surprise that students sometimes have to pull strings hard to get interesting paid work. Use every family connection or friend of a friend that you can muster.

Try contacts first: if you know someone in TV, for example, and want to get a foot in the door by manning the phone in a studio, make sure you go and see your best friend's second cousin who splices and subtitles film. You can ask for advice and names and addresses, make notes of what the expert friend tells you and act on the advice. Don't wait for something to happen, because often nothing materialises — look for advertised jobs at the same time.

WORK UK

You can use a home or school computer to produce a spotless and well organised CV and take at least one copy for the contact. Few instructions here: if you have not been shown how to prepare a CV at school, your parents should be able to help you. Remember to include everything relevant to the area you are looking at (for example, your photographic work for that TV job) and fit in all your other school and outside achievements (prizes at St Cuthbert's, money raised on Red Nose Day, successful stint selling home-made bikinis as a Young Enterprise marketing director). Experience with computers will score highly (see CHAPTER 4: OFFICE SKILLS).

When you have sent off your perfect CV, whether it is to a contact who might have a job or in response to an advertisement, make sure to follow up. If a contact suggests you ring studios A and B, say, and speak to X and Y at the end of July after you have sent them each your CV with a covering letter, don't call Y at the beginning of July before you have written. Never be afraid to persist or try a 'passing visit'. There may be no job now, but if they like you, they may remember you when there is one.

Be informed. Do you know about sound studio mixing equipment? Or engineering widgets? Read the trade magazines before you meet someone for a job interview, because even knowing a bit about the business will make them feel happier about employing you.

The open market

Most of the above advice also applies to getting jobs advertised in the open market. Sadly there are still many areas (for example, film companies, TV studios, merchant banks and law firms) where long-term jobs appear to be given only to personal contacts or graduates (with at least an upper second-class degree) from a 'restricted' list of universities. Their loss? But if during your year off you can get inside an organisation where you would like to work when you graduate, your chances of going back there are much improved. And, to repeat, computer skills will get you almost anywhere for a short-term job, through the better-known 'temp' or 'computer temp' agencies.

122

MY BRILLIANT COURIER

"I spent a large part of my gap year working as a cycle courier in London. I've been a keen cyclist for a while and so being a courier made sense for me. The big advantages are that it's a very flexible job and the pay is good. You can more or less choose which days you work and can often cancel at very short notice. However, it's very unusual to work five days a week as it's extremely hard work. You get paid according to how many packages you deliver, so your pay depends a lot on how quickly you work. In an eight and a half-hour shift I earned an average of £50-£60, but on a really good day I could earn nearly £100. Also I met lots of interesting couriers, including students, out of work actors and Australians, and flirted with a lot of secretaries — I rode in Lycra.

There were bad sides to the job, however. After a full day at work I was almost too tired to go out, particularly if I was working several days a week. It's also pretty dangerous; one day I was knocked off my bike three times, and I had many collisions with cabs, pedestrians and buses. Once I was whizzing down Oxford Street and smacked into a bloke who stepped out in front of me. I found myself on the ground and saw a big puddle of blood between my feet. Luckily (for me) it wasn't mine but came from the bleeding nose of the man I'd just hit.

The things couriers deliver vary widely. One of my colleagues once had to deliver keys to someone who had locked himself out of his house and was supposed to be waiting outside. Unfortunately the man went to the shops for five minutes and when the courier arrived to find no-one around he posted the keys through the letter box... I once had to deliver a Barbie doll, and on another occasion a pair of cowboy boots with a message attached which the sender had asked me to read out "Bill, you were wonderful!"

Sam Armour, Classics at Trinity College, Cambridge, 1998

WELFARE-TO-WORK

If you have been resident in the UK and unemployed for six months you can qualify for paid work under the Welfare-to-Work scheme. Find out more at your local Job Centre.

WORK UK

Advertisements

The first good candidate often gets a job. Act quickly. Buy your local newspaper or magazine as soon as a new edition comes out on the news stand; be the first to get on the telephone; ask only essential questions; speak clearly and take down necessary directions to get to the place where you may be recruited. Most national newspaper advertising is for full-time 'permanent' jobs.

So it is usually quicker to try local newspapers and specialist trade magazines. Good for London students, for example, are the pages of adverts in the *Evening Standard*. Keep phoning: after 'no's from 21 advertisers you may get a 'yes' from the 22nd. Or ask the refuser if he knows other firms to try.

Employment agencies

There are two types, the public Job Centres (with local authority careers centres) and the private employment agencies. These used to be very different, with the state-owned employment centres known for low-wage, hard-labour jobs (building sites, lifting crates of beer, cleaning offices at 5.00 in the morning), while the private agencies specialised in office jobs — for women. Now the difference is not so clear-cut. Everyone knows the names of the work agencies with branch networks: Manpower, Brook Street Bureau and others. Agencies provide factory work (Manpower, which also provides office work), clerical and reception work, and if you can keyboard (touch-type) text or numbers into a computer, you have an instant passport to office work. The work may be boring, but the company could be fun, and it tends to be well paid. Try local agencies first, look smart, and take every certificate and reference you can lay your hands on.

Do-it-yourself

If contacts, advertisements and agencies all fail, there is always DIY job-hunting. Just walk into shops and restaurants to ask about casual work or use Yellow Pages to phone businesses (art galleries, department stores... zoos) and ask what is available. Ring up, ask to speak to the personnel manager, and ask if and when they have jobs available for school-leavers with A-Levels

124

PERFECT MATCH

"I spent twelve weeks working at two companies in the City with two bosses from hell. First were six awful weeks when I was filing for seven hours at a time in a freezing basement: there was no natural light, I could see my breath in the air, and by the end of the day my hands were cracked from all the filing.

And that was nothing compared to what I had to put up with from my boss. She was obsessed with time, commenting crudely if my trips to the toilet exceeded five minutes. Not the sort of person you'd want to spend an evening with.

Next came six hellish weeks at another company in the same building working under [sic] a terrifying nymphomaniac. She was really aggressive, hung over me all the time, and was as clock-obsessed as my first boss. Luckily I avoided her clutches, but several of my colleagues didn't...

I also caused a fair bit of havoc with the computers in the second company. I crashed the computers of both the other people who worked in my office, and damaged mine so severely that it had to be thrown away. I also nearly brought the entire company to its knees when, switching off the computers for the night, I nearly switched off the central server, which would have crashed the entire system. I think both the boss and I were happy when I left."
Daniel Metcalfe, Oxford University, 1998

and how you should apply. If they ask you to write in, you can do it after the call.

Interviews

The common-sense points have already been made in this section. Parents can give extra help, by giving you 'practice' job interviews at home. Friends who have jobs already will give more tips. Be positive. Above all when you talk to employers, look interested, sound sensible and show that you are bright but not rude. You are not expected to turn up dressed like a member of the Royal Family, but T-shirts and Timberlands will ruin your chances with most pin-striped bosses.

WORK UK
Accepting the job

If a job is offered, make sure you know the terms: what type of work, how much per hour pay, if lunch breaks are included, hours of work, how and when you will get paid and whether you will have tax deducted or not. If you think you could get injured on the job, say, by heavy lifting, check also that you are covered by your family insurance policies, although the employer may be technically liable for damages.

PAY, TAX AND NATIONAL INSURANCE

You can expect to be paid in cash for casual labour, by cheque (weekly or monthly) in a small company and by bank transfer in a large one. Always keep the payslip that goes with your pay, along with your own records of what you earn (including payments for casual labour) during the tax year: from 6 April one year to 5 April the next. You will have to list your income when you (or your parents) file your tax return at the end of the financial year: 5 April 1999 or 2000.

If you are out of education for a year you are not treated as a student but as a normal taxpayer. So you can earn up to £4,195 a year (1998/9 single person's allowance) tax free. (If you end the year having earned less than this but have had tax deducted during the year, you can claim a rebate from the Inland Revenue.)

The £4,195 is, obviously, an average **£80.67 a week free of income tax** or £349.58 a month. You need to ask your employer for a P46 form when you start your first job and a P45 form when you leave (which you take to your next employer.)

Unless you are self-employed, you start to pay National Insurance (**NI**, a taxpayer's contribution to the country's health and social welfare system) when you get to **£64 a week**. So if you are employed on the PAYE (Pay As You Earn) system you will find NI money has been deducted from your pay as well as tax. Always keep a note somewhere safe of your NI number.

If you are not a gap-year student (if you are still at school, college or university) and you are doing casual work in your holidays the rules are different. You need to ask your employer for a P38(S) form, on which you declare that you are in full-time education and that you will not be earning more than a certain amount of money during the tax year.

Big business and small business

Each year we ask Britain's biggest companies what employment they can offer to post A-Level students. Jobs can can take the form of organised schemes or occasional short-term work. Chances of work are better with companies with large chains of shops or offices. Your chances will be even better, however, with growing small and medium-sized businesses, and we have slipped a few of these into the list (in italics), including ours. You can identify others through your local recruitment advertising columns. Also identified are companies which offer a pre-university placement under the Year in Industry (YII) scheme. Many thanks to personnel people who gave us helpful and honest answers about the prospects for the coming year. Students who want to make it in business, test yourselves — how many of these companies do you know anything about?

HO   Head Office.

N/a   Information not available

YII   Member company of Year in Industry, which arranges pre-university industrial placements.

E   Number of UK employees.

A

Abbey National
For jobs in branches check the local press or ask your local branch about short term employment opportunities. For advertised vacancies, contact Customer Services for an application form. (E: 25,464).   *www.abbeynational.co.uk*

Arcadia Group plc
For jobs in our branches (Burton Menswear, Dorothy Perkins, Evans, Hawkshead, Principles, Racing Green, Topshop/Man), apply directly to your local branch.

Arthur Andersen
This big accountancy firm runs a 35-week integrated work and training programme between September and May, taking about 60 gap-year students. Requirements: solid GCSEs with Maths GCSE A-Grade, and at least three Grade Bs predicted at A-Level. Candidates must have a strong interest in business and

DEGREE SPONSORSHIP

Although the number of fully-sponsored degrees on offer from the public or private sector has declined in the 1990s, many organisations still offer sponsorship to students to study for a degree, sometimes on condition that they join the sponsoring company or institution for a period when they graduate. The Army is one example in the public sector (see box opposite). Some sponsorship schemes, however, involve making long-term commitments during the year off between school and university. For those who want a year of variety and discovery, spending most of the year tied to one job will defeat the objective. If you don't mind doing this, and you are interested in spending a year in industry, you could start by contacting YII, the organisation of that name (see following pages).

finance and want to work in that environment after their degree. The placement starts in September and is paid, with students receiving a travel bursary of £1,500 at the end of the gap year. Each year of university the student will receive sponsorship of £1,500 and further summer paid employment. There is no obligation to return to the firm afterwards, but they hope you will. Apply before April for a September start. Contact Liz Coombs. Arthur Andersen Graduate Recruitment, 1 Surrey St, London WC2R 2PS. Tel: 0171-438 3000

ASDA

There are alot of employment opportunities within ASDA stores on a temporary or part-time basis under the 'Flying Start' scheme. If your are keen to work with customers and you are a 'team player', apply to the Store Personnel Manager of the store in which you wish to work. Work would include shelf stacking, working at the checkout and meat packing, and within this scheme it is possible to begin work at your local store and later transfer to one local to your university if you wish to continue on a part-time basis while studying. ASDA also runs formal industrial placements at their HO. These are for students at the universities of Leeds and Manchester, wishing to take a gap year within their course. Selection is made through the universities.   *www.asda.co.uk*

B

Bank of Scotland

A vacation placement scheme is run every year from June to September. To apply, send your CV and a letter by December to Sandra Lindsay, Orchard Brae House, Level 4, 30 Queens Ferry Road, Edinburgh, AH4 2UZ. (E: 10,500).

www.bankofscotland.co.uk

WORK UK/BIG BUSINESS

THE ARMY

You can get a short service commission with the Army, which does not necessarily commit you to joining the Army when you leave university. Commissions last from four to eighteen months 'where mutually convenient to the Army's and the individual's requirements.' Women can apply as well as men.

Contact: Army Short Service Limited Commission, Recruiting Group, Army Training & Recruiting Agency, Ministry of Defence, Room 1, Building 165, Trenchard Lines, Upavon, Pewsey, Wilts SN9 6BE. Tel: 01980-618 142

Bass
Bass has a group-wide graduate business management scheme, but placements and opportunities for gap-year students are limited. Best to approach local Bass establishments (pubs, Holiday Inns, Gala Clubs etc.) (E: 85,000 incl. overseas).

Blue Circle Industries
Possibility of some clerical/WP/DB/DTP work for a few weeks at a time. Send a CV and letter to Graham Tricker, Group Personnel Manager, Blue Circle Industries plc, 84 Eccleston Square, London SW1V 1PX.

Bierrum and Partners
A civil engineering firm which takes one gap-year student a year through YII. For other short-term work contact the Personnel Manger, Bierrum & Partners, Barwythe Hall, Pedley Hill, Stakham, Dunstable, Bedfordshire. (E: 100).

Boots
Recruitment of post GCSE and A Level students is undertaken with a view to long term employment within the company for which full training is given. However, eight week vacation placements are offered to university students. The best approach is to contact your local store and enquire about temporary employment opportunities.(E: 80,000)   *www.boots.co.uk*

BP
Eight week placements are offered to generalists in their second year and vacation or one year placements to technologists in their second and third years. For more information contact: Jill D. Bradshaw, HR Adviser, Graduate Recruitment, The British Petroleum Company p.l.c., Britannic House, 1 Finsbury Circus, London EC2M 7BA. For temporary employment opportunities, contact your local BP Centre for information.   *www.bp.com*

WORK UK/BIG BUSINESS

British Steel

British Steel takes on a small number of gap year students who are intending to study mainly Engineering/Scientific courses with a view to undergraduate sponsorship. The gap year is spent working in a department related to the course of study you intend to pursue. Please write to the Graduate Co-ordinator at your nearest British Steel business or Graduate Recruitment, British Steel plc, Ashorne Hill Management College, Leamington Spa, Warwickshire CV33 9QW. (E: 39,000). YII. *www.britishsteel.co.uk*

C

Cadbury Schweppes

Cadbury Schweppes places people on work experience in response to specific business needs. The best approach is to contact the business units direct.

Carlton Communications

Holding company for Carlton Television. There are few opportunities and they are inundated with applications, so preference is given to those who specifically want a career in TV. Write to Personnel Manager, Carlton Television, 101, St Martin's Lane, London WC2N 4AZ. (E: 550) *www.carltonplc.co.uk*

Coats Viyella

Speculative applications are welcomed, but success depends on company needs. Send a CV and letter to: The Graduate Recruitment Advisor, Coates Viyella, 28 Saville Row, London W1X 2DD. *www.coats-viyella.com*

WORK UK/BIG BUSINESS

Commercial Union Assurance

There are opportunities for sandwich course placements within the IT division, and for actuarial vacation placements. Applications should be sent to the UK Human resources Office, Exchange Court, 3 Bedford Park, Croydon, Surrey CR9 2ZL. There is also a graduate scheme: application forms/brochures may be requested using the 24-hour answerphone (Tel: 0181-688 5872). Jobs are also advertised in the national press. (E: 9,000)   *www.cu.com*

D

Data Connection

This company has an unusual success story: one of its former gap year student trainees is now a director of the company. It runs a scheme for a minimum eight weeks, fitting it around the individual. Pay is about £800 a month with sub-sidised accommodation. The student is placed in a software development team and trained in the same way as a new graduate. It is possible then to be sponsored through university. Contact Justine McLennan, Graduate Recruitment, Data Connection Ltd, 100 Church Street, Enfield, Middlesex EN2 6B. Tel: 0181-366 1177 Fax: 0181-363 1533   *www.datcon.co.uk*

WORK UK/BIG BUSINESS

De la Rue
Makes banknotes, but don't let that give you ideas. There are occasionally opportunities for gap-year students those these are very limited. There is, however, a graduate training scheme. For details write to Helen Wright, Personnel Officer, De la Rue, Jays Close, Viaboles, Basingstoke RG22 4BS. (E: 4,000).

Demos
Independent research institute, specialising in research into public policy issues. Occasional vacation work available. CV and letter to Richard Warner, Demos, 9 Bridewell Place, London EC4V 6AP. (E: 10). www.demos.co.uk

E

Eastern Group plc
One year placements are offered to undergraduates each year. These incorporate training in the summer vacation which can be followed up by an invitation to work during the Christmans and Easter vacations covering staff holidays, though opportunities are very limited. For speculative applications contact the Personnel Department, Caxton Road, Bedford MK41 0EW. (E: 6,000). YII.

East Midlands Electricity
Sandwich placements are available for undergraduates and some limited opportunities for gap-year students aswell as occasional summer jobs. For speculative applications contact HO at 398, Coppice Road, Arnold, Nottingham NG5 7HX, stating whereabouts in the country you would like to work and they will refer you to the relevant manager. (E: 4,000).

WORK UK/BIG BUSINESS

EMI Group plc

Short term employment is made available according to company demand. Contact individual businesses such as EMI Music International (Tel: 0171-467 2000) or EMI Records UK (Tel: 0171-605 5000) or HO (Tel: 0171-355 4848).

Enterprise Oil plc

For recruitment purposes, the company is divided in to two sections. If your interests are on the financial/accountancy side, contact Ian Charmers. If you are interested in technical experience with geologists or geophysicists, contact Alison Ames. Send a CV and letter stating exactly what you want to do to Enterprise Oil plc, Human Resources Department, Grand Buildings, Trafalgar Square, London WC2N 5EJ. (E: 450).

G

Galerie Moderne

Gain invaluable work experience in a Knightsbridge twentieth century decorative arts gallery. Send CV to Galerie Moderne, 10 Halkin Arcade, Motcomb Street, London SW1X 8JT.

General Accident

Short-term contract opportunities do exist at General Accident sites across the UK. Students interested in working for GA should contact their local branch, or, for specific interest areas (e.g. statistics, human resources, marketing) contact Resourcing Manager, General Accident Head Office, Pitheavlis, Perth PH2 0NH.

WORK UK/BIG BUSINESS

Granada Group

Holding company for many individual firms. Each subsidiary has its own HO, so donít contact Granada Group. Advice is to establish your interests and contact the appropriate company: Granada TV Rental (Tel: 01234-355 233), Granada TV (Tel: 0161-832 7211), LWT (Tel: 0171-620 1620), YTT TV (Tel: 01132-438 283), Granada Hospitality, (Motorways, Little Chef and Travelodge) (Tel: 01525-873 881), Granada Food Services (Tel: 0181-995 8200), Granada Entertainments (Tel: 0161-832 9090) and Forte UK and London Hotels (0171-301 2000). (E: 92,000).

Great Universal Stores (GUS)

Advice is to write early on stating your preferred area of work (such as customer services, merchandise, IT, Marketing, poersonnel). GUS also recruits through colleges of further education in the local area, (Manchester), taking on students in their 2nd and 3rd years. For speculative applications send a CV and letter to Graduate Recruitment, GUS Home Shopping, Universal House, Devonshire Street, Manchester M60 6EL. Tel: 0161-277 3172. (E: 19,000).

H

Halifax plc

For temporary vacation work contact regional offices. (E: 30,000) *www.halifax.co.uk*

Hongkong and Shanghai Banking Corporation

Speculative applicatons are not discouraged, but success depends on company needs. Contact Graduate Recruitment, HSBC, 10 Lower Thames Street, London EC3R 6AE. Tel: 0171-638 2366.   *www.midlandbank.com*

I

IBM

IBM aims to take at least 50 gap-year students into its UK pre-university employment programme. Most successful candidates have at least two As and a B at A-Level. It does not always matter what the subjects are, but many jobs require 'aptitudes found in those planning to read subjects like computing, engineering and science'. The programme opens in September with a three-week training course covering computing office systems, marketing, communication and presentation skills. Closing date for applications is 28 February 1999. IBM also considers students who apply after their A-Level results, but there is inevitably less flexibility. Students are asked their preference for locations, and the most strongly technical placements are in Warwick and Hursley, near Winchester. Accommodation needs seem to sort themselves out. Some students return to IBM in vacations afterwards and on graduation. Contact Student Employment Officer, IBM UK Ltd, Recruitment Dept, P.O Box 41, North Harbour, Portsmouth, Hants PO6 3AU. Tel: 01705-561 000

WORK UK/BIG BUSINESS

> ### *PHOTOCOPIERS I HAVE KNOWN AND LOVED*
> *"I worked at IBM Basingstoke as part of the IBM gap-year scheme for four months before teaching English in Malawi, although the scheme is supposed to last 10 months. First came a very intensive three-week training programme, run by students who had done the scheme before, where we learnt all sorts of skills. An important part of this was putting on presentations, including an unprepared three-minute talk where you were only given the title a minute before you went on — one friend of mine had to give a talk on 'Photocopiers I have Known and Loved'. The training was hard work, but I learnt useful skills and met some really cool people. Once I was actually working the job was intense, with constant deadlines, but being part of a team means that your contribution is important and it is a great buzz when everything goes right and you see your hard work and preparation pay off. As compensation for the hard work, all of us on the scheme made sure our social life was healthy, with lots of house parties. The pay wasn't amazing, but I had lots of fun and learnt loads of new skills. The time was a really great experience and it also looks great on your CV. I'd definitely recommend it."*
> *Charlotte Westley, Maths, Sidney Sussex College, Cambridge, 1998*

Johnson & Johnson

Manufacturer of hospital products, with a factory in Yorkshire. Possible places are subject to availability and would be advertised in the national press. (E: 2,000)

K

Kwik Save

Possibility of admin work at HO in Clwyd or vacancies in local stores. Send a CV and letter stating what sort of work you are looking for to Sharon Duffy, Kwik Save Stores Ltd, Warren Drive, Prestatyn, Clwyd L119 7HU. Tel: 01745-887 111. Your application will then be forwarded to the relevant Human Resources manager. (E: 30,000)

St.Michael

Do you have what it takes to fill our GAP?

Starting in September, around 40 students taking a break between school and university will have the chance to gain a real insight into retail management careers, with the world's leading retailer. Not only will we pay you while you learn, but if it suits both parties this can lead to a more lasting relationship in a number of different ways.

You'll be joining us for a six-month period, gaining valuable first-hand experience and retail training in a Marks & Spencer store near you. At the end of this period you may feel the experience and money have been useful, but it is not for you. In this case you leave to pursue your other interests with no obligations. On the other hand, you may like it so much you decide to change your plans and stay. If you've got what it takes, and there's a suitable vacancy, you can join our Young Management training scheme there and then. You may, on the other hand, really like what we have to offer, but want to take some time off before embarking on a retail management career. If so, the same offer stands, but you apply after having taken the remaining six months of your break.

You may, of course, be keen to join us, but after graduating. Having proved your worth working with us already, this could lead not only to a place on our graduate programme, but also to a commitment from us to support you with Saturday and vacation work, providing useful earnings and valuable experience while you study.

If you feel you would like to fill our GAP, call 0171-268 3195 for an application form and GAP leaflet.

We are an equal opportunities employer.

MARKS & SPENCER

L

Land Securities

Although Land Securities doesnít offer placements to gap-year students, graduates who have taken a year out are looked on favourably for recruitment. Enquiries to the Personnel Department (Tel: 0171-413 9000)

London Electricity (Entergy)

Industrial placements are available for undergraduates as poart of their course. Send a CV and letter to Personnel Division, London Electricity, Templar House, 81-87 High Holborn, London SC1D 6NU. (E: 4,000).

M

Marks and Spencer

Marks and Spencer runs a gap-year business placement scheme (see advertisement opposite) which took 40 candidates in 1998. Starting in September each year, the programme provides six months practical experience and gives students and insight into the world of retailing. Candidates achieving the required standard will have the opportunity of employment within M&S during their subsequent studies and vacations. The places available are additional to the 200 places on the Business Placement Programme which M&S offers to undergraduates in their penultimate year of study. Even if retail is not for you, participating in this gap-year scheme should help you to make a more informed decision about your future career. Closing dates for applicaitons for the September 1999 intake is likely to be Friday 2nd July 1999. For an application form call (after April 1999) the Marks and Spencer Recruitment Department, 47-67 Baker Street, London W1A 1DN. Tel: 0171-268 3195.

Midland Bank

There may be vacancies at regional branches. Check the local press or ask your local branch about short term employment opportunities. Posts generally arise on an ad hoc basis. (E: 55,000)   *www.midlandbank.com*

N

Nortel Telecommunicaitons

Operates through the Year in Industry Scheme, but also welcomes speculative applications from gap year students. Send CV and letter to The Resourcing Group, Nortel Ltd HQ, Stafferton Way, Maidenhead, Berkshire SL6 1AY. (E: 6,000)

WORK UK/BIG BUSINESS

BOSCH SANDWICH

"Because I wasn't totally sure if I wanted to go to university, I decided to work to gain experience in industry. I worked for the thermotechnic division of Bosch for a year. I got the job through a school placement scheme and started the August after A-Levels. I spent a month in each department until Christmas, getting experience in areas such as production and marketing. I then worked in accounts for the next eight months (which I had originally applied to do). The company was very much in the learning stages of working with students which was a good thing. They employed quite a few sandwich course students and I didn't have a particular job, so I could easily push for what I wanted to do. I earned £125 a week but I didn't really do it for the money. There are plenty of advantages to working in industry for a gap year. I am sponsored through university and receive a substantial cheque at the beginning of each term. I gained excellent business training and now I have the opportunity to work in any Bosch site in the world, although I'm not contracted to work for them when I graduate. Of course there were times when I hated it, but on the whole it was a good experience and I'd do it again."

Scott Auty, Economics at Exeter University, 1998

Northern Electric

Considers applications for unpaid work experience. Write to Mrs K. Gardener, Personnel Services Section, Northern Electric plc, Carliol House, Market Street, Newcastle upon Tyne NE1 6NE quoting the reference GOP. Other opportunities limited but would be advertised in job centres. (E: 3,500). YII.

P

P&O

Holding company for subsidiaries including P&O Containers, P&O Ferries, Bovis Homes and Bovis Contruction (Tel: 0181-422 3488). Although there is not an official gap-year placement scheme run by P&O, it is worth contacting some of its other companies. For P&O Cruises, write to Personnel Department, Richmond House, Terminus Terrace, Southampton SO14 3PN.

138

WORK UK/BIG BUSINESS

Peridot Press

Publishers of THE GAP YEAR GUIDEBOOK, THE INTERNET GUIDEBOOK and other books. We offer a few paid research assignments for gap-year students or graduates for short periods between March and July. Some other casual work available in the holidays. If you are quick-thinking with interviewing, writing or computer skills, send your CV (for 1999 work) and follow up with a phone call after October 1998. Address inside this book cover. Tel: 0171 221 7404. *www.peridot.co.uk*

R

Reuters

Gap-year placements are rare and competition is intense, but interested candidates should send their CVs to the Personnel Department Reuters, 85 Fleet Street, London EC4P 2AJ. (E: 3,000). *www.reuters.com*

Royal Bank of Scotland

Vacation work is available. Contact the personnel department of your local branch or HO at P.O. Box 31, 42 St Andrew's Square, Edinburgh EH2 2YE. (E: 20,000) *www.royalbankscot.co.uk*

Royal Sun Alliance

Gap-year students are taken on according to business needs. Send a CV and letter stating what experience you whish to gain to Personnel Department, P.O. Box 144, New Hall Place, Liverpool L69 3HS.
(E: 25,000) *www.sunalliance.co.uk/sunalliance*

S

Scottish Hydro-Electric

Recruitment generally takes place by direct approach to the local Hydro-Electric Manager. Speculative Applications for specific training placements, however, should be sent to the Personnel Officer, Scottish Hydro-Electric, 10 Dunkeld Road, Perth PH1 5WA.

Scottish Courage Brewing

Recruiting is done locally on an ad hoc basis. For work placements specifically in production, write to the Production Personnel Director, Scottish Courage Brewing Ltd, Fountain House, 160 Dundee Street, Edinburgh EH11 1DQ.

WORK UK/BIG BUSINESS

T

Tesco

There are plenty of short term employment opportunities withing Tesco stores, apply to the Store Personnel Manager of the store in which you wish to work. In addition to this, Tesco has a programme called 'Excel in industry' which is for sandwich course students, and a programme caleld 'Excel for graduates'. For further details, contact HO on tel: 01707-350 472. YII.

SMELLY

"I had heard about the Year in Industry scheme by word of mouth. The application process is fairly easy. The Zeneca site I was at was in Bracknell, and the company paid for my relocation until I could find a place to stay so I lived in a hotel for a month. In the end I shared a house with three other people on the scheme. We threw a party every month or two and generally had a good time.
The company you are sent to is supposed to provide you with three weeks training. I chose three weeks of management training. The course was good. We learned about health and safety in the workplace — all commonsense stuff really but it was great to meet the other people on the course and to discover that I actually got on with some of them really well. I think all the people on the scheme had assumed that everyone else would be boring (stereotypical engineer thing) and we were all pleasantly surprised to find that we actually liked each other.
The work I was doing was chromatography — essentially the analytical work to back up research. The research people would work out new conditions under which chemicals might be made, and I would assess the various products for purity in order to work out which the best method was. I also did some characterisation of chemicals which involved testing them for their boiling point, melting point, etcetera, and amusingly enough, smell; even though under the standard operating procedure for smell the advice was not to smell any chemicals under any circumstances. We were supposed to record what the chemicals smelled like through 'incidental observation' — in other words, by chance."
Alex Thomson, Zeneca & Cambridge University, 1997

WORK UK/BIG BUSINESS

Thames Water Utilities

Year in industry places are open to young people who have completed their A-Levels or GNVQs and are looking for a years work experience before starting their degree. For further information contact Year in Industry (quote Thames Water reference), Thames Valley Director, School of Engineering, Oxford Brookes University, Oxford OX3 0BP. Final year sponsorship with vacation work experience is also available to engineering students. Candidates should apply during their penultimate year. For information contact Graduate Recruitment, Thames Water, Napier Court, 4, Vastern Road, Reading, Berkshire RG1 8DB. YII.

Thorn plc

Possibility of some vacancies, though opportunities are limited. Speculative letters to Thorn Europe, Baird House, Arlington Business Park, Theale, Reading, Berkshire RG7 4SA. YII.

U

Unilever

This highly decentralised business has summer placements available for penultimate-year undergraduates. Advice to gap-year students is to approach some of the largest subsidiaries: Bird's Eye Walls, Walton-on-Thames, Surrey; Lever UK, Kingston-upon-Thames, Surrey. ìIt is my opinion that graduates who have taken a year out at the age of 21 are more likely to do much more daring and ambitious things in that year out - all of which contribute to their personal developmentî. Dr M.J. Duffell, former Head of Graduate Recruitment, National Personnel Department. (E: 22,000)   *www.unilever.com*

MUSHROOM-STYLE MANAGEMENT

"During my year out I tried to restructure a company called ADA Valley Foods. At first I had little idea of what running a business entailed. ADA sold the waste product from a local mushroom farm. This waste mushroom mulch was mixed with horse manure to form a slightly alkaline compost mixture. I bought the waste product from the farm and then outsourced another firm to bag the material, which was sold in lots of 35 bags to a pallet, to garden centres and commercial gardens. At first everything was an uphill struggle. I had to cold-call all our old customers who had stopped ordering and try to sell them something they didn't really want. I found that in spite of having a good product potential buyers were asking questions that I didn't have the answer to and consequently I wasn't selling anything. Gradually, I started to hit back. It was all about pretending to be bigger than you really are. I was really working out of my bedroom at home, but to give this impression to potential customers would be commercial suicide. I invested in some headed paper, asked my bagger to print a logo on the compost bags and gave myself the title 'Managing Director' or 'Area Sales Manager' on any correspondence I wrote. Sales started to pick up. It was a constant juggling act to ensure that suppliers worked to meet targets and that the customer believed his compost was being supplied, packaged and delivered by a unified commercial whole. The fact that I was only really a middleman did have its drawbacks. Once a customer rang up to make a very large order which I knew that I couldn't deliver because my packager was going on holiday. I used my, by now, well-honed management technique and said that we had been snowed under with orders and couldn't possibly supply any compost until the following week. Impressed with our 'success' the customer decided he could wait. I was lucky that the business was to an extent already set up for me. When a customer asked for an analysis of what was in the compost, I borrowed some PH paper from school and did an acidity test as well as using some Chemistry A-level so that by next morning I could ring the customer and say that scientists from our 'lab' had just come up with the latest chemical breakdown."

Andrew Barkly, Newcastle University, 1995

WORK UK/BIG BUSINESS

JOBSEEKER'S ALLOWANCE

Thinking of long-distance skiving? Blowing your savings on a round-the-world trip and sending a friend to collect unemployment benefit for you while you're on Bondi beach? Think again. If you are 18-24 and have been unemployed for six months, you can sign on for the state-funded Jobseeker's Allowance (JSA) benefit — a basic £39.85 a week if you have savings of less than £3,000 and no other income (you can earn £5-a-week without affecting the benefit, but anything you earn over that gets knocked off). But you have to check in to your Job Centre and sign a Jobseeker's agreement to look actively for work, and then check in regularly once a fortnight to collect the benefit until employment is found. Washing bottles at £3 an hour? Of course, if you are difficult or act stupid employers won't want you, but that could show up on your work record later, when you really need to work. Tough, isn't it?

Unipart

Speculative applicaitons for their YII project should be sent to: DCM Human Resources, Unipart House, Unipart, Cowley, Oxford OX4 2PG. YII.

United Biscuits

Although there are no gap-year placements, sandwich (degree) students should contact Graduate Recruitment Dept, United Biscuits Ltd, Church Road, West Drayton, Middlesex UB7 7PR, for an updated list of placements.

www.unitedbiscuits.co.uk.

V,W,X,Y,Z,

Whitbread

Contact restaurants and pubs individually for holiday work. (E: 80,000)

Yorkshire Water

Some opportunities for work experience. Contact Yorkshire Water Services: Tel: 0113-244 82201. (E: 3,500). YII.

Vacation work

Here are a few vacation work employers (see also CHAPTER 7: BIG BUSINESS), with reports from students who took their own initiatives.

Waitressing, fruit-picking, keying information into computers: the jobs you can do are there if you know where to find them and what skills pay most. Dont' let an employer kid you that the minimum £3.00 wage for 18-20 year-olds is a 'norm': pay should depend on how good you are. Work you enjoy will probably pay less well. Summer camp work in Britain is available through companies like Kingswood (see below), Eurocamp and PGL.

Camp Beaumont (Kingswood Group)   Tel: 0171-922 1234
Linton House, 164-180 Union St, London SE1 OLH

You may remember going to Camp Beaumont summer camps as a teenager. Well, now you can go back and work there. Summer rates with free accommodation and food are: group leaders £45-60 a week; instructors £60+; senior group leaders £75.

Town and Country Catering   Tel: 0181-998 8880
Manor House, Manor Farm Road, Alperton, Middlesex HA0 1BN

This agency recruits for a variety of jobs for big events such as Ascot, Henley (Regatta), Wimbledon and the Chelsea Flower Show. The number for Wimbledon recruitment is: 0181-947 7430.

144

WORK UK/VACATION WORK

HOUSE OF MAGGOTS

"I've had quite a few crappy jobs during this year, the worst of which was being a dustman (I'm retaking chemistry and politics to get the three As I need for medical school). I arrived at the site and was asked if I'd ever done it before. I said no, and it was suggested that I wouldn't be much use, in rather more colourful terms. It was interesting to see what people had been eating all week — there were maggots everywhere. The first large bin I picked up I managed to tip accidentally into the next garden which had just been cleared. The whole day was a nightmare: it was hot and on my five-minute break I was burning up and dying for a drink. Ahead of us during our round was a milk float, so I decided to get a drink from it. Unfortunately I ended up chasing it for three streets before it pulled over and I could get one. By the time I got back to the dustcart I was more knackered than when I started..."

Simon Croker, 1997

HOUSE OF COMMONS

"The best way to get a job in the House of Commons as an assistant secretary is through contacts. The second best way is through 'The House' magazine, which really is the house magazine. This is circulated to nearly all MPs and is the best place to advertise your skills or see whether there are any suitable jobs available. Typing is almost obligatory for this kind of job, but when I worked there part-time, my duties varied from answering the telephone and sorting letters to listening to debates, writing press releases and helping with office moves, so it is worth applying even if you can't type. It is a great deal of fun — there are often other young researchers in the office and is brilliant for picking up obscure facts that you can amaze your politics tutor with when you get to university."

Sarah Parsons, Bristol University, 1995

Voluntary work

If you are kind-hearted and like helping other people, why not contribute to the community by offering to do voluntary work for a charity? There will not be much material reward but your help could make a huge difference to someone else's happiness. An umbrella group or national agency could find a suitable project for you to work on, or you can contact organisations direct. We give just a few suggestions here. Overseas voluntary work details follows in Chapter 8.

Government policy

The Labour government's five-year, £3 billion, *Welfare to Work* programme for 18 to 24-year-olds who have been out of work for six months came into force in April 1998. Also known as the 'New Deal', it offers four options. One of these is to work for a voluntary organisation and another to join a national Environmental Task Force — where pay of basic unemployment benefit plus £20 was proposed. (For information about the proposed *Millenium Volunteer Programme* see the Internet Website *http://www.open.gov/dfee/millen/index/htm*). Jobcentres and voluntary organisations will be able to give you more details about the complexities of pay, tax and benefits under the *Welfare to Work* arrangements, and a useful leaflet called *Voluntary and Part-Time Workers* (FB26) is available from the Benefits Agency.

Umbrella groups

There are a number of organisations which place people with other charities or with a wide national network of their own.

BRITISH TRUST FOR CONSERVATION VOLUNTEERS

BTCV, 36 St Mary's Street
Wallingford, Oxon OX10 0EU

Tel: 01491-839 766
Web: *www.btcv.org.uk*

This organisation runs week-long working holidays doing conservation work in England, Wales, Scotland and Northern Ireland (as well as abroad, see Chapter 8: Voluntary Work Overseas). Accommodation varies according to the project (usually a youth hostel) and the cost ranges from £35-£90 a week. Training courses are available. To get experience of publicity,

146

administration and fund-raising work you can go along to your local BTCV office and volunteer.

COMMUNITY SERVICE VOLUNTEERS (CSV)

CSV   Freephone: 0800-374 991
237 Pentonville Road   Fax: 0171- 837 962
London N1 9NJ   Web: *www.csv.org.uk*

CSV is an agency which matches a volunteer place to every volunteer who applies and who can go away from home. About 3,000 volunteers aged 16 to 35 every year take part in this scheme and about a third of them are 17-19. CSV finds posts lasting from 4 to 12 months, helping people in the community under the wing of another charity or organised by CSV itself. Full board, accommodation and travel costs are provided plus weekly allowance of £24. CSV is exempt from minimum wage laws.

NATIONAL ASSOCIATION OF VOLUNTEER BUREAUX

National Association of Volunteer Bureaux   Tel: 0121-633 4555
New Oxford House, 16 Waterloo St   Fax: 0121-633 4043
Birmingham B2 5UG   E-mail: *navbteam@waverider.co.uk*

NAVB can put people in touch with their local volunteer bureau, which matches people wanting to volunteer with local and national voluntary or community groups that are looking for help. Contact the address above or your nearest NAVB volunteer bureau. Length of work depends on the individual's interests and commitments. Necessary expenses of volunteering are met.

Useful information

Youthnet is the charity that runs *The Site* on the Internet: "the first step for anybody looking for an opportunity, help or advice on a wide range of topics anywhere in the UK." Lots of youth work and voluntary organisations listed.

Individual charities

If you feel passionately about helping children or the disabled, for example, why not get in touch with a charity directly? Here are some which would be very grateful for your help.

CHILDREN AND YOUTH

FASIC - Overcoming Speech Impairment   Tel: 0171-236 3632
347 Central Markets, Smithfield   Fax: 0171-236 8115
London EC1A 9NH

Break   Tel: 01263-823 170
20 Hooks Hill Road, Sheringham   Fax: 01263-825 560
Norfolk NR26 8NL

Centre for Alternative Technology, The   Tel: 01654-702 400
Machynlleth, Powys SY20 9AZ   Fax: 01654-702 782

Children's Country Holidays Fund,   Tel: 0171-928 6522
First Floor (Rear), 42-43 Lower Marsh   Fax: 0171-401 3961
London SE1 7RG

Children's Trust, Tadworth Court   Tel: 01737-357 171
Tadworth, Surrey, KT20 5RU

Grail, The 125 Waxwell Lane   Tel: 0181-866 2195
Pinner, Middlesex HA5 3ER   Fax: 0181-866 1408

Great George's Community Cultural Project   Tel: 0151-709 5109
Great George Street, Liverpool L1 5EW

Hothorpe Hall (RELIGIOUS), Theddingworth   Tel: 01858-880 257
Leicestershire LE17 6QX   Fax: 01858-880 979

Monkey Sanctuary, The, Murrayton, Nr Looe   Tel: 01503-262 532
Cornwall PL13 1NZ

National Trust for Scotland (Thistle Camps)   Tel: 0131-226 5922
5 Charlotte Square, Edinburgh EH2 4DU   Fax: 0131-243 9444

Pax Christi
Christian Peace Education Centre   Tel: 0181-203 4884
St.Joseph, Watford Way, London NW4 4TY   Fax: 0181-203 5234

WORK UK/VOLUNTARY WORK

Quaker Youth Theatre (The Leaveners)   Tel: 0171-272 5630
8 Lennox Rd, Finsbury Park, London N4 3NW   Fax: 0171-272 8405

Tent City, Old Oak Common Lane   Tel: 0181-743 5708
East Acton, London W3 7DP (SAE needed)   Fax: 0181-749 9074

Time for God, 2 Chester House, Pages Lane   Tel: 0181-883 1504
Muswell Hill, London N10 1PR   Fax: 0181-365 2471

Shaftesbury Society, The   Tel: 01666-822 685
Burton Hill School, Malmesbury, Wilts SN16 0EG

Simon Community, The   Tel: 0171 485 6639
PO Box 1187, London NW5 4HW

Whizz-Kidz   Tel: 0171-233 6600
1 Warwick Row, London SW1E 5ER

WORK WITH THE SICK AND DISABLED

Churchtown Field Studies Centre   Tel: 01208-872 148
Churchtown, Lanlivery   Fax: 01208-873 377
Bodmin, Cornwall PL30 5BT

Queen Elizabeth's Foundation for the Disabled   Tel: 01702-431 725
Lulworth Court, 25 Chalkwell Esplanade
Westcliff-on-Sea, Essex SS0 8JQ

Ritchie Russell House Young Disabled Unit   Tel: 01865-225 482
The Churchill Hospital, Headington, Oxford OX3 7LJ

SHAD Haringey, Winkfield Resource Centre   Tel: 0181-365 8528
33 Winkfield Road, Wood Green, London N22 5RP

SHAD Wandsworth   Tel:0181-675 6095
5 Bedford Hill   Fax:0181-673-2118
London SW12 9ET

Sue Ryder Foundation   Tel:01787-280 252
Cavendish, Sudbury, Suffolk CO10 8AY   Fax:01787-280 548

Useful reading

A Year Between, Central Bureau for Educational Visits and Exchanges, 10 Spring Gardens, London SW1A 2BN, £9.99.

Overseas Voluntary Work: Placements and expeditions

Here we list postings and expeditions arranged by overseas voluntary work agencies or commercial organisations. (We charge a small fee for including entries in this list.) Demand for the most popular assignments is greater than supply, so you will need to be a good candidate. We stress again that size is no indication of competence. More are listed in the detailed OVERSEAS VOLUNTARY WORK section which follows this.

KEY	
Africa and Asia Venture	AV
BSES Expeditions	BSES
Coral Cay Conservation	CCC
Crusaders (Crusoe)	C
Earthwatch	E
Friends Of Israel Educational Trust	FI
GAP Activity Projects	G
Gap Challenge (World Challenge)	GC
Health Projects Abroad	HPA
Interserve	INT
Project Trust	PT
Quest	Q
Raleigh International	R
Right Hand Trust	RT
Students Partnership Worldwide	SPW
Teaching Abroad	TA
Trekforce	TF
United Nations Association International Youth Service	UN
Village Education Project	VE
Visitoz	V

Placements   Organisation

From September 1998. Other organisations offering projects in these and other countries appear in OVERSEAS VOLUNTARY WORK.

Africa

Botswana	PT, UN
Burkina Faso	UN
Cameroon	E
Egypt	CCC, PT
Gambia, The	E, RT
Ghana	TA
Ivory Coast	UN
Kenya	AV, BSES, C, E, RT, TF, UN
Lesotho	G, UN
Madagascar	E
Malawi	AV, GC, PT, RT
Morocco	G, UN
Mozambique	UN
Namibia	E, PT, R, SPW
Seychelles	CCC
South Africa	C, E, G, GC, PT, SPW, UN
St Helena	RT
Swaziland	G, RT, UN
Tanzania	E, G, GC, HPA, SPW, VE, UN
Togo	UN
Tunisia	UN
Uganda	AV, C, PT, RT, SPW, UN
Zambia	G, UN
Zanzibar	GC
Zimbabwe	AV, C, E, PT, RT, SPW, UN

America (North)

Canada	BSES, E, G, GC, UN
USA	BSES, E, G, UN

OVERSEAS ASSIGNMENTS

America (South, Central and Caribbean)

Argentina	E, G
Bahamas	E
Barbados	UN
Belize	CCC, E, GC, R, TF
Bolivia	C, E, Q, UN
Brazil	C, E, G, PT, TA, UN
Chile	G, PT, Q, R, UN
Costa Rica	C, E, GC, Q, UN
Cuba	PT, UN
Dominica	E, UN
Ecuador	E, G, GC, Q, UN
El Salvador	C
Falklands	G
Grenada	RT
Guatemala	C, E, Q, UN
Guyana	PT, R
Haiti	E
Honduras	PT
Martinique	UN
Mexico	C, E, G, TA, UN
Paraguay	G
Peru	E, GC, Q
Sao Tome	E
St Vincent	RT
Uruguay	E
Venezuela	E

Antarctica

Antarctica	BSES

Asia

Bangladesh	INT, UN
China (including Hongkong)	E, G, PT, TA, UN
India	AV, BSES, C, E, G, GC, INT, TA, UN
Indonesia	CCC, E, TF
Japan	G, PT, UN

OVERSEAS ASSIGNMENTS

Korea	PT
Kyrgyzstan	BSES, E
Malaysia (*Sabah)	G, GC, PT, *R
Mongolia	R
Nepal	AV, G, GC, INT, SPW, UN
Pakistan	INT, PT
Philippines	CCC, E, UN
Sri Lanka	E, PT
Thailand	E, PT, UN
Vietnam	G

Australasia

Australia	E, G, GC, V
Easter Island?	E
Fiji	G
New Zealand	E, G

Europe

Armenia	UN
Belarus	UN
Belgium	UN
Bulgaria	UN
Czech Republic	E, G, UN
Cyprus	E
Denmark	UN
Estonia	UN
Finland	UN
France	C, UN
Greece	E, UN
Greenland	UN
Ireland (Eire)	UN
Latvia	C, UN
Germany	G, UN
Hungary	E, G, UN
Iceland	E
Italy	E, UN
Lithuania	UN
Netherlands	UN

OVERSEAS ASSIGNMENTS

Poland	G, UN
Portugal	C, UN
Romania	C, G, UN
Russia	E, G, TA, UN
Serbia	UN
Slovakia	G, UN
Slovenia	UN
Spain	E, UN
Switzerland	UN
Turkey	E, UN
Ukraine	TA, UN

Middle East

Israel	E, FI, G
Jordan	G, PT
Lebanon	PT
Palestine	UN
Oman	R

Overseas projects

Applications for overseas voluntary work places need to be made, in some cases, as soon as you have filled in your deferred-entry university application form. We hope those who usually read books from the beginning won't get caught out by not turning to this chapter quickly. We list here organised overseas projects ranging from short-term teaching posts to one-year placements and challenging expeditions. You will already have seen the country-by-country list of OVERSEAS ASSIGNMENTS (pages 150-54). Details about VOLUNTARY WORK ORGANISATIONS and feedback about their postings follow here, then a section on OVERSEAS VACATION WORK.

Volunteer abroad

Voluntary work overseas is one of the most rewarding ways of spending all or part of a gap year. Those who do it come back with memories they never lose.

By winning a place on an organised voluntary work project, students soak themselves in another culture. They may find themselves working with people who know only poverty, disease, hunger and monotony. Away from Western influence, 18-year-olds can see the world from a different point of view.

OVERSEAS VOLUNTARY WORK

Conscience tourism

Since the first edition of this book came out in 1992, however, the idealism associated with voluntary work has come under severe commercial pressure. Some organisations are offering packages that are little more than tourism dressed up as voluntary work — at a price. If students want to spend a few weeks helping the underprivileged before boredom sets in and they want to move on, it can be arranged. And while some 'expeditions' involve genuine exploration or scientific research, others are just a trek.

Idealist or hedonist? Whatever your reason for going abroad, one thing is absolutely essential: **talk to others who have been on that particular voluntary work assignment/expedition** as well as to the organisation supervising it. Even this can fail, if your contact turns out to be someone on a completely different wavelength to you. Volunteers have to take some risk.

More than 4,000 places on overseas volunteer projects could be filled (with the organisations we list in this section) for the gap year 1998/9. Students should have at least 109 countries to choose from for 1999/2000 and with a growing number of organisations offering gap-year programmes, pressure on places has eased. A look at the COUNTRY INDEX before this section will show the choice now open to students and their parents. Lists can close early however, and planning should start now (autumn term, Upper 6) for posts starting in the autumn of your gap year. Ranging from three-month jobs to teaching that lasts the whole academic year, most placements provide only free accommodation and food — very few provide pocket money.

True grit

For genuine voluntary work schemes, students who expect only TV, tapas and tequila are out; ones who can teach, build, inspire confidence and share what they know are needed. Physical and mental fitness, an ability to get on with people and adapt oneself and staying power are essential: the student will have to go through a series of hurdles: application, raising funds from hard-pressed sponsors, selection or training, and work on the project itself overseas.

OVERSEAS VOLUNTARY WORK

A-Levels under your belt

It helps to have core A-Levels for teaching posts (like English, maths, history, geography and sciences) because subjects like ancient history and politics are a luxury that many schools in developing countries cannot afford to teach. However, what you are providing is as much to do with a different style of teaching (more enquiring and creative) as with specific knowledge, so don't worry too much about what you don't know; focus on what you can do or what skills you can teach.

Your university situation is a factor as well. Students who find out in August 1998 that their A-Level grades are not good enough for a university place may have to withdraw from project places. If you plan to resit an exam it cannot be done from a *felucca* in Aswan. If reapplying is necessary, it will also need to be fitted into your timetable.

On your own

Some other points are worth emphasising. Parents often favour big voluntary organisations because they think that under the umbrella of a large organisation their child will be assured of help in a nasty situation. Experience is certainly important. But often a specialist organisation is more knowledgeable about a country, a school, or other destination for a volunteer. Size and status have no bearing on competence. A charity can be more efficient than a commercial company, and a company can show more sensitivity than a charity. There are few general rules.

Second, the truth is that over in Tanzania or wherever you are sent, you can't count on much. Regardless of the reputation of the voluntary work organisation you choose, it's the luck of the draw whether the school you are put in, for example, needs you — or if a family you stay with treats you well. We have had countless stories of students being given information by organisations about school postings which has turned out to be wrong. It is worth checking what training is given and what support there is in-country, but be aware that you may not get what you expected.

The advice is to be ready for this, and — yes, here it comes

OVERSEAS VOLUNTARY WORK

again — talk to people who have been on the assignment you are going to (ask the organisation to give you phone numbers).

Show me the money

Many organisations ask you to raise substantial funds. It can be hard to combine raising money with studying for A-levels, but there are a lot of ways to do it. As usual, the earlier you start, the easier it will be. One way is to work and save, but you may find it more fun if you do something different. The organiation that you go with should be able to give advice, but options include organising sponsored events, writing to companies or trusts asking for sponsorship, car-boot sales and just plain scrounging. Your old school might agree to give you money if you go back and give a talk about your trip. The last resort is to go cap in hand to your parents, either for a loan or a gift, but this can be unsatisfying as you feel less independent and may get into debt.

Riot gear

If you think you will be visiting a politically volatile country call the Foreign Office's Travel Advice Unit on 0171-238 4503/4504 (Fax: 238 4545) before you leave. If you do go to a troubled area, it is advisable to register with the British Embassy, High Commission or Consulate there and give them a rough itinerary.

Organisations

AFRICA INLAND MISSION (AIM)

Africa Inland Mission   Tel: 0171-281 1184
2 Vorley Road, London N19 5HE   Fax: 0171-281 1184
E-mail: *africa.mission@ukonline.co.uk*

AIM looks for volunteers with a specifically Christian outlook, to teach in Africa (mainly Kenya: check out political stability before you go). The volunteer needs to raise money for living expenses as well as the airfare before starting work. Placements are normally for a full year, with time off to travel, but they will also take people for eight months (starting January). The cost is around £4,000. For more information contact Angela Godfrey at AIM.

AFRICA AND ASIA VENTURE

Africa and Asia Venture   Tel: 01380-729 009
10 Market Place, Devizes,   Fax: 01380-720 060
Wiltshire SN10 1HT   Web: *http://members.aol.com/aventure*

Africa and Asia Venture (AV) is a voluntary work organisation started in 1994 by ex-Army officer Peter Bell and Nigel Warren, who had teenage children of their own and got fed up with backpackers arriving on their doorsteps in Africa 'without a clue about what to do'. AV now takes parties of school-leavers to teaching placements (three months in a secondary school with a month's travel afterwards, including a safari) in Kenya, Malawi (also for graduates), Uganda, Zimbabwe, India and Nepal. AV provides a training course first, including advice on teaching and lifestyle, and full back-up in each country. Cost is about £2,075 including insurance and a small contribution towards educating an African child. Departures (for over 350 placements in 1999/2000) in September, January and April. More boys would be welcome. (See advertisement overleaf.)

OVERSEAS VOLUNTARY WORK

BTCV

British Trust for Conservation Volunteers
St Mary's St, Wallingford, Oxon OX10 0EU   Tel: 01491-839 76636
Web: *www.btcv.org.uk*

This charity runs working conservation holidays in Britain (see CHAPTER 7: WORK UK: VACATION WORK) and also in many parts of Europe, Japan, Australia, Senegal and beyond. In Britain the trips last a week or a weekend, overseas two to three weeks.

BRATHAY EXPLORATION GROUP

Brathay Exploration Group Trust   Tel: 015394-33942
Brathay Hall, Ambleside
Cumbria LA22 0HP   Web: *freespace.virgin. net/Brathay.exploration/*

This charity provides 'challenging experiences for young people' (aged 16-25). It runs a range of expeditions from one to five weeks long which vary each year. Shorter programmes offer, for example, an introduction to mountaineering in Scotland. Students can remain

OVERSEAS VOLUNTARY WORK

> ### DURACELL BATTERIES JUST GO ON AND ON
>
> *"I taught English and sport at the Kavarnet High School in Kenya for four months. It was fantastic. They played football to a high standard and were naturally incredibly fit. I played in the teachers' team and when we practised they all went on for three to four hours without stopping, like Duracell batteries running up and down the pitch. We taught volleyball, tennis and hockey as well, but the equipment was very old. One day when I was teaching English I had to explain how to have a telephone conversation, so I brought in one I'd mocked up with two plastic bottles and a piece of string. They all stood up and cheered because they were so happy that one of their teachers had made an effort — some of them don't bother to turn up. Africa Venture looked after us in small groups so it was like being part of a family. Coming back to do telesales work in Tunbridge Wells was boring."*
> *Stephen Axten, Economics at Manchester University, 1997*

in the UK or travel as far as Belize, Nepal, Murmansk in Russia, Siberia or Vietnam: the 1999 programme was due to be launched in October 1998. Brathay has a strong fieldwork background, and often publishes results from field trips in journals. Placements have included researching glacier retreat in Norway and working in conjunction with the Natural History Museum on studying flora and fauna in Belize. Students could be sent out to work on an on-going survey: no experience or specific skills are required, and Brathay takes a wide variety of people. Programmes run between July and early September (no application deadline). Costs vary from £200 for UK-based programmes to over £2,000 for placements abroad.

BSES EXPEDITIONS

BSES Expeditions
at The Royal Geographical Society
1 Kensington Gore, London SW7 2AR

Tel: 0171-591 3141
Fax: 0171-591 3140
E-mail: *BSES@RGS.org*

This charitable organisation runs six-week expeditions in the summer and three- to four-month ones in the spring to wilderness areas abroad to conduct scientific fieldwork on behalf of universities,

OVERSEAS VOLUNTARY WORK

research institutes or host nations. Age: 16 years 6 months to 20. The main recruitment period is between September and February, but do feel free to contact them at other times. There will be BSES expeditions to Kenya, Alaska and Kyrgyzstan in summer 1999 and probabilities for 2000 are an expedition to Arctic Canada and a 'Post-monsoon' one to the Indian Himalayas. Sponsorship costs £2,200-£2,900. (See also advertisement in CHAPTER 9: TRAVEL.)

CHURCH MISSION SOCIETY

Church Mission Society (CMS) Tel: 0171-928 8681
Partnership House, 157 Waterloo Road Fax: 0171-401 3215
London SE1 8UU E-mail: *jeremy.thompson@cms-uk.org*

Offering more of a learning experience than a giving one, the CMS runs three to five-week 'Project Experience' programmes in Africa, Asia, the Middle-East and Eastern Europe for Christians aged 18-30. The projects are 'an opportunity for Christians to discover what it means to be a Christian in another culture', and involve meeting and occasionally working alongside local people. Costs vary from £550 to £950 depending on the country. Applications by mid-April to Experience Programmes Adviser: Jeremy Thompson.

CONCORDIA

Concordia (Youth Service Volunteers) Tel/Fax: 01273-422 218
Heversham House, 20-22 Boundary Rd
Hove, East Sussex, BN3 4ET

Concordia organises placements for volunteers aged 18-30 on international work camps throughout Europe and the USA; plus Turkey (including teaching English), Morocco, Tunisia, and Japan if you are aged 20+. Projects include conservation, children's summer camps, restoration of old buildings and social work with the mentally or physically disabled. Volunteers often work on projects with local people, and groups are led by locals. There is a registration fee of £70 and volunteers pay their own travel expenses and insurance, but board and lodging are free. Camps last two to three weeks and run mainly in June to September, although they do run at other times. Farmwork (with accommodation and a small wage provided by the

OVERSEAS VOLUNTARY WORK

farmer) is available in Switzerland and Norway for 3-8 weeks or 1-6 months respectively. Contact the Overseas Coordinator (before Easter if possible) for further information.

CORAL CAY CONSERVATION

Coral Cay Conservation　　　　　　　　　Tel: 0171-498 6248
The Ivy Works, 154 Clapham Park Road　　　Fax: 0171-498 8447
London SW4 7DE　　　　　　　　　　Web: *www.coralcay.org*

It's probably easier to get to Belize than to find Coral Cay's HQ in a south London yard, but it's worth the trip to hear about the work they are doing. In Belize Coral Cay provides the government with information about the Belize Barrier Reef in the hope of being able to set up more marine reserves. Since 1986 it has helped to establish eight new 'Marine Protected Areas', and it has now extended its work into the Philippines and Asia Pacific (see COUNTRY INDEX). The work supports long-term conservation only: a project in Honduras was turned down by CCC because it was not considered sustainable. Up to 40 volunteers are sent out each month to undertake surveys of coral reefs and/or tropical forests. The Belize and Philippines expeditions are popular with those hoping to study marine biology. Free scuba diving tuition is provided on site for volunteers requesting it. They will have to pass a stringent medical examination (for diving up to 28 metres deep) before leaving the UK, and work pretty hard to finance the trip: costs vary from £650 (two weeks) to £2,550 for a 12-week expedition, excluding airfare.

CRUSADERS

Crusaders　　　　　　　　　　　　　Tel: 01727-855 422
FREEPOST 544, St. Albans,　　　　　　　Fax: 01727-848 518
Herts. AL3 4BR　　　　　　　　　　Web: *www.crusaders.org.uk*

This is a Christian organisation which offers young people the chance to 'work for God'. Crusaders runs a variety of programmes, one of which is CRUSOE (Crusaders Overseas Expeditions). Volunteers, who must be committed Christians, stay for three to five weeks in South America, Africa or India. (Locations change slightly each year.) Also programmes for 14-15 year olds in Europe. Projects

OVERSEAS VOLUNTARY WORK

involve practical work (such as building) and working with street children, orphans and other evangelistic projects. Information about the 1999 programme was due to be be available in November 1998, with a selection weekend in February 1999. Successful candidates chosen need to raise £600 to go to Europe or £1,300 to cover costs if going to other continents (this includes a contribution to the project you will be working on). Contact CRUSOE for more information.

EARTHWATCH

Earthwatch   Tel: 01865-311 600
57 Woodstock Road   Fax: 01865-311 383
Oxford OX2 6HJ   Web: *www.earthwatch.org*

Conservation charity which supports research and exploration projects worldwide by finding paying volunteers to act as field workers. Trips are usually for two weeks and prices can get quite high for the more exotic trips. Some are cheaper: for example 'Mammoth Caves' costs £370 excluding air fares. There are more than 130 projects, ranging from 'Land of the Snow Leopard' and 'Indonesian Sun Cooking' to 'Komodo Dragons in Indonesia', where you could find yourself dealing with 'small dinosaurs' more than two metres long which can outrun and outswim you. Fortunately you'll only be freeing them from traps for tasks like blood-sampling for genetic testing (£1,870 for this three-week trip). Earthwatch insists that these are real scientific expeditions, but you don't need special qualifications. Contact Laura Morrison or Alison Bartlett for more information.

OVERSEAS VOLUNTARY WORK

ENGLISH-SPEAKING UNION (ESU)

ESU
Dartmouth House
37 Charles Street, London W1X 8AB

Tel: 0171-493 3328
Fax: 0171-495 610
Web: *www.esu.org*

The ESU is a charitable organisation which organises educational exchange posts in high schools in the US and Canada, awarding up to 40 scholarships a year to gap-year students. Assignments are from two to three terms. Tuition and board are free, but you need to allow around £2,000 for fares and pocket money. (See advertisement opposite and CHAPTER 5: LANGUAGES for more information.)

FRIENDS OF ISRAEL EDUCATIONAL TRUST

Friends of Israel Educational Trust (FOIET)
25 Lyndale Avenue
London NW2 2QB

Tel: 0171-435 6803
Fax: 0171-794 0291
E-mail: *foi_asg@msn.com*

FOIET is a British foundation, founded in 1976, which has developed link-ups between Israel and the UK. Its programme 'Bridge in Britain' was started in 1980. Each year up to 12 'Bridge in Britain scholarships' are made available to British school-leavers. Award winners spend six months in Israel, working on a *kibbutz* (this involves working in a factory, on the land, or teaching); or teaching in an Israeli-Arab village; teaching English and running youth programmes in a *moshav* (a smallholders' co-operative) and in an Israeli new town.

Participants are sent to destinations in groups but are given different assignments individually or in pairs. Airfare, insurance, board and lodging is provided, though students need around £600 in spending money. All participants are encouraged to travel extensively in the area; within Israel, Palestinian areas, Jordan and Egypt. There is six months' structured work with weekends off and at least a month's worth of days off and holidays. The number of participants varies a great deal because many people are wary of travelling to the volatile Middle East. Director John Levy assures us that 'safety is absolutely paramount.' For more information write with an SAE.

OVERSEAS VOLUNTARY WORK

FRONTIER

Frontier Ltd   Tel: 0171-613 2422
77 Leonard Street   Fax: 0171-613 2992
London EC2A 4QS   Web: *www.mailbox.co.uk/frontier*

Non-profit organisation. Some 200 'flexible and committed volunteers', usually aged between 18-25, are sent each year on 10-week environmental research expeditions to Mozambique (diving), Tanzania (rainforest), Tanzania (diving), Tanzania (savanna), or Vietnam (rainforest). Usually run in conjunction with a university or government department in the host country with the aim of helping long-term conservation projects. This is a scientific survey but it is open to everyone. Training is given in the first week in the form of lectures and techniques are shown in field. The work is rigorous but done as a group which can ease the strain a bit. While you are doing this there is not a great deal of opportunity to move around and most people tend to stay in the area they are working in for the duration. Field work from January-March, April-June, July-September, October-December. Applications should be made six months to a year in advance. Cost: £2,900 including your visa, and a non-returnable £200 deposit which can be rolled over to another expedition if you don't raise the funds in time. A bit of extra petty cash is advisable for treats. Fundraising advice provided. Contact John Ramsay.

GAP ACTIVITY PROJECTS (GAP)

GAP Activity Projects (GAP)   Tel: 01189-594914
GAP House, 44 Queen's Road   Fax: 01189-576634
Reading, Berkshire RG1 4BB.   E-mail: *volunteer@GAP.org.uk*

GAP (no connection with this book) says it arranges more gap-year attachments than any other voluntary organisation, and its short-term teaching, social work and conservation assignments are heavily oversubscribed. Critics describe it as 'just a student job agency.' Fans believe short postings make sense for 1990s teenagers, many of whom want to pack as much as they can into a year off. In 1997/8, 1,970 candidates applied and 1,262 were placed.

OVERSEAS VOLUNTARY WORK

GAP's volunteer project managers stress that they consider the needs of the overseas host as well as the student looking for a job. 1998 school-leavers should send for a full brochure and application form at the beginning of their final A-Level year. Interviews begin in October and run until all the places are filled in the summer, and the earlier you apply, the better your chances of getting the assignment you want. The cost of going on a GAP assignment varies from £1,000 to £2,500 depending on the destination. It breaks down like this: non-refundable registration fee £35 (which gets you an interview); GAP fee £490 (including non-refundable deposit £75); insurance about £125 for nine months worldwide cover (you can arrange your own); a TEFL course, if necessary, from £120 for a one-week course. Add airfares. A word of warning from returning 'gappers': don't expect everything always to go smoothly or to be picked up by a representative if you have trouble. They are not always available.

GAP CHALLENGE

Gap Challenge Tel: 0181-537 7980
  at World Challenge Expeditions Tel: 0181-961 1122
Black Arrow House, 2 Chandos Road Fax: 0181-961 1551
London NW10 6NF E-mail: *welcome@world-challenge.co.uk*

World Challenge Expeditions has now been running its 'Gap Challenge' programmes for five years. Students of 18-25 are sent in small groups to Belize, Costa Rica (working with a leather-back turtle conservation group), India, Malawi, Malaysia, Nepal, Peru. South Africa or Tanzania. Placements last three to six months and include

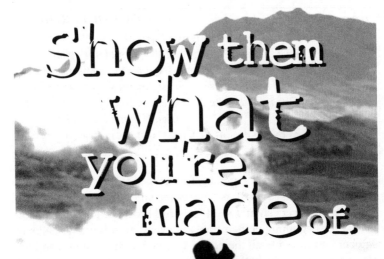

show them what you're made of.

Gap Challenge can provide you with the experience and education of a lifetime.

See another side of the world with our voluntary work placements. It's challenging and highly rewarding.

For over ten years, we've been organising placements and expeditions to some of the most fascinating places on earth.

From conservation projects in Belize and teaching in Tanzania to care work in Southern India.

Voluntary placements run from 3 to 6 months. And with a 12 month return flight there's plenty of opportunity and flexibility to travel on independently afterwards.

The cost of a placement ranges from £1,500 to £2,500. This includes training, flights, transfer to the destination, in-country support and a 24 hour emergency back-up from Gap Challenge HQ in London.

So show yourself what you're made of. Contact our young, friendly team on 0181 537 7980 for a comprehensive information pack and application form.

Email: welcome@world challenge.co.uk

Gap Challenge, World Challenge Expeditions, Black Arrow House, 2 Chandos Road, London NW10 6NF. Tel 0181 961 1122

AUSTRALIA • BELIZE • CANADA • COSTA RICA • ECUADOR • INDIA • MALAWI • MALAYSIA • NEPAL • PERU • SOUTH AFRICA • TANZANIA

teaching, social work, conservation, eco-tourism and agricultural work with local conservation groups. With a 12-month return flight, there is plenty of time for independent travel afterwards. In India and Nepal an introductory week is organised by World Challenge, when the group stays together and sees a bit of the country before volunteers go to their posts. Paid work is available in Canada (in hotels or mountain lodges). Placements start in January and September and although you can apply as little as a month before the starting date, it is better to do so as far in advance as you can. Placement costs range from £1,500 to £2,000, which includes the training course, return flight, transfer to the destination, in-country support from appointed representatives and 24-hour emergency back-up and support from Gap Challenge in London.

GLENCREE CENTRE FOR RECONCILIATION

Glencree Centre for Reconciliation   Tel: (00 3531) 282 9711
Glencree, Enniskerry, Co. Wicklow, Ireland

This centre is an autonomous non-governmental organisation working together 'with everybody who tries to bring peace in whatever area of society'. Contact Naoise Kelly (that's a man) for information about short-term volunteer posts (two months in summer, if you like gardening, cooking, arts, crafts, computing) or one-year posts.

HEALTH PROJECTS ABROAD (HPA)

Health Projects Abroad (HPA)   Enquiry Line: 01629-640 053
PO Box 24, Bakewell   Tel/Fax: 01629 640 051/4
Derbys. DE 45 1ZW   E-mail: *hpauk@dialpipex.com*

A charity started in 1989 that channels aid to Tanzania through a health volunteer scheme. The rural communities they help identify the health facilities that need to be improved. HPA takes about 120 people aged 18-28 (more men desired as the majority of volunteers are female) out for three months' manual labour in the dry season each year. There are three three-month sessions, starting in late April, late June and late August. There is no pretence that volunteers

OVERSEAS VOLUNTARY WORK

are going to teach or train — they are more likely to be digging or plastering alongside local people. Volunteers need to raise £3,000 to cover all travel and in-country costs, medical insurance, the cost of the three residential weekends in the UK, and a contribution towards the development programme. Apply 10 months before the departure date. Write to Cath Rowlatt (Volunteer Programme Manager) at HPA.

INTERSERVE

Interserve
325 Kennington Rd
London SE11 4QH

Tel: 0171-735 8227
Fax: 0171-587 5362
Web: *www.interserve.org*

This organisation is a self-financing international missionary society, which runs a programme for school leavers in Asia and the Middle East called 'On Track'. Working with members of the local churches, volunteers tackle projects like work with street children or deaf people. Placements last 2-12 months. Volunteers must be 18+ and active members of their local church. Applications should be made as early as possible. The cost is around £1,500 depending on where you are going, including air ticket and board and lodging. Orientation/training weekend before you go, a week's in-country training and debriefing when you get back. Contact Dave Taylor.

JACOB'S WELL

Jacob's Well Appeal
2 Ladygate, Beverley,
East Yorks HU17 8BH

Tel: 01482-881 478
Fax: 01482-865 452
E-mail: *100575.2205@compuserve.com*

About 60-80 people go to Romania each year with Jacob's Well to do work in the community and in a hospital and a day centre for mentally handicapped children. 'Work' involves loving, caring and playing. Volunteers must be 18 or over and pay their own travel costs (around £250) and living expenses while living with a Romanian family ($20 a week in summer, $25 a week in winter to include fuel). Placements 1-3 months; some people go back again. Contact Agnes Perry; telephone as above or write to 57 Cherry Garth, Beverley, E. Yorks HU17 0EP.

OVERSEAS VOLUNTARY WORK

KIBBUTZ REPRESENTATIVES

Kibbutz Representatives   Tel: 0181-458 9235
1a, Accommodation Road   Fax: 0181-455 7930
London NW11 8ED   E-mail: *enquiries@kibbutz.org.uk*

A *kibbutz*, for those who don't know, is a farm that operates as a self-contained community, in Israel, and Kibbutz Representatives is officially part of the *kibbutz* movement. If you are 18-32 and both physically and mentally fit, KR will organise a place for you (hard manual work, which could be 'light industrial', farming, cooking or worling with children) either as an individual or as a group. Eight hours a day working pays for your board, lodging and laundry. You must apply and be interviewed, and if successful you will be guaranteed a placement. Cost: £330-£350 including year long open return air fare and insurance. Minimum stay eight weeks (six in summer).

MARLBOROUGH BRANDT GROUP

Marlborough Brandt Group   Tel: 01672-514 078
1a London Road, Marlborough,   Fax: 01672-514 922
Wilts SN8 1PH   E-mail: *mbguk@compuserve.com*

This organisation was set up as a link between Marlborough and the village of Gunjur, in the Gambia, and has been sending volunteers (from all over the UK and beyond) to teach in the middle school there since 1984. Three to four people go out in September and stay until the following August. They live with a family in the village (you get given a Gambian name) and food and accommodation are free, though conditions are basic. Selection is by interview, two training weekends are held to prepare people, and there is an induction course on arrival in Gunjur. There are opportunities to travel in West Africa in the school holidays, and 'you experience total immersion in African culture'. The registration fee of £200 covers training expenses and you need to raise about £3,000 to cover your fare, insurance, travelling and pocket money. There is often significant help (in the form of sponsorship) available from charities. Write a letter explaining why you want to apply, to the director at the above

OVERSEAS VOLUNTARY WORK

KIBBUTZNIK

"There are two companies that organize kibbutzes, Kibbutz Representatives or Project 67, which I went with. There's a short introductory talk in England and once you're in Israel you get randomly allocated to one of 200 kibbutzes. I was up in the north, but some people landed up in the desert.

This was the basic working day: Up at six or earlier, depending on your job, then work until lunch. The rest of the day you have free. There were lots of different jobs, for example in the kitchens, preparing food (which was a drag). The main two things at my kibbutz were avocados and fish. Picking avocados was brilliant because you just lounged in the sun all day and picked the occasional avocado. You get full board, and a bit of money: if you don't smoke or drink it is possible to make money, but basically don't expect to. I went in March when there was really nice weather, and sometimes there were trips organized for us – we visited Jerusalem and the Sea of Galilee.

No girls ever worked in avocados or anything really physical because they're traditionally men's jobs: most of them worked in the guest houses. I was never in one job for long time, which is a good thing because if you've got a nightmare job, you know you're not going to have to hack it for long. The afternoons were spent relaxing — we had an indoor pool, basketball courts, and played a lot of frisbee. Mostly kibbutzniks were really nice, but the older citizens tended to look down on us and treated us as second-class citizens. However, in the pubs I got to know some of the younger, more sociable kibbutzniks, who were really friendly. About a third of the 30 workers were on their gap year. The rest had either just finished uni and didn't want to settle down yet or made up the surprising amount of unemployed people taking breaks. I had one day off a week, and each month we were allowed about three days off, during which I went to Jerusalem with a couple of other guys and had a really good time. The living accommodation was pretty basic with two or three to a room. We complained at the time but it wasn't really that bad. We also had MTV so I watched Beavis and Butthead every day."

Roddy Black, Oxford University, 1998

OVERSEAS VOLUNTARY WORK

address attaching a typed CV and the names and addresses of two referees, by the end of November.

PROJECT 67

Project 67
10 Hatton Garden, London EC1N 8AH

Tel: 0171-831 7626
Fax: 0171-404 5588
E-mail: *project67@aol.com*

This company organises working holidays on *kibbutz* and *moshav* in Israel, mostly in summer. On a *kibbutz* the student is expected to blend in with the community, working with the members in the fields, factories or with animals. Food and accommodation is provided. On a *moshav* the students live with a family and work on the farm and are paid. The cost is £230-300 including a return flight, guaranteed placement, and a night in Tel Aviv if needed. Those going to a *moshav* are usually older than the average gap-year student (20-35), but there are exceptions. The old image of volunteers working in the fields from sunrise to sunset is a misconception; it is more likely you will be doing mundane jobs, and have a lot of free time. This free time usually has to be spent on the farm, with one day off a week. However subsidised beer flows freely and people seem very relaxed.

PROJECT TRUST

Project Trust
The Hebridean Centre, Ballyhough
Isle of Coll, Argyll,
Scotland PA78 6TE

Tel: 01879-230 444
Fax: 01879-230 357
Web:*www.projecttrust.org.uk*

Project Trust offers long-term gap-year posts — for those who want to do voluntary work for twelve months. Fans say that this length of time is necessary to really understand appreciate another culture, and that employers will be impressed by you spending a whole year away. Critics say a whole year in one place is too long for an 18-year-old to be away from home, and fear it can disconnect them completely. Run by the no-nonsense MacLean-Bristols from the Isle of Coll near Mull, PT sends some 200 students away each year. Posts include Africa, Thailand and others. Apply up to December 1998 for

OVERSEAS VOLUNTARY WORK

BAA, BAA, BAA, BAA, BAA, BAA, BAA, BAA, BAA, BAA

"I spent five and a half months in the Falkland Islands sheep farming. The farm I was working on had 70,000 sheep, give or take a couple. One thing I did was sorting the wool, as it varies a lot in type and quality. Some of this involved picking maggots, boils, skin and dung out of the wool, and eleven hours of that got a bit much by the end of the day. The other main thing I did was pressing the wool. This involves chucking fleeces into a pit and then jumping on them. They compress massively, so you end up underground and wait for people to chuck more fleeces down at you. This was very hard work, but got me really fit."

James de Ville, Buckinghamshire University College, 1998

1999/2000 places. You will be invited to a one-week selection course on Coll, then successful candidates go on a training course on Coll in July/August 1998. Student is expected to raise £3,250 from sponsors, including £110 in deposits (£50 back if you don't get a place). PT gives fund-raising guidance including local workshops. Total covers project fees, airfare and medical insurance but not UK travel.

QUEST OVERSEAS

Quest Overseas
25 Storey's Way,
Cambridge CB3 ODP

Tel: 01223-462 932
Fax: 01223-575 514
Web: *www.quest-overseas.co.uk*

Quest Overseas runs projects in Central and South America (£3,300-600 excluding return airfare). Departures summer and Jan/Feb; apply as early as possible, but some places may be available three months beforehand. The Latin American project starts with a language course in Quito, Ecuador, followed by four weeks either in Lima, Peru, working in orphanages, or doing rainforest conservation in Ecuador or working on the Yavari: this is a boat built in 1862 which was sailed from London to Lima and then taken apart, transported by mule up to Lake Titicaca (the highest navigable lake in the world, and put back together again). After one of these projects you do a six-week expedition through the Andes. Alternatively, you could do the Central America project (language course followed by

174

OVERSEAS VOLUNTARY WORK

conservation work such as saving turtles on Costa Rica's beaches) or the other Latin American programme which has a language course followed by a 12-week journey from the equator to Tierra del Fuego. Quest has stopped sending people to South Africa as it is considered too dangerous.

RALEIGH INTERNATIONAL

Raleigh International   Tel: 0171-371 8585
Raleigh House, 27 Parson's Green Lane   Fax: 0171-371 5116
London SW6 4HZ   Web: *www.raleigh.org.uk*

The organisation that sends people on expeditions rather than arranging overseas voluntary work placements. During the expedition you do three projects (community, environmental and adventure) with the emphasis on personal development (leadership, teamwork, communication). Raleigh insists the projects usually benefit host communities. Open to anyone from 17-25 who can swim and speak English. Raleigh has about 1,000 places on offer each year (including young people from other countries and the expedition host countries). In 1999 expeditions will include Belize, Chile, Namibia and Mongolia. Starts with a challenging assessment weekend, including lots of group work. Most expeditions last 10 weeks and there is at least one starting most months between January and October. Apply at least six months ahead of the expedition start date. Costs: Registration and assessment £25, and the recruit must raise £2,995 in sponsorship fees for expedition, which includes all transport and insurance costs. Fund raising support is given, including nationally organised events. Contact Information Desk.

RIGHT HAND TRUST

Right Hand Trust   Tel: 01938-810 215
Gelligason, Llanfair Caereinion   Fax: 01938-810 215
Powys SY21 9HE

The Right Hand Trust is a Christian organisation which sends gap-year students and graduates to Africa, and recently to the Caribbean. Its work in Africa is mainly in Gambia, Kenya, Malawi,

OVERSEAS VOLUNTARY WORK

WORM GOES TO NEPAL

"In October I decided to go to Nepal to work on the Environmental Education programme with Schools Partnership Worldwide (SPW). Two of my friends were going in November, and another one who was leaving in February wanted me to go with her. Once we arrived in Kathmandu we were taken to a place 40 minutes away called Dhulikel. We stayed there for two weeks, generally adjusting and also having intensive language training every morning. We then used to walk about town speaking to the locals, and attempting to shop, although all you could buy was chillis, shawls, Dettol and cigarettes (the Nepali brand cost 11p for 20). In the second week of our stay there, we met our Nepali counterparts: 12 of them, about the same age as us. I'll never forget first meeting them. I just wondered how on earth we would be able to communicate. We did however understand that the more effort we put in into getting along with them, the more successful the programme would be. One of the unique things about the SPW environmental programme is the fact that you worked alongside Nepalis your own age for four months, making brilliant friends with them and using this bond to motivate other young people into doing something to improve their standard of living.

So after our first two weeks we went to Chitwan National Park, which is a protected jungle and home to many endangered species. Considering the week was supposed to be training, we had the biggest laugh. We went on a jungle walk to 'observe the ecosystem' that involved spotting crocodiles, parrots and monkeys. The work we did on training included interviewing local people about their problems, such as ecotourism (loads of tourists whose money goes to emigrant hotel owners from Kathmandu rather than the true local people who need the money) and also the people-park conflict.

If a rhino destroys an entire village's crops in one night, the villagers get no compensation and have no money to build a fence. So we talked them through with our our Nepali counterparts to find out what solutions they could think of. This would help us when we were working on outreach in smaller groups in really rural villages, trying to help the villagers solve their problems...

OVERSEAS VOLUNTARY WORK

WORM GOES TO NEPAL

... In the evenings we interviewed local people again, to give us some more ideas about possible ways of income generation. There is an organisation called ACAP (Annapurna Conservation Area Project) that makes sure money made from tourism is channelled into raising the standard of living in the area and conserving the local environment. We learnt about the problems of deforestation — ACAP has very strict rules on not using the trees for firewood, but none of the villagers can afford kerosene gas so there is a lot of conflict there. One of the most memorable moments was being invited into the home of three women and their husbands and children. The home consisted of one room and by the light of a single candle, we could make out two wooden beds with no mattress and a few pots and pans. This was all these people possessed : two of the women had had children by the age of sixteen, and they had no skills whatsoever. The literacy rate in Nepal was 37 per cent and only 1 per cent of women could name the Prime Minister. We then spent three weeks in a true Nepali village. One Nepali volunteer and one British volunteer lived in the same house together, so it wasn't such a culture shock. We ate daal bhat in our individual families, sitting on the mud floor and eating with our right hands, and then we all met up at the tea shop for a cup of tea. In the training village we learnt how to build smokeless stoves because 97 per cent of mothers suffer from respiratory diseases, (hardly surprising as none of the lower caste houses have chimneys) and they just inhale all the smoke from the fire they're cooking on. Our main focus was learning how to build low-cost technology that would benefit the villagers, such as how to plant a vegetable garden that enables a variety of vegetables to grow, and we supplemented it with nutritional advice for the mothers.

Despite the fact that Nepal is the third poorest country in the world, you come away feeling that it is much richer than the West. You go into the home of a family that materialistically speaking has nothing, yet they have so much to offer, amd you learn so much just being there. It is an education that no school can give you."
Hermione ('Worm') Love, Music at Manchester University, 1998

OVERSEAS VOLUNTARY WORK

Swaziland, Uganda, and Zimbabwe. The students are usually involved in teaching and social work, with another student, in a rural community. The training process begins in July with an induction course (five days). Students then have until Christmas to raise around £2,300 (which covers flights, insurance, training and accommodation). In December there is a cross-cultural training course in conjunction with USPG (United Society for the Propagation of the Gospel) for eight days. Around the New Year participants are sent to Africa for a five-day acclimatisation course, after which they are sent to their teaching posts to begin the school year in January. The posts run until August. Contact Mark Wright.

SHORT TERM EXPERIENCE PROJECTS (STEP)

Latin Link   Tel: 0171-207 5880
325 Kennington Road   Fax: 0171-207 5885
London SE11 4QE   Web: *www.latinlink.org/latinlink*

As part of the missionary society Latin Link, this organisation sends up to 180 volunteers on projects to central and south America. There is an orientation weekend in England, training in-country, and debriefing on return. The work is with local churches, building schools, health centres and orphanages or doing evangelical work. There are two projects: the first runs from mid-March to mid-July (four months: £1,580), and the second from mid-July to September (six to seven weeks: £1,280). You can do both (nearly six months) for £1,940. The cost includes food and accommodation, a first-aid course, equipment and travel. Volunteers must be over 17 and active members of their local church. Apply by end of November for projects the following spring and May for posts the same year. Contact Simon Walsh.

OVERSEAS VOLUNTARY WORK

STUDENTS PARTNERSHIP WORLDWIDE (SPW)

Students Partnership Worldwide   Tel: 0171-222 0138
17 Dean's Yard   Fax: 0171-963 1006
London SW1P 3PB   Web: *www.spw.org*

SPW sends about 300 students aged 18-25 abroad each year to work on various projects, and the majority of these now come from outside its 40 sponsoring schools. (Check if your school is one that will give you help towards the costs by sponsoring you). You can teach in Namibia, Nepal, South Africa, Tanzania, Uganda or Zimbabwe, or work on environmental projects in Nepal, Tanzania, Uganda or Zimbabwe, and there are also social work placements in India. You could help start chicken farms, build stoves in remote villages, or help with AIDS awareness. In all destinations apart from India, there is an SPW office, staff and local volunteers and you get between three and seven weeks' training. The India programme is quite separate from the rest of SPW, and although we have heard good things about the Nepal programme, reports from India are less good. Applications are on a first come first served basis, so apply early in your final year at school, although places may be available up to a couple of months before departure. Costs for teaching projects are £2,100-300 and include travel, insurance, a living allowance, training and administration overseas. The environmental programmes cost £2,400-600 inclusive.

ST DAVID'S (AFRICA) TRUST

St David's (Africa) Trust   Tel: 01873-810665
St David's House, Rectory Road   Fax: 01873-810665
Crickhowell, Powys, NP8 1DW   Web: *www.gibnet.gi/~stdavids*

This mix of language learning and voluntary work looks ideal for post-A-Level students (18 or over) with an interest in Arabic and Islamic culture and history — several students have been out to Morocco on a six-month placement with St David's Trust before starting a degree in Arabic. You can work with children and animals. Reasonably good conversational French is needed; GSCE will probably do but A-level preferrred. St David's Trust will be taking

OVERSEAS VOLUNTARY WORK

volunteers to its traditional Moroccan house in Taroudant at the foot of the Atlas Mountains for three months from September 1998 and 1999, and six months from January 1999. Also placements with the Leprosy Rehabilitation Centre in Cape Coast, Ghana (useful for people wanting to work later for development organisations such as Oxfam, Save the Children or United Nations agencies). Full cost varies from £1,250 to £2,500 but director David Denison says two thirds of his placements are partially funded from other sources.

TEACHING ABROAD

Teaching Abroad Tel: 01903-859 911
Gerrard House, Rustington Fax: 01903-785 779
West Sussex BN16 1AW Web: *www.teaching-abroad.uk.com*

Another agency which organises teaching placements for a fee, this one puts volunteers in Brazil, China, Ghana, India, Mexico, Russia and Ukraine. Charges range from £745 to around £1,700 and include food, lodging, travel and local back-up. Also Projects Abroad, which covers many projects including unpaid work experience in business or medicine, and also social work, conservation and architecture. Business placements include journalism (with the Institute of Journalism in Ghana, and allocated to radio stations and the press), accountancy and finance. The medical placements include anything from dentistry to being a vet, and you may even find yourself attending an operation — something to impress medical school with? These start any time and last from as little as one month to as long as a year. See advertisement opposite.

TREKFORCE EXPEDITIONS

Trekforce Expeditions Tel: 0171-824 8890
138 Buckingham Palace Road Fax: 0171-824 8892
London, SW1W 9SA Web: *www.ds.dial.pipex.com/town/parade/hu15*

Trekforce is the expeditionary arm of the International Scientific Support Trust. It takes groups of 17-year-olds and upwards on conservation-based expeditions to the rainforests of Indonesia and Kenya. The projects last for six weeks. Applicants have to raise £2,350 — presenting a tough target as all expeditions do — but

OVERSEAS VOLUNTARY WORK

Trekforce says it offers copious advice and training weekends as well as a one week jungle 'familiarisation' on arrival. Also a five-month 'gap' programme in Belize which includes a six-week expedition and learning Spanish in Mexico to teach English in Belize (£3,500). There is no official cut-off date for applications but it is best to have them in as soon as possible so that there is time for raising the sponsorship funds. Neither price includes air fares. (See advertisement on page 180.)

UNITED NATIONS ASSOCIATION INTERNATIONAL YOUTH SERVICE

UNAIYS, Temple of Peace   Tel: 01222-223088
Cathays Park, Cardiff CF1 3AP, Wales   Fax: 01222-665557

UNAIYS is affiliated to the United Nations Association and is for people who believe in the principles of the United Nations charter. It organises work camps for two to three weeks for about 350 volunteers each year, ranging from archaeology and arts and cultural work to work with refugees and children's play projects. You pay for travel and a £80-£120 registration fee, but board and lodging are provided. Over 60 countries worldwide, from Albania to Zimbabwe.

VILLAGE EDUCATION PROJECT

Village Education Project   Tel: 01732-459 799
c/o Niss K J Allen, Mint Cottage,
Prospect Road, Sevenoaks, Kent TN13 3UA

Teaching children in rural primary schools in the Marangu region of Mount Kilimanjaro in Tanzania. Age 18 or over. Cost £1,575 excluding visa, pocket money, food and insurance. Two weeks pre-departure training in Sevenoaks learning some basic Swahili and English teaching skills. January to August/September.

OVERSEAS VOLUNTARY WORK

NEOLITHIC NON-DIG

*"I went on an archaeological dig for two weeks in Argos, Greece.
There were quite a few people from different units and loads of
museum people. There are loads of digs in Argos because it's the
only place that has evidence from Neolithic times, and the city itself
is expanding so fast that every time they build something they have
to excavate. Argos is quite a small city and during the time we
were there, there were seven digs going on. We just sat in the shade
while all the builders dug. There is some law in Greece that means
archaeologists can't do the actual digging, which believe you me is
a godsend when it's an absolutely scorching 30 degrees."*
Emma Ahlas, Manchester University, 1998
(See CHAPTER 6: OTHER EXTRAS)

WILDLIFE VOLUNTEERS

Wildlife Volunteers   Tel: 01449-720 820
Alder Carr Farm   E-mail:*hardingham@aldercar.keme.co.uk*
Creeting St Mary, Ipswich, Suffolk

This organisation has recently been started up by Joan Hardingham,
who was born in South Africa (graduating in Zoology) and hopes to
bring together wildlife conservation projects in Southern Africa and
volunteers from the UK. She explains that because farmers are turning their farms over to nature reserves in South Africa, some will
provide food and lodging in exchange for volunteer labour, with the
placements varying from one place to another. In July 1998 she was
looking for an assistant to an archaeologist or ecologist working on
a 'Veld Assessment' and students for game and plant surveying and
patrolling on reserves. Check out safety thoroughly first.

WORLD CHALLENGE EXPEDITIONS

Organisers of Gap Challenge, page 167.

OVERSEAS VOLUNTARY WORK

YWAM

Youth with a Mission   Tel: 01332-360 987
Year for God   Fax: 01332-299 658
Overdale House, 96 Whitaker Rd   Web: *www.ywam-england.com*
Derby DE23 6AP   E-mail: *yfg@compuserve.com*

Youth With a Mission (YWAM) is a Christian organisation which sends people to serve overseas for a year starting in September. Mature 18-year-olds are considered. After some orientation to the locality (including a week in the UK), you get stuck in to a development project, doing, say, work with street children or AIDS sufferers, in teams of 2-8 people. During the year you complete a 'discipleship training school' (DTS) which consists of three months of lectures and two to three months on a field assignment. The DTS can be done at any time during the course. In 1998/9 teams are going to Albania, Argentina, Brazil, India, Kazakhstan, Russia and Uganda. The cost is about £3,500, including air fare, food and accommodation, DTS and insurance.

WWOOF

WWOOF   Tel/Fax: 01273-476 286
PO Box 2675, 19 Bradford Rd, Lewes, E. Sussex BN7 1RB

An organisation which places volunteers on organic farms in the UK or abroad: for example, working weekends or longer stays. Voluntary work is unpaid, usually on small farms that cannot afford to take on employees but like having volunteers to stay. You work for your board and lodging having paid a small (£10) joining fee to WWOOF, who can give you a list of WWOOF hosts and contact organisation in Europe or further afield. Write for info: SAE 9" by 4".

Useful information

Youth for Britain is a database (PC floppy disks £95) of information for 16-25 year olds, listing organisations offering international volunteer projects. If your school careers office doesn't have it you can contact YfB for a questionnaire which you fill in with your requirements and they will do a search for you for £15. (Tel: 01963-220 036)

DRUGS

Medicines Act 1968

This regulates the manufacture and supply of certain substances, many of which are used as medicines. It does not criminalise the use or possession of these substances.

Misuse of Drugs Act 1971

This places restrictions on what can be done with substances which are defined as 'controlled drugs'. Offences created by the Act include the possession (including past possession), supply, possession with intent to supply, production or cultivation, importation or exportation of some or all of these drugs. It is also an offence to offer to supply or be concerned in the supply of a controlled drug. The legal definition of 'supply' is very wide. It covers any form of distribution including the selling, giving and sharing of drugs to or with others. So if, for example, you are looking after drugs for someone, intending to return them, or if you buy drugs for distribution among friends who have contributed to the price, or if you share joints with people, you may be charged with a supply offence. The police have the power to stop and search you on the street if they have a 'reasonable suspicion' that you are in possession of a controlled drug. Controlled drugs are divided into three classes, A, B, and C, and five schedules. The class which the drug is in will dictate how serious the penalty will be for crime involving it. Class A includes heroin, cocaine, ecstacy, LSD, opium, cannabis oil and amphetamine which has been prepared for injection. Class B includes cannabis and amphetamine. Class C includes the benzodiazepines (valium, temazepam) and anabolic steroids. The schedule which the drug is in will dictate, amongst others things, the circumstances in which it can be lawfully possessed or supplied, and whether it can be prescribed or not. What penalty you get will depend upon the seriousness of the offence. As a general rule, you will get a non-custodial sentence, such as a fine or a community service order, for an offence of simple possession, but any offence involving an element of supply will carry the risk of a prison sentence.

Release (Advice Line 0171-729 9904) July 1998

Drugs overseas

You think that's tough? In some foreign countries (for example, Malaysia and Singapore) the penalty for importing drugs is death.

OVERSEAS VOLUNTARY WORK

Feedback

Feedback from gap-year students circulates all year round. Mothers swap early news over Christmas drinks; friends meet over *fajitas* to exchange anecdotes, experiences, and real horror stories. Some gossip is true, some half-true, and some comes at the end of a chain of Chinese whispers bearing little relation to fact. Two years ago one girl was tragically killed by a crocodile. But sleeping students having their kidneys removed on Chinese trains? No evidence yet.

Even parents who think they are well-informed should sound out returning students and question voluntary organisations about their track record in a country or with a special project. The number of serious accidents is small and many of them could just as easily have happened at home. But students have died on projects abroad, most often in road accidents, by drowning, or as a result of taking drugs. Backpacker havens such as Zippolite in Mexico, East London beach in South Africa and Kovalam beach near Trivandrum in South India are said to have particularly dangerous sea currents: it cannot be emphasised enough that students should take care where and how they swim. Drugs, disease (including sexually transmitted diseases) also find easy prey in students abroad, and some volunteers have come back pregnant. More than one student has been suffocated by leaking fumes from old gas water heaters: windows should be kept open when using gas water-heaters, because in poor countries basic maintenance does not always get done.

The most frequent cry from parents, after a child returns from an overseas project, is that they did not realise the part they should have played themselves — to give their children as good a briefing as possible about foreign travel (including the country, language, customs, transport, clothes, food, risks) before departure. The overwhelming message is to prepare for the trip well in advance and give children the means (credit card and contact list at the very least) to keep in regular contact. Generally the credit card should not be used to spend more than £50 — not for trading jewels in Bangkok.

Overseas paid work

Overseas voluntary work has been dealt with, and those who want to travel without necessarily looking for work can turn to CHAPTER 9: TRAVEL. Here we give a few tips about paid vacation work abroad and guide you to some of the organisations and publications that already cover this area well. Favourite ways of paying your way include au pair and ski chalet jobs, waitressing and bar work, teaching English — and private initiatives.

Plan ahead

It's no good getting a visa to work abroad if there are hardly any jobs available in the country you are going to. Just after we went to press last year Thailand's currency and stockmarket collapse began to spread to the rest of Asia, leading from boom to bust across the region a year later. No jobs? A lot depends on how well a country's tourism industry is doing, and when that's going well there is always work for English-speakers.

Finding work in Europe is easier if you plan to stay there some time — if you're in Paris as an au pair you get to know your way about and it's easier to pick up restaurant work, for example. Bear in mind that in some less-developed countries paying for working visas can be a waste of money unless you have a job lined up in advance. And make sure any work you do is legal in that country — you do not want to be deported. It is a good idea to check laws and student employment information with the relevant embassy department in London if you are interested in finding work abroad. Well-staffed embassies can be very helpful: there are lists in CHAPTER 5: LANGUAGES..

Au pair

The Louse Woodward case (the conviction of an English nanny in the USA for the murder, later reduced to manslaughter, of a baby in her charge) has made people more cautious about taking on au pair work, and au pair agencies are now having to give a lot of legal advice. However, if you want to get to grips with a

OVERSEAS PAID WORK

foreign language but don't fancy forking out for food and a dismal flat, consider being an au pair. It involves living with a foreign family, often in Europe, for several months.

In return for board, lodgings and pocket money (around £40 per week in Europe in local currency depending on the exchange rate against sterling) you will be expected to look after the children and do light domestic chores like ironing, cooking, tidying their bedrooms and doing their washing, for six hours a day, five days a week, as well as spending two or three evenings a week baby-sitting. If you are asked to work more than this then technically you are not doing the work of an au pair, but of a mother's help (which pays more). Being an au pair is a good way to immerse yourself in a different culture, learn a new language and hopefully save some extra cash.

A good starting point for finding reputable au pair agencies is to see if they are members of FRES (the Federation of Recruitment and Employment Services), which has a Website listing all its members and covering au pair employment in many countries (see below). If you have a complaint against a member agency you can take it up with FRES.

FRES (Federation of Recruitment and Employment Services)
36-38 Mortimer St, London W1N 7RB

Tel: 0171-323 4300
Fax: 0171-255 2878
Web: *www.fres.co.uk*

The agency should ask for an interview and references, and maybe a medical certificate. It's illegal for them to charge you any money before they've found you a place, and even when you've accepted a place the registration fee should not be more than £40. Make sure the agency has connections where you'll be working, get a list of other local au pairs so you have support when you're out there, and take your time finding a suitable family. The fewer children the better, and you should expect your own room. It's also worth checking what there is to do in your free time — you don't really want to spend every weekend in your bedroom because there's nothing else to do.

Before you leave, check you have written confirmation of the hours, duties and pay agreed as well as photocopies of all important documents such as passport, birth certificate, and translations of any academic certificates to prove your student status. Extra passport photos are a good idea (even if they're not needed, the chronic pose usually gets a good laugh from the children). Also worth a thought is the number and address of the local British Consulate If you hold a British driving licence it's a good idea to translate the details so you can apply for an international driver's licence. (See CHAPTER 8: TRAVEL for more information on driving abroad.) Additional agencies can be found in *The New Good Nanny Guide* (£14.99, published by Vermilion, Random House) and *The Au Pair and Nanny's Guide to Working Abroad* (£10.95, published by Vacation Work.)

Au pair in France

If you fancy sipping a cappucino on a Parisian boulevard you can try working in France as an au pair. In exchange for about 30 hours work a week (leaving most evenings and weekends free to

OVERSEAS PAID WORK

enjoy the nightlife) you receive full board and accommodation, as well as about £40 pocket money a week. Fluent French isn't necessary. GCSE standard will do, as many parents want you to speak English with the kids. Demand for au pairs in Paris is high all year, but obviously it rises at the beginning of the summer, and if you live in Paris, you'll probably get a chance to see another part of France when you accompany the family on their summer holiday. Living with a French-speaking family will improve your French out of all recognition, particularly your accent. If you hear it from dawn to dusk, you'll pick it up more effectively than from any textbook.

It is important to complete all the necessary paperwork for living and working in another country. If you are planning on staying for more than three months in France you need to apply for a *carte de séjour* which is valid for a year. This is obtained from the *mairie* (town hall) of your place of residence in France. Most agencies will organise the paperwork side for you, and make sure the legal documents are in order before you leave.

Au Pair Contact   Tel: 0181-748 2657
50 Ullswater Road, Barnes   Fax: 0181-563 0367
London SW13 9PN

This small agency, run by Michelle Webb, places au pairs in France. She has long-standing contacts with good French agencies who will organise the placement for you.

French Consulate   Tel: 0171-838 2000
21 Cromwell Road, London SW7 2EN   Fax: 0171-838 2001

Consulat Britannique   Tel: (00 331) 44.51.31.00
9 Avenue Hoch, 75008 Paris

Alternatively you may prefer to go direct to a French agency. The enrolment procedure is similar although there may be extra requirements: One such agency, *Accueil Familial des Jeunes Etrangers,* asks that applicants pay a Fr680 registration fee on joining the agency. If you drop out Fr400 of the fee will be reimbursed as long as the agency has been given one months' notice.

OVERSEAS PAID WORK

Most French agencies require a set of passport photos, with translations of two references, and your most recent academic qualifications, as well as a hand-written letter in French to your prospective family which tells them something about you, your reasons for becoming an au pair and any future aspirations. The agency may also ask for a medical certificate, again translated into French. The French consulate advises you to check that the family you will be staying with obtains a mother's help work contract (*accord de placement au pair d'un stagiaire aide-familial*) before you leave for France. (The employing family applies to the *Main d'oeuvre Etrangère*). You can expect to earn around Fr1,650, a month being a *jeune fille au pair*, and get a free orange card in Paris — valid for travel on the metro and buses and medical insurance.

Accueil Familial des Jeunes Etrangers   Tel: (00 331) 42.22.50.34
23 Rue du Cherche Midi, 75006 Paris   Fax: (00 331) 45.44.60.48

This agency places girls with families in the suburbs of Paris as well as in the city itself and in other towns throughout France.

Alliance Culturelle Internationale (A.C.I.)   Tel: (00 334) 93.13.44.13
4 Avenue Felix Fauré, 06000 Nice   Fax: (00 334) 93.92.58.85

ACI places au pairs between 18 and 30 years old. Telephone interviews are possible. It can also accept girls for a month or two in the summer as paying guests in families (no charge if the stay is in July or August). ACI operates within a large catchment area in the South of France, from Menton to Marseille, Aix-en-Provence, Arles, Montpellier, Toulouse, Var, St Tropez and Corsica. In touristy areas of the Cote d'Azur placements last for six months, and at other times of the year from six months to a year.

Comité Parisien de L'Association Catholique
    des Services de Jeunesse Feminine   Tel: (00 331) 44.32.12.90
63 Rue Monsieur le Prince, 75006 Paris   Fax: (00 331) 44.32.12.91

Worth checking out, but only open from 2pm-6pm Monday to Wednesday. Does help if you speak French.

OVERSEAS PAID WORK

Language classes

These are a definite must and if the family you are staying with
has not already allowed for this, it is worth making the time.
There are a number of good language schools serving most of
Paris. It is advisable to start researching the possibilities early on
in your stay, as places tend to fill up quickly. Expect to sit a short
written and/or oral test, set by the school so that it can assess
your proficiency in French. Usually lessons last for a couple of
hours at most and are run on a twice-weekly basis. Language
classes may have to be paid for up front, but they do provide a
chance to meet other au pairs of different nationalities and it is
amazing how quickly vocabulary and comprehension improve.
At the end of the course you may have to sit a short exam so that
you can be awarded a certificate of achievement.

Au pair in Italy

Similar requirements apply to au pairs in Italy. The average
wage for an au pair working five hours a day is about £50 a week,
but it could be as much as £100 a week for a mother's help working 10 hours a day. Within three days of arriving in Italy you will
have to register with the police to get a *permesso di soggiorno* (permit to stay), which lasts for three months.

Au Pairs Italy
46, The Rise, Sevenoaks, Kent TN13 1RJ   Tel: 01732 451 522

Italian Consulate   Tel: 0171-235 9371
38 Eaton Place, London SW1X 8AN   Fax: 0171-823 1609

Italian Consulate (visas)   Tel: 0891-600-340

... and across Europe

Au pairs should have some childcare experience, possibly speak
a European language, and usually be 18 years or over.

Au Pairs of Surrey Group   Tel: 01344-778 246
7 Highway, Edgecumbe Park   Fax: 01344-778 246
Crowthorne, Berkshire RG45 6HE   Web: *www.yell.co.uk/sites/aupair*
                                    E-mail: *aupair.surrey@mcmail.com*

OVERSEAS PAID WORK

An established agency which places au pairs throughout most of Europe. Having initially applied to Au Pairs of Surrey, your application is sent to approved agencies (also available for support once you're overseas) in Europe who vet the families. Language courses can be done at nearby language schools.

Solihull Au Pair & Nanny Agency   Tel: 0121-733-6444
1565, Stratford Road, Hall Green   Fax: 0121 733 6555
Birmingham B28 9JA

Mainly places au pairs in France, Italy, Spain, Switzerland, Belgium, Austria and Germany.

England & Overseas Nanny/Au Pair Bureau   Tel: 0171-494-2929
87, Regent Street, Piccadilly, London W1R 7HF   Fax: 0171 494 2922

This bureau has 28 overseas representatives and places au pairs aged 17 upwards.

...or au pair in America

You may be handed a car for your own use in the USA, but the word 'au pair' has a very different connotation in America and there has been a more cautious approach since the trial of English nanny Louise Woodward. The working hours are 45 hours a week, rather than the 30 or so expected in Europe. It is considered to be a full-time position, and the au pair is often in sole charge of the children. All au pair programmes are legislated and regulated by US law, which means (at the time of going to press), that all au pairs receive $139.05 (about £84) pocket money in return for 45 hours work a week, regardless of the agency. You can expect a good standard of living, full board and a room and use of a car. There are support networks for au pairs, once they arrive in the US: agencies should provide assigned co-ordinators who will act as mediators between au pair and family if difficulties arise — and it is possible to be reassigned to a different family.

Work with under-twos is more demanding and therefore most agencies ask that you have at least 200 hours of experience with that age group and are at least 19 years old.

OVERSEAS PAID WORK

The USA has a confusing bureaucratic system, and if you do not
follow the proper channels you risk earning money illegally and
even being deported. It is therefore important to go to an agency
that runs a bona-fide scheme. British and English-speaking
Europeans can go to the USA on a 'cultural exchange' with a J1
visa which is valid for a year. Candidates must be between 18
and 26 years of age, have a secondary education, experience or
training in childcare, hold a full driver's licence and be in good
health.

According to APIA, US government regulations stipulate that
au pairs must attend education courses (because au pair work is
seen primarily as a cultural exchange) "putting in a minimum of
three hours a week during term-time. This is financed by the host
family up to a limit of $500."

OVERSEAS PAID WORK

Au Pair in America (APIA)   Tel: 0171-581 7322
37 Queen's Gate,   Fax: 0171-581 7345/55
London SW7 5HR   Web: *www.aupairamerica.co.uk*

APIA has a freephone advice line (0800 413116) and a video about life as an au pair. A $400 'good faith deposit' (about £250) is payable when you are matched with a host family, and candidates will be reimbursed their deposit after completing the 12 months. (If you don't finish the programme, you break your agreement and lose the good faith deposit and the free flight home.) If you are aged between 18 and 26, APIA directs you to an appointed interviewer near you and your application is passed to its US office. Then families will get in contact and you will be expected to settle with the first family you feel comfortable with — not everyone can go to California. The APIA scheme includes medical insurance towards which candidates are required to contribute $100 and a four-day orientation course near New York which deals with first-aid, culture shock and what is expected in general child care. You get the statutory $139.05 a week in pocket money. There is now more demand for qualified childcarers so if you are 20 or over and have a childcare qualification or two years childcare experience under your belt, you could earn $190 a week (for the same hours work) with APIA's new programme 'Au Pair Extraordinaire', plus a $1,000 'completion bonus'.

AuPairCare Cultural Exchange   Tel: 01273-220 261
101 Lorna Road, Hove, Sussex BN3 3EL   Fax: 01273-220 376

AuPairCare is organised by Challenge Educational Services (with a head office in San Francisco) and gives British 18 to 26-year-olds the chance to be an au pair for an American family for a year. With AuPair Care, you can work with under twos if you're 18, provided you supply references, and have had 200 hours experience. You are not allowed to request a particular area in the US: AuPair Care says it prefers to match the character and needs of the family with yours and place you in an area where a local counsellor can keep in touch with you. (See CHAPTER 5: LANGUAGES for more information on Challenge.)

OVERSEAS PAID WORK

AuPair Homestay   Tel: 0345-626 984
287 Worcester Road   Fax: 01684-562 212
Malvern, Worcs. WR14 1AB

Au Pair Homestay (EIL) offers a one-year programme for male and female non-smokers between 18 and 26 who hold a clean driving licence and have child care experience. Au pairs lodge a £350 training fee deposit pre-departure, which is fully refunded on successful completion of the programme year. Air tickets for the whole journey are included in the programme at no cost. Au pairs receive a one-day pre-departure training day in the UK as well as three days of child care training in the USA on arrival which focuses on looking after American children and how to motivate difficult children. AuPair Homestay doesn't usually place au pairs younger than 21 with under-twos.

US Embassy   Tel: 0171-499 9000
24 Grosvenor Square, London W1A 2JB

The embassy is very longwinded if you're trying to find out about au pair work. It's better to contact an agency direct.

US Embassy (Visas)   Tel: 0171-499 684
5 Upper Grosvenor Street, London W1A 2JB

OVERSEAS PAID WORK

Teaching English as a foreign language

Teaching English as a foreign language is known as TEFL, and there are a lot of organisations happy to persuade you that a TEFL qualification is a very useful thing to have. Probably too many, in fact, because it's quite difficult for under-21s to get TEFL work abroad. Don't fork out a lot of money in vain.

Formal TEFL courses are available at colleges throughout the UK, but there is only one TEFL qualification recognised by the British Council and open to 18-year-olds, and that is the Trinity College Certificate in TESOL (Teaching English to Speakers of Other Languages). Courses that do not lead to this qualification are probably only worthwhile doing if linked to a voluntary work placement, and for voluntary work a short course will usually be recommended by the organisation concerned.

But you don't have to have any certificates to teach English informally abroad, and a short course will give you some idea of how to teach and increase your confidence. Weekend courses tend to focus on theory and longer courses usually involve some sort of teaching practice.

How to find work

There are always fluctuations in the availability of work for people who can teach English, particularly outside the EU. It used to be easy to find work in Japan, but more and more qualifications are now required there, and demand may be falling off in Eastern Europe since the rush into capitalism left everyone with a nearly redundant second language (Russian).

In most countries, however, it is possible to give private lessons. The best way to find out more about individual countries is to contact the relevant embassy in the UK, which will give you up-to-date details of visas, salaries, qualifications needed and a view about the availability of work. TEFL jobs are advertised in *The Times Educational Supplement* (on Thursdays and Fridays), *The Guardian* (on Tuesdays), in the education section of *The Independent* and in *The English Language Gazette*. Overleaf are some of the centres that run courses.

OVERSEAS PAID WORK

English Worldwide   Tel: 0171-252 1402
The Italian Building, Dockhead   Fax: 0171-231 8002
London SE1 2BS

Most places on this course are for GAP (GAP Activity Projects) participants who already have a teaching placement, and you don't come away with a recognised qualification. However, although GAP students will take priority, others are accepted if there are places. It costs £110 for one week and you practise teaching on your peers. The two week course costs £ 175 and you get to practise teaching foreign students.

Grove House Language Centre   Tel: 01322-386-826
Carlton Avenue, Dartford, Kent DA9 9DR   Fax: 01322-386-347

Inlingua (ITTR)   Tel: 01242-253-171
Rodney Lodge, Rodney Rd
Cheltenham GL50 1JF

Multi Lingua   Tel: 01483-535-118
Abbot House, Sydenham Road
Guildford, Surrey GU1 3RL

OVERSEAS PAID WORK

Teacher Training International Tel: (9.30 - 1.30)0800-174 031
3 Queensberry Place, London SW7 2DL Fax: 01491-411 383

TTI runs a TEFL course (three times a week for six weeks: £550) at the end of which you gain a TEFL certificate. The course includes grammar awareness, teaching practice and written assessments. You can make up your mind about the course at a 'taster day' costing £35, which counts towards the overall cost if you decide to take the course.

TEFL Training Tel/Fax: 01993-891 686
Friend's Close, Stonefield, Witney
Oxon 0X8 8PX

TEFL Training runs an intensive study weekend (£160 or £130 with student card) and a follow-through course (£65) which consists of 80 hours of home study. Together they result in a certificate for 100 hours. It also produces a self-study pack for £160 which includes a video.

Trinity Tesol Training Tel: 0171-734-3889
Oxford College House, 3 Oxford St, London W1R 1RF

Teaching English in private lessons

Private tuition is a good way to earn extra cash. Advertisements can be placed in local schools, universities, papers and shops. But be careful about wording your advertisement, particularly if you are young and female. Do not give any indication of your gender, and never write: "Young English girl gives English lessons" — you could get some heavy-breathing phone calls. Try to meet prospective students in a public place before inviting them to your home or going to their home. Interesting magazine and newspaper articles can be used as teaching aids.

Useful reading
Booklets available from AGCAS: *Teaching English as a Foreign Language* and *Teaching Abroad*. Send £2.65 to: Higher Education Careers Service Unit, Prospects House, Booth Street East, Manchester M13 9EP.

OVERSEAS PAID WORK

Headway A series of course books, tapes and workbooks that are both teacher and student friendly (Oxford University Press).

Practical English Usage A grammar reference book to answer all those tricky grammatical questions. Price £11.95 (Oxford Paperbacks).

Teaching English Abroad Includes a country-by-country guide and a directory of courses. Price £9.99 (Vacation Work, Oxford).

Skiing and tennis

There are several ways to earn your way through a season's skiing in Europe, although you are not likely to save much money to come back with. At 18 you can't expect jobs much more glamorous than a chalet person at best. Kitchen porter and general dogsbody is quite likely to be your lot. Other options include working as a ski instructor: BASI (see below) runs a £3,600 course from February to April for good skiers who want to get a ski instructors' licence. Whatever you do, most companies offer ski perks like a lift pass, and if you are a ski fanatic this is your ticket to get away.

Being a chalet girl involves cooking (and other duties that can vary from light tidying up to heavy-duty cleaning, so check the job specification) for ski parties in apartments or chalets. In return you get pocket money. Not all ski travel agencies will take students under 18, so remember to check this out. One route for gap-year students to get a chalet girl job is to do a cookery course first at a cookery school or college that is known to place its students with chalet-girl employers afterwards. The course need not be long, and some cookery schools worth contacting are listed in CHAPTER 6: OTHER EXTRAS. For thorough coverage of ski opportunities try the book *Working in Ski Resorts, Europe & North America (£9.99)*, Vacation Work Publications

British Association of Ski Instructors (BASI) Tel: 01479-861 717
Glenmore, Aviemore Fax: 01479-861 718
Invernesshire PH22 1QU

Mark Warner, George House Tel: 0171 393 3178
First Floor, 61-65 Kensington Church Street Fax: 0171 393 0088
London W8 4BA

OVERSEAS PAID WORK

Simply Ski   Tel: 0181 742 2541
Chiswick Gate, 598 - 608 Chiswick High Rd   Fax: 0181 995 5346
London W4 5RT

The Ski Company   Tel: 0181-858 9535
4a Nelson Rd, Greenwich, London SE10 9JB   Fax: 0181-858 5511

Vacation work Europe

No-one needs a permit to work in another EU country, and there are countless jobs available to students who can speak the right languages: usually low-paid like waitressing (see also CHAPTER 5: LANGUAGES). For those who like to join a group doing organised work in a camp, there are many choices. One French vacation work (strictly speaking, voluntary work) scheme has been recommended to us, organised by *Rempart*, a union of conservation associations in France which has been going for 32 years. *Rempart* aims to restore historic monuments or buildings across France, through various stages or two-week courses. It gives European students an opportunity to travel to all corners of the country.

Rempart   Tel: (00 331) 42.71.96.55
1 rue des Guillemites, 75004 Paris   Fax: (00 331) 42.71.73.00

There are also British companies that organise camp work in Europe. Check out that they comply with new minimum pay laws so you won't become slave labour. Eurocamp organises camping holidays throughout Europe (not in the UK) and employs people of 18 and over to help from April to September. You can be a courier, help clean vans, put up and take down tents or supervise. Pocket money £95 a week (1998).

Eurocamp   Tel: 01565-650 022
Overseas Recruitment Dept, Eurocamp   Fax: 01565-625 517
Canute Court, Tost Road,
Knutsford, Cheshire WA16 0NL

PGL is a children's adventure holiday programme employing about 2,000 young people in Britain, France and Spain each summer at its camps. You need to be a minimum 18 years old. Pay isn't excessive at £60 a week (1998) for support staff and group

OVERSEAS PAID WORK

leaders and £50 for activity instructors. And these rates only apply to people who start work before 22 June. After that the pay falls to £36 a week for everyone. (You may get more if you work for them a second time around.) There is, however, free food and accommodation. You don't have to be experienced in a specific field, unless you are going to teach sailing, canoeing, wind-surfing or pony-trekking, and PGL provides instructor training for all activity instructors and group leaders. Vacancies also for couriers and 'support staff'. Most staff are employed between March and September: apply before October of the year before.

DANCING ON THE TABLES

"I travelled for a year round Australia, having arrived in the country with £250 in my pocket. I earned and spent as I went, getting jobs all over the place, mostly waitressing and working in hostels. Hostel work is the best because you get accommodation and food for free, plus a bit of extra money. I worked in a restaurant on the seafront where we did all the cleaning in the morning and waitressed at night. We used to sit on the balcony drinking coffee and watching the sunrise, getting paid ten bucks an hour. In Melbourne I lived in the quite rough Global Backpackers hostel, and one night the police came round looking for a couple of skinheads. They weren't happy to find that out of the 40 lads there, 30 had gone skinhead the week before. I also worked in a café in Melbourne Central. In Cape Tribulation I got a job working in 'PK's Hostel'. There was this really bad smell and no-one could work out what it was. Eventually a seven-foot dead python was discovered rotting under my bed. I also worked in the Beachey Hostel in Harvey Bay. All six of the staff shared a room and we had a 24-hour alcohol licence so when I got up at 7.00 a.m. to sort out breakfast there'd still be people dancing on the tables from the night before. Travellers would arrive planning to stay only for a day, but the lifestyle was so good in the hostel that a week later they'd still be there, having spent half the money they were going to be travelling round Australia with!"
Ellie Pearch, University of Life, 1998

OVERSEAS PAID WORK

PGL (Seasonal Personnel Dept)
414, Alton Court, Penyard Lane
Ross-on-Wye, Herefordshire HR9 5NR

Tel: 01989-767 833
Fax: 01989-768 769
Web: *www.pgl.co.uk*

Solaire Holidays organises camping holidays in France and Spain and needs help during the summer — especially general couriers, children's couriers and bar staff. Pay about £85 a week (1998) with free accommodation and travel.

Solaire Holidays
1158 Stratford Road, Hall Green
Birmingham B28 8AF

Tel: 0121-778 5061
Fax: 0121-778 5065

Vacation work Australia

Final scorching destination of backpackers heading east. To find out what type of visa you need, you will have to listen to up to 10 minutes of information from the Australian High Commission's robot telephonist (like many other information services you pay 50p day rate and there's no human being at the end of the line). Key points are that to do casual work in Australia you will need a 'working holiday visa' which allows anyone from 18-25 to travel and take occasional work there for up to a year. You will also have to give evidence of £2,000 of financial support, and you won't be allowed to work for any employer for more than three months. In June 1998 the visa cost £65 ('visa application fee') and allowed people to take up to three months' work with any single employer in Australia during the year. Once you have used up

OVERSEAS PAID WORK

> *HOSTESSES AND CHAMPAGNE ON THE WIDE OPEN SEAS*
> *"I went to Australia with a sailing organisation called Leisure Management International. I paid them about £3,000 to cover the training, accommodation and flights. The training lasted six weeks, beginning in January, but I stayed in Australia until August. There were about nine people on the training course, all from completely different backgrounds. I was the only one on a gap year; others were doing it for fun or maybe to improve their qualifications. Everyone was of a different standard, and we sailed anything from dinghies to 42-foot yachts. Leisure Management helps to organise placements after the course, but some of the crewing companies want commercial qualifications, so the easiest thing to do was go to a marina and see what was available. I ended up sailing two amazing boats. One was called 'On the Edge' and is the fastest catamaran in the southern hemisphere. The other boat was an eight-foot maxi called 'Matador' that cost $22 million to build. We were involved in three-day trips on boats with hostesses and amazing food. At seven in the morning we'd get the boat ready for sailing, have breakfast at about eight, sail all day and moor wherever we liked at about 4.30 p.m. Then we'd lounge on the boat and crack open a beer as the sun went down, before helping to cook supper. The sailing course meant we were in a really good position to get sailing jobs around Europe. Companies like Sunsail in the UK will pay you to skipper a yacht with a crew of 18-25-year-olds. Basically, you have an incredible time on the sea."*
> *Rupert Stevenson, Newcastle University, 1998*

your working holiday visa you will never be allowed another one. Apply for visa application form 147 (enclosing 9" x 12" envelope and 55p stamp) to: **Australian Outlook**, 3 Buckhurst Rd, Bexhill-on-Sea, E. Sussex TN 40 1QF.

Australian High Commission
Australia House
Strand, London WC2 4LA

Visa enquiries: 0891-600333
Information : 0171-379 4334

OVERSEAS PAID WORK

OVERSEAS PAID WORK

Australian Consulate   Tel: 0161 228 1344
Chatsworth House, Lever St, Manchester M1 2QL

There are also organisations like the **Visitoz** Scheme, which allows gap-year students or graduates with a working holiday visa to get short-term jobs in Australia to earn money so that they can continue their travels. On arrival in Australia students are taken to the Burnet family's house or associate farm and given basic training. Jobs range from working on a cattle ranch as a jilleroo or jackeroo to being a mother's help. They even have places on a crocodile farm. Visitoz says it has a wide network of farm contacts in most parts of the country and can guarantee work, each job usually lasting between one and three months. Arrangements are made for bank accounts, Medicare cards (Australian Health Service) and tax file numbers. Reassuring for worried parents but perhaps irritating for independent-minded students is the stipulation that when travelling the Burnets make people phone them regularly. Pay rates vary but are usually good (typically A$200 a week in hand), and free food and accommodation are often included. Contact William Taunton-Burnet (at the address below). Application fee to Visitoz is £10, and the Visitoz Scheme charge is £340.

Visitoz UK   Tel: 0181-748 0046
1A Benbow Road, London W6 0AT   Fax: 0181-748 0046
                                                E-Mail: *WDTB@aol.com*

Vacation work India

With several hundred million people already milling around India, prospects for paid work are poor. Voluntary work is a more realistic aim. The Indian High Commission's rambling recorded message about visas now has a rewind button so you have time to write things down. There are more than 10 different visas (you can even get a 'yoga study' visa), but the one most students want is a tourist visa. Visas can be obtained either in person or by post from either its Birmingham, Glasgow or London offices: you can write off for an application form (sending an SAE) or dial a fax-back service from your fax machine (0891-44

OVERSEAS PAID WORK

45 43) Postal processing takes at least four weeks. Three-month tourist visas start from the date of entry into the country and six-month tourist visas start from the date of issue. Both cost £19.

Postal Visa Section   Visa enquiries: 0891-444 544
High Commision of India   Switchboard: 0171-836 8484
India House, Aldwych, London W62B 4NA

Postal Visa Section   Visa enquiries: 0891-444 544
Consulate General of India,   Switchboard: 0121-212 2782
20 Augusta St, Jewellery Quarters, Hockley, Birmingham B18 6JL

Vacation work USA

There are a few organisations that will get you a job and a visitor's working visa too. Camp America is a very large organisation that can get you a job and a visa to work in an American children's summer camp — contact them before May. Placements are for nine weeks and applicants could earn (June 1998 rates) from $260 (for an 18-year-old counsellor) up to $800 (for a life guard). Because you get free room and board you can earn enough to travel for one month afterwards. Camp America has also just placing applicants as staff at American summer resorts where families go for tennis, golf and other sporting activities.

Camp America   Tel: 0171-581 7373
37A Queens Gate, London SW7 5HR   Web: *www.campamerica.co.uk*

BUNAC (British Universities North America Club) and its summer camp affiliate can get you a visa for most temporary casual jobs you might be able to find in Canada, the USA and Australia. BUNACAMP offers summer camp counselling jobs for people over 19 years old on 1 July, and sends about 4,000 people to summer camp each year. If you have experience with groups of children, this could be your ticket to the USA. (See advertisement on next page.)

BUNAC   Tel: 0171-251 3472
16 Bowling Green Lane   Fax: 0171-251 0215
London, EC1R 0BD   Web: *www.BUNAC.org*

OVERSEAS PAID WORK

Girdling the earth

This section covers travel with no particular purpose in mind — in other words, not to do prearranged voluntary work or some other organised project. We have broken it up into two parts. First, there is general advice for those who have not been on long trips abroad before. Second, there are TRAVEL REPORTS from gap-year students about their experiences in different parts of the world.

Getting away

If you spend all 15 months between A-Levels in June and university in October the following year on British soil, something must be wrong. You can't take your double-bass to Belize? Why not?

Go away for longer than a few weeks if you can, because after university you might start work which you can't afford to leave... then you might get married... then you might have children. After that (although employers' attitudes to career breaks are changing) you may not be able to take more than a few weeks away from all your responsibilities for 20 years or more.

TRAVEL

After retakes (if necessary), a job, and the office skills, language, driving or other courses you want to fit in, you could start out on a long, hot, not-very-grand tour in the spring, spinning it out until late summer. Or, if you can arrange a loan with parents (or anyone else), you could head off in September (once A-level results are out of the way) and do the serious stuff when you get back.

If you go travelling in the summer straight after A-levels — and you are not one of those with an unconditional offer, a brain vast enough to promise you three or four certain 'A' grade A-Levels (triggering an electronic confirmation that your parents can simply notify you about) — you may have to come home in time for the crucial A-Level results in mid-August to enter clearing. And if you apply for university entrance while on your gap year, you may need to apply before you go travelling and/or return in time to make decisions. (Check with UCAS.)

Rehearsal: inter-railing

One well-tried formula is to break travel up into two trips. First, perhaps, unwind completely by going inter-railing straight after finishing A-Levels — travelling round Europe on a single ticket for one month on European trains.

Going inter-railing used to be the first and favourite activity of Europe's crumpled school-leavers, and it is still well worth considering. Prices fell in 1998 and the ticket now represents pretty good value for money, particularly if there are a lot of places you want to visit. You can order the ticket from British Rail International on the phone (still sometimes a long wait) or you can get it from international stations: the International Rail Centre in Victoria (see address opposite) or the Rail Europe Centre at 179 Piccadilly, London W1.

The Inter-Rail pass allows you to travel second-class on national railways in up to 27 countries, and what you pay for the pass depends on how many countries you want to visit. Students may have to pay supplements to travel on express inter-city trains, and definitely to go on Eurostar. An option worth considering is spending nights on trains; you can get flip-down beds, which are surprisingly comfortable, or seats, which are not. Either way, it's cheap and saves you time.

For the purpose of the ticket, Europe is divided into zones: Zone A: Republic of Ireland; Zone B: Norway, Sweden and Finland; Zone C: Austria, Denmark, Germany and Switzerland; Zone D: Croatia, the Czech and Slovak Republics, Hungary and Poland; Zone E: Belgium, France, Luxembourg, Netherlands; Zone F: Spain, Portugal, Morocco; Zone G: Italy, Greece, Turkey, Slovenia (including a return sea ticket from Brindisi, Italy, to Patras, Greece); Zone H: Bulgaria, Romania, Macedonia and Yugoslavia. You can't include the UK unless you get the ticket in another country. A ticket for any one zone valid for 22 days costs £159. For any two zones you can get a one-month ticket for £209; for any three zones a one-month ticket for £229; for all zones a one-month ticket is £259. You need a valid passport to buy the Inter-Rail pass and you should arrange insurance. Remember that getting to the continent (by rail or ferry) will cost extra: Stena Line (0990 70 70 70) charges only £24 if you have an Inter-Rail pass.

British Rail International   Tel: 0990-848 848
International Rail Centre,   Brochure: 01420-22902
Victoria Station, London SW1V 1JY   *www.britrail.com*

Be prepared

As with most aspects of a gap year, planning ahead is a good idea. The more you know about your destination, the easier your trip will be: India, for example, is unbearably hot in April and May.

Before visiting any country that has recently been politically volatile or could turn into a war zone (or whose status you're unsure about) check the current situation by calling the Foreign Office Travel Advice Unit •Tel: 0171-238 4503/4504

If you have not travelled before, you will need a full valid passport before you go. If you already have one, do not make the common mistake of not checking the expiry date. It's not unusual for people to open passports at an obscure foreign airport an hour before catching the flight home to find it is no longer valid.

If you do need a passport for the first time, application forms are available from post offices. A full ten-year passport costs £21 and you will need your birth certificate and passport photos. It can take as long as a month from the time you apply to the time you receive your passport, although there are procedures for getting one quicker if there's a big rush.

If you have to apply in person (at passport offices in Belfast, Glasgow, Newport, Liverpool, London or Peterborough) it costs £10 extra (bring a book to read: the queues can be horrendous). If you have more than a month in hand, you can send the application to the address on the form or hand it in at various places: see the form. It is a good idea to leave a complete photocopy of your passport at home before you go travelling and to keep a photocopy with you, as it makes it a lot easier to cope with a lost or stolen passport.

It is useful to join the international Youth Hostels Association (YHA): the membership card is accepted as proof that you are a YHA member when you stay in hostels in almost all countries. YHA membership for one year costs £10 for 18-year-olds and over, and £5 for under-18s.

An ISIC (International Student Identity Card) at £5 from Campus Travel or STA (see list of travel companies) identifies you as a student and entitles you to a few freebies, as well as discount fares at STA. Buy one before you leave school, because they are issued only to full-time students (studying at least 15 hours a week). If you don't have one of these, you can get a 'Go25' Card (anyone under 26, available from same places as for an ISIC) for £4 which offers similar discounts.

Passport Agency (08.15-16.00 Mon-Fri)   Tel: 0171-279 3434
Clive House, 70 Petty France   Telerobot: 0990 210 410
London SW1H 9HD

Youth Hostels Association (England & Wales)   Tel: 01727-855 215
Trevalyan House, 8 St Stephen's Hill   Fax: 01727-844 126
St. Alban's, Herts AL1 2DY

TRAVEL

216

Plan the route

Do you feel lured to a particular continent? Latin America? A particular climate? Snow? Unexplored territory? Mongolia via the Trans-Siberian Express? A particular purpose? Surfing? An Italian girlfriend, or just Roman remains? Or all these ingredients, wrapped up in one journey?

You need to get a framework clear in your mind. Bear in mind that it is much better (most parents would say essential) to go with a friend, and having contacts lined up along the route is a big help. The more remote a place is, the more useful it is to have company. If you have six months or so to spare, you can arrange travel that takes you all the way round the world, although you will probably spend more than half your time in one region, like Africa or the USA.

There are good travel guides for almost every destination. Both the *Rough Guide* and *Lonely Planet* series are excellent for budget travel, and also have useful cultural sections to help you get to know the places you are going to.

If you're focusing on one place (rather than going round the world, in which case you usually book a definite route) it's a good idea to plan the main leg of the journey and pay for the air, sea or rail ticket out and back in advance but leave the bits in between flexible. Flights inside the USA and CIS (former USSR) are cheap, for example, and (since the collapse of their currencies) flights between almost any country in Asia. If you have booked a series of flights through a travel agency, you may be able to change the dates directly with the airline when you are abroad, though the route the flight takes usually has to stay the same. Check before you leave how you can alter bookings once you are abroad: you may have to allow 72 hours when making later changes.

Combinations

There are well-trodden backpacking routes: through south-east Asia and Australia; across Russia to China and Hongkong by rail; from the USA to central America; or through Spain and Africa and back to the UK. You can try countries that have

TRAVEL

recently opened up to foreign visitors, like Vietnam (though you pay a lot for visas). A one-month visa for Vietnam, for example, is available from the embassy (Tel: 0171-937 1912) at £40. But avoid danger zones and check with contacts who know a country before even thinking about getting a visa: your family would rather not have a bloodstained postcard from a war-torn Balkan village. Ring embassies if you are in doubt: Afghanistan, for example, is still not issuing tourist visas. The Foreign Office regularly updates its danger list as new areas of unrest emerge.

Travel agents and tour organisers

The names of exotic travel agents can be found in advertisements in the national daily and Sunday newspapers. Voodoo Ventures, say, may promise three weeks of throbbing thrills in Haiti. Gap-year students can rarely afford these exotic holidays, unless there is a cheaper version (typically a trek) that can be a short preamble to several months' travel or part of a big-discount airfare package. It's worth trying out the bargain flight agencies, though the safety records of obscure airlines are not always comforting. Also of interest may be the many airlines offering budget fares to European destinations: such as *Go, Easyjet, Debonair* and *Ryanair*. The following travel companies are used to dealing with independent travellers and/or students:

Bridge the World   Europe, USA & Canada: 0171-916 0990
47 Chalk Farm Road   Australia & New Zealand: 0171-734 7447
Camden   Worldwide: 0171-911 0900
London NW1 8AN   Web: *www.btw.co.uk*

Bukima Africa   Tel: 0181-451 2446
55 Huddlestone Road   Fax: 0181-830 1889
London NW2 5DL   E-mail: *bukima@compuserve.com*

If you're interested in organised trips, Bukima Africa runs overland tours in Africa, South America and the Middle East. You travel in groups of about 20 people (mostly students and backpackers) with a leader, and it's mostly camping. You're largely self-sufficient, doing your own cooking, and the itinerary is fairly flexible to take into account things people may want to do.

TRAVEL

Trips last from 25 days up to a mammoth 30 weeks, and sample routes include Istanbul-Cairo and Cairo-Mombasa.

Campus Travel
52 Grosvenor Gardens
London SW1W 0AG

Europe: 0171-730 3402
North America: 0171-730 2101
Long-haul: 0171-730 8111
Web: *www.campustravel.co.uk*

Also at: 105 St Aldate's, Oxford OX1 1DD   Tel: 01865-242 067

Council Travel
28a Poland Street
London W1V 3DB

Europe: 0171-287 3337
Worldwide: 0171-437 7767
Summer Study USA: 0171-478 2000

Council Travel is part of the Council on International Educational Exchange, which organises study placements and work placements in more than 30 countries (see Chapter 5: Languages: Chinese, English).

Encounter Overland
267 Brompton Road
London SW5 9JA

Tel: 0171-373 1433
Fax: 0171-244 9737
Web: *www.encounter.co.uk*

TRAVEL

ROUND THE WORLD TICKET
London-Delhi-Bangkok-Sydney-Los Angeles-London
There are many different routes round the world. We asked for a
ticket which involved starting at the beginning of September 1998
and spending a month in each of the places visited. Prices depend
on season and which stops you choose to include. Here are some
estimates from different travel agents; some involve slightly different
routes such as going via Bombay not Delhi. Don't forget to add
between £40 and £50 airport tax.

Bridge The World	£905
Campus Travel	£899
Council Travel	c£1,000
STA Travel	£931
Thomas Cook	c£1,000
Trailfinders (before 16/9)	£977

**Return flight London-Delhi, leaving September 1997 and staying out
there for six months.**

Bridge The World (after 16/9)	£420
Campus Travel (4/12 mos)	£387/£435
Council Travel	£435
STA Travel	£426
Thomas Cook	c£500
Trailfinders	£391

Prices at May 1998

Encounter Overland (see address opposite) also organises overland trips in groups of 8-23 people, usually with a wide spread
of nationalities. Your main mode of transport is a truck, which
you could ride all the way from London to Kathmandu via
Nairobi (you get to fly back). It's mainly camping, with hostel
stays in big centres. Also available are shorter programmes, such
as whitewater rafting in Nepal or the 'Mountain Gorilla' programme in East Africa.

Exodus Travels
9 Weir Road
London SW12 0LT

For brochure: 0181-673 0859
Switchboard: 0181-675 5550
Web: *www.exodustravels.co.uk*

TRAVEL

STA Travel   Telesales Europe 0171-361 6161
Priory House   Rest of the world: 0171-361 6262
6 Wrights Lane   International helpdesk: 0171-361 6123
London W8 6TA   Tours, accomm., car hire, insurance: 0171-361 6160
                           Web: *www.statravel.co.uk*
Also at: Manchester   Tel: 0161-834 0668

Thomas Cook   Web: *www.tch.thomascook.com/*
(Branches in most cities)

Trailfinders   European/transatlantic flights: 0171-938 3232
194 Kensington High Street   Long-haul flights: 0171-938 3939
London W8 7RG

Trek America   Tel: 01295-256 777
4 Waterperry Court, Middleton Rd,   Fax: 01295-257 399
Banbury, Oxon. OX16 8QG   Web: *www.trekamerica.co.uk*

Trek America organises treks or van tours in different areas of
the USA, and also Canada, Guatemala, Belize, Hawaii, Mexico
and Alaska. These range from tours lasting a week (£382) to nine-
week trips right across the USA and Canada (£1,800). Groups are
usually made up of 10-13 people (lots of different nationalities)
and a guide/driver. You do all the work: cooking, setting up
camp at nights, and so on. But it is remarkably difficult to get into
the National Parks without a driver as the Greyhound routes
stick to the major inter-city highways, so if you are a lone traveller and unable to hire a car (hiring age is at least 21) it is useful
to have a travel company like Trek America organise the transport. You can include things like tandem skydiving in the trek
but that might give your parents heart failure.

Shipping lines

Airspace would start emptying fast if students flew as working
crew members on planes — but you can sail free as a working
crew member on ships. Contact head offices of shipping companies to find out the procedures before you leave the UK and find
out how to book a passage from a foreign port. The best book is:
Working on Crew Ships, published by Vacation Work Abroad, 9

DRIVING IN EUROPE

"My friend and I were travelling round Europe in a car; I hadn't passed my test yet so she was driving and I was attempting to navigate. We were exploring Prague and every time I misread the map, we ended up in a one-way street going in the wrong direction, and had to go through a 'No Entry' sign to avoid a collision. Eventually the police started following us and pulled us over. They demanded to see our passports and driving licence and made us pay a fine of about £20.

A few days later we returned from shopping to discover our car had disappeared from the parking space where we left it, complete with all our gear. We were convinced it had been stolen and eventually found a tiny police station but the officers didn't speak a word of English. While my hysterical friend tried to explain the situation with pictures, I wandered the streets until I found a Czech girl who'd lived in London for two years. She managed to charm the police into telling us our car had been impounded, and we'd have to go across town to get it. After a hair-raising journey at 70 miles an hour in a police car through Prague we managed to get our car released for the paltry fee of £6.60, which weirdly was the total sum of money we had on us at the time."

Hermione Love, Music at Manchester University, 1998

Park End Street, Oxford OX1 1HJ, Tel: 01865-241 978, Fax: 01865-790 885. Price £8.99 (plus £1.50 p&p).

Travelling by car

Another popular option is to travel (mostly around Europe) by car. It means you can kip in it when necessary, save money on train fares and you don't have to lug your rucksack into cafés. Make sure you know the motoring regulations of the countries you'll be visiting — they vary from country to country. It's a good idea to put your car in for a service a couple of weeks before you leave, carry a warning triangle in it and fit headlamp beam converters if needed.

The AA advises that you carry your vehicle insurance and

TRAVEL

vehicle registration documents and a current tax disc in the car. Take your passport, driving licence and international driving permit (if required in the countries you are visiting). If you need to obtain an international driving licence, take two passport photos, your driving licence and your passport to your nearest major driving centre. This costs about £4.

The Automobile Association   Tel: 0990-448-866
Norfolk House, Priestley Road, Basingstoke
Hampshire RG24 2NY

Kit

MAPS AND DIRECTIONS
Students (and, yes, captains of industry too) have been known to leave Dover or Heathrow without a single map. Unless you're going trekking you won't need anything too flash: the ones in guidebooks are usually pretty good. And you could persuade

one of your parents to buy you a good pocket business diary to take with you, one with information about different countries, that gives dialling codes, time differences, local currency details, bank opening hours, public holidays and other information. You can copy into it essentials like directions to voluntary work postings, key addresses, medical information, credit card numbers, passport details, contact numbers in case of loss of traveller's cheques and flight details. (Panic move for absent-grey-cell types: if you are in a plane when you realise that you forgot to pack any maps, ask if you can tear the route maps out of the in-flight magazine. That way at least you will know if Chile is on the left or right-hand side of South America.)

You think this advice is patronising? You'd be surprised what people do...

CONTACT LIST

Parents often spend weeks writing to contacts and phoning friends and relations to ask if they can have Johnnie to stay en route or rescue Kate from a truly terrible fate. So a contact list is something not to get wet. (Travel gadgets like plastic zip folders to keep lists and other key paperwork dry are available at chemists and airports.) Assume the worst: that when you phone your uncle's business contacts the person on the list has probably forgotten who your uncle is. The contact might still be helpful, and it's a relief to have somewhere comfortable to stay for a day or two when you're sick of hard beds and ham and cheese sandwiches.

TRAVEL

TICKETS AND MONEY

It is a good idea to leave photocopies or serial numbers of tickets, passports and credit cards at home. It's also worth keeping copies on you, separate from the rest of your valuables, and also one traveller's cheque separate from the others (useful if all the rest get stolen). Waist money pouches worn under clothes are recommended: not the height of fashion, but everyone wears them.

Take widely accepted traveller's cheques like those issued by big international banks and don't carry much cash. Cheques in pounds sterling are widely accepted, but US dollars more so. If you take cash, dollars always go down well, and a some local currency may help you find your feet at first. (The first time travellers get stung is often when the driver who has taken you to your hostel says he hasn't got any change.) It is also worth recording the numbers of the traveller's cheques that you spend, as it helps if you need to replace lost or stolen ones.

CREDIT CARDS

Essential back-up. Both Visa and Mastercard are useful for getting cash advances at banks abroad, which you can then use to buy more traveller's cheques (safer than walking around with suitcases of money). Credit card transactions are also a good way of leaving a trail: they often show up miraculously quickly on the monthly statements that arrive at home. You should be able to get a card in your name but on your parent's account if you are unable to get one yourself. Remember to keep a note of the numbers and how to report the loss of the card.

WHERE TO BUY

Some overseas voluntary organisations (such as SPW) arrange for their students to have discounts at specific shops: worth a check if that's what you're doing. Best advice on equipment usually comes from a specialist shop, although these may not be the cheapest: these include YHA shops, Blacks, and Camping and Outdoors Centres.

RUCKSACKS

Advice from students who have collapsed under the weight of 65 to 70 litre rucksacks; think carefully before buying so big. There is no need to look like a walking sack of coal, sweating under the weight of bottles of shampoo that will take two months to use. Thailand does have shampoo. For hot countries a 30 to 35 litre rucksack (excluding sleeping bag) is big enough for some. Rucksacks that take a sleeping bag at the bottom are popular, and so are ones that open laterally like suitcases. You might want to go for one with zips and tiny padlocks for security, but remember that this doesn't give real protection, as a determined thief will happily slash your bag open. You can get all sorts of trendy attachments such as 'an integral pocket for your hydration bladder' but don't hand over money for stuff you won't need. In cold countries you are obviously going to need a bigger rucksack, but you can keep bags light by packing clothes made of special lightweight fabrics. •A well-stitched 65-litre rucksack will cost between £40 and 100, and a 35-litre rucksack between £20 and £50.

A must is an extra small day bag or rucksack to carry valuables and things you need in a hurry, as well as bottles of water, guidebooks, camera and so on. You should be able to leave your rucksack in most hostels or guest houses if you are staying for more than a day (most thieves won't be interested in nicking your socks), but **take camera, walkman, passport and money with you everywhere, zipped up.**

FOOTWEAR

It's worth investing in something comfortable if you're heading off on a long trip. In hot countries, a good pair of sandals is the preferred footwear for many. Sports sandals such as *Teva* ones are pricey (£30-£70) but strong. If you're going somewhere cheap, you could just pick up a pair out there, but check that there aren't any nails coming through the soles before you buy. If you're going to shoes territory, wear what you'll feel OK in for six months. Some people like chunky walking boots, others just their trainers, but it's best to get something that won't fall apart when you're halfway up Mount Kilimanjaro.

TRAVEL

SLEEPING BAGS

Not strictly necessary: it depends where you go. For hot countries you may just want to take a sheet (or a sheet sleeping bag, which is basically just a sewn-up sheet), although a sleeping bag does stop you from having to come into contact with the sheets in that dodgy budget hotel... If you do take a sleeping bag, think about what you'll be doing (the more active your holiday, the more you need a decent bag) and go to a specialist shop where you can get good advice. Take into account weight and size and the conditions you'll be travelling in (you might want to go for one of those dinky compression sacs that you can use to squash sleeping bags into). Sheet bags are useful, and you can rent down bags for treks in, say, Nepal, but don't assume you'll always be able to do this. For cold countries, you need bulky heat-retaining materials. If you're going to be doing a lot of sleeping outdoors, a roll-mat is probably a good idea too.

•Sample prices (bottom end); sheet bag: around £7; one-season sleeping-bag (suitable to 5˚C): £30, two-season sleeping-bag (suitable to 0˚C): £35; three-season sleeping-bag (suitable to -5˚C): £40. (You can pay two or three times as much for better gear.)

HANDY ITEMS

The list of useful things to take varies from person to person, but the following are generally considered very helpful: string that can double as a washing line and is handy for putting up mosquito nets; a universal sink plug; and a padlock and chain to secure your rucksacks on long journeys and double-lock hostel rooms. A penknife with different functions is also extremely useful. Water purifying tablets are handy, although bottled mineral water is usually available (check that the seal is intact). Masking tape has also been recommended to us as a vital piece of survival kit: apparently handy for mending slashed rucksacks, sealing ant nests, fixing doors, sticking up mosquito nets and more.

CAMERAS

Being able to record a trip is for most people a vital part of the experience. Remember to be very careful to keep cameras and film safe from damage (usually sand and water) and theft. Keep

---

MORE VITALS

*"One bit of advice that may seem glaringly obvious: when you
come to Customs and are given stacks of annoying bits of paper,
keep them! I was convinced when I was travelling [through Mexico
and Belize to Guatemala] that the whole lot were totally irrelevant
and chucked them away. It later transpired that one little scrap
was my visa and I ended up having to bribe an official at the
Guatemalan border to let me into the country."*
Tiff Garside, Birmingham University, 1998

---

all your negatives in a safe place because most travellers agree
there is nothing more gutting than losing either your developed
photos or undeveloped films — they're irreplaceable. Getting
photos developed as you go along is an option worth considering; it may work out cheaper, and stops you looking at stacks of
photos long after taking them and asking yourself "Which
mountain is that?" The downside is that you'll have to carry
them about; you may not want the extra weight.

Health

Note: Although we make every effort to be as up-to-date and
accurate as possible, the following advice is intended to serve as
a guideline only. It is designed to be helpful rather than defini-
tive, and you should always check with your GP what *you* need
for *your* trip.

You need to get advice at least six weeks before going away: six
months in five-bottle-top hostels puts people at higher risk than
two weeks in a five-star Mandarin Hotel. Tell your doctor your
proposed travel route and ask for advice not only about injections and pills needed, but possible symptoms. You may now
have to pay for your jabs, and some, like the Hepatitis A vaccine,
are very expensive. Don't skimp on grounds of cost.

Describe the things you may be doing as well as the places you
are going to. And if you are going abroad to do voluntary work,
don't assume the organisation will give you medical advice first
or even when you get there (though they often do). Find out for

TRAVEL

yourself, and check if there is a medically qualified person at or near the institution you are going to be posted with. People who've been to the relevant country/area are a great source of information.

Try to keep a record of any treatment that you have when overseas, such as courses of antibiotics; this information can be important. Also be wary of needles and insist on unused ones; it's best if you can see the packet opened in front of you, or you could take a 'sterile kit' (containing needles) with you.

Some airlines offer an advice line. British Airways has local travel clinics in Britain where you can get jabs: contact the Location Line to find out the nearest one to you (Tel: 01276-685 040). The Medical Advisory Services for Travellers Abroad (MASTA) has a Travellers' Health Line for advice on vaccinations, malaria, the latest health news and important political news (Tel: 0891-224 100, 50p per minute, or if for advice on travel to more than six countries Tel: 01705-553 933). Also useful is the Department of Health Freefone Health Information Service (Tel: 0800-665 544).

Chronic conditions

Asthmatics, diabetics, epileptics or those with other conditions should always wear an obvious necklace or bracelet or carry an identity card stating details of their condition. Tragedies do occur due to ignorance, and if you are found unconscious, a label can be a life saver.

DIABETICS

Keep ID as above. Take enough insulin for your stay, which must be kept in the passenger area of a plane, not the aircraft hold where it will freeze. Write to the British Diabetic Association for travel information (booklet £1.80) saying which country you plan to travel in — different travel packs are available for about 70 countries. The Careline gives advice, and details of travel insurance covering diabetes are also available from the BDA.

British Diabetic Association   Tel: 0171-323 1531
10 Queen Anne Street, London W1M 0BD   Careline: 0171-636 6112

TRAVEL

> ### BRA-LESS WITH WORMS
> *"We were about to go trekking and it looked like I had a huge verruca on my foot, so I wasn't sure if I'd be able to walk. I got it checked out at a clinic in Kathmandu, and as they'd never heard of a verruca, they just decided to chop the dead skin off. I sat there as they sawed and proceeded to pull out a huge sack of worms from inside my foot. The Western doctor said he'd never seen anything like it and he later told me that I must have picked it up from sandflies on a beach in Zanzibar.*
>
> *While we were trekking I got severe fever which turned out to be typhus contracted from my nits. While I was lying semi-delirious in the lodge, the owner's daughter came into my room and started rummaging under my bed. I was too ill to do anything and I later discovered she'd nicked my bra. I had to trek all the way home bra-less, because being a minimalist trekker I'd only brought one with me."*
> Catherine Hinds, Human Sciences, Oxford University, 1998

ASTHMA AND ALLERGIES
Whether you are an asthmatic or have an allergy to chemicals in the air, food, stings, or antibiotics, ask your GP for advice before you go. You will be able to take some treatments with you.

DENTIST
Pretty obvious but often forgotten: get anything you need done to your teeth before you go.

EYES
Wearers of contact lenses should stock up on cleaning fluid before going, especially if venturing off the beaten track, and be careful what water is used for cleaning; ask your optician for advice. It's also worth making sure you have glasses as a back-up, as it's not always possible to replace lost or broken contacts. Off-the-peg spectacles are now available from chemists for less than £10.

TRAVEL

FIRST AID KIT

There is no need to take a whole chemist's shop with you. Ask your GP for advice, but useful basics are rehydration sachets (to use after diarrhoea); waterproof plasters; TCP; corn plasters for sore feet; cotton buds; a small pair of straight nail scissors; safety pins; insect repellent; antiseptic cream; anti-diarrhoea pills (only short term; they stop you up but don't cure you); and anti-histamine cream. •You can get a medical pack from Boots or travel shops, or by mail order from MASTA (Tel: 0113-238 7575).

CONTRACEPTIVES

If you are on the pill, take enough to last a few months. Condoms: unprotected sex can be fatal, so everyone should take them even if they are not likely to be used (not everyone thinks about sex the whole time). Keep them away from sand, water and sun. If buying abroad, make sure they are a known make and have not been kept in damp, hot or icy conditions.

Contagious diseases

AIDS

The HIV virus that causes AIDS is caught from: injections with infected needles; transfusions of infected blood; sexual intercourse with infected person, or possibly cuts (if you have a shave at the barber's, insist on a fresh blade, but it's probably best to avoid the experience altogether). Protection: condom, safe needles, treated blood. •Fatal disease. No preventive vaccination available yet, but Aidsvax vaccine started drug trials in mid-1998.

MALARIA

Caught from bite by infected mosquito, and mosquitos are getting more vindictive. In 1997 there were 2,364 reported cases in the UK, slightly down from the year before, according to figures from the Malaria Reference Laboratory. Highest risk areas are hot, swampy or tropical regions like West Africa and Asia, and in early 1998 numbers rose sharply in East Africa — thought to be due to heavy rains caused by 'the El Nino effect'. •No jab, but your GP will give you a course of pills to take during your trip and after your return. Mosquito nets are useful in some areas, but they can be hard to put up correctly. For a long trip, the pills can cost a lot. And some people, particularly on long trips, stop taking their pills, especially if they're not getting bitten much. Don't. Malaria can be fatal.

Your GP should know which of a variety of anti-malarials is best for you, depending on your medical history (e.g. for epileptics) and the countries you are visiting. A GP will also be able to tell you what the symptoms of malaria are, and that you must seek treatment quickly. There is a choice between traditional paludrine plus chloroquine and the more powerful mefloquine (also known as Lariam) which can have side effects (dizziness, anxiety, depression) but is suitable for resistant strains. MASTA recommends that you start a course of mefloquine two to three weeks before departure as this will allow time for side effects to develop and therefore to alter your prescription in time. For paludrine and chloroquine start the course one to two weeks before you leave and with all pills continue it for four weeks on your return.

CHOLERA, HEPATITIS (A & B), MENINGITIS, POLIO, RABIES, TETANUS, TUBERCULOSIS, TYPHOID, YELLOW FEVER
Ask your GP for advice on vaccinations/precautions at least six weeks before you go (some may be available on the NHS). Keep a record card on you of what you've had done.

SUNBURN
Avoid over-exposure, especially on first arrival in a sunny country, and use sun creams and sun-block frequently. More than 40,000 new cases of skin cancer are reported in Britain every year (1,500 die each year), and half your exposure to direct sunlight usually happens in your first 20 years.

Medical insurance
There are reciprocal agreements between EEA (formerly EU) member states to treat each other's medical emergencies free or at a reduced cost, usually where sudden illness or an accident

TRAVEL

means an immediate operation. You may need to take an E111 form with you, which entitles you to free or reduced state medical care while you are abroad, so check with your travel agent or pick one up from a post office where it must be stamped. But wherever it happens (especially in the USA) a serious illness, broken limb or injury you cause someone else can be very expensive. Insurance cover against these risks is vital.

Travel insurance

Travel insurance costs vary widely by company, destination, activity and level of cover (see box opposite). Shop around by phone but do make sure you know what you're covered for and when you've got the policy read the small print carefully (for example, transport home if you need an emergency operation that cannot be carried out safely abroad). Some policies don't include cover for loss of cash, as one girl we heard of found out to her cost when $1,400 was stolen from her hotel room...

Medical insurance is usually part of an all-in travel policy. Unfortunately many travel policies weight the compensation heavily in favour of death (not much use) and exclude obvious

WORLDWIDE TRAVEL INSURANCE

Here are quotes from insurance companies showing what 'dangerous' sports they include in a cheap six-month round-the-world travel policy. Check for things like whether baggage is included, cancellation cover, and whether medical costs are paid directly by the company or whether you have to pay yourself and then claim later.

Barclays £415 Tel: Local branches
Most beach watersports, but premium doubled for winter sports.

Campus £165 Tel: 0800-214 638
"Go Bananas" policy: includes baggage, and £25 gives you cover for all dangerous sports. Excluding baggage: £123.

Endsleigh £176.60 Tel: Local branches
No cover for hazardous or winter sports; if you want cover, premium doubled for the time you do the activity

Europ Assistance £217 Tel: 01444-442 442
Scuba to 30m, most water sports but not winter sports. Offices in every country in the world, and connections with the Home Office

Inter Assurance £95 Tel:01252-747 747
OK for one-off sporting activities but not sustained periods. No baggage cover

Midland £188.44 Tel: Local branches
Double for skiing, snowboarding £20 extra, beach watersports; scuba diving (down to 9m; down to 30m £20 extra).

STA Travel £123 Tel: 0171-465 0484
Covers temporary work, £45 extra for hazardous sports. Easily extendable when you're travelling, and refund possible if you come back early. *May 1998*

things students might do — scuba diving, parachuting or bungee jumping. Make sure you have generous cover for injury or disablement if you plan high-risk activities. If you have a condition that is likely to recur, you may have to declare this when you get the insurance and it is important to find out where hospitals are in the area you are travelling through. If you are going to a volunteer post, you need to know the name of the medically responsible person there and the procedures for getting to a doctor or hospital, and to make sure that person is fully briefed about your condition as soon as you arrive.

TRAVEL

Some banks provide cover for a holiday paid for with their credit cards, but the cover may not include all the essentials. If you book a holiday using a Barclaycard, for example, you get free travel accident insurance but nothing else. Banks also offer blanket travel insurance (medical, personal accident, third party liability, theft, loss, cancellation, delay and more). You may be able to get reductions if you have an account with the relevant bank or buy foreign corrency through them. Travel agents often automatically include insurance with the fares you book, but remember you don't have to take the policy your travel agent recommends; you may be able to find a better deal yourself.

On the road

MEETING PLACES

Your first impression of a some countries will be the locust-swarm of people that descends on you, all hassling you to take a taxi or buy something. At night, it can be quite scary. Anyone can get lost, and this can be the first place. When you are on the road, don't panic. Always agree meeting places before you go somewhere, and you can play safe by having a double back-up plan: "If I don't see you outside the Latino Roxy cinema at 1.00, I'll see you at the Lufthansa office at 4.00. Then I'm going back to the hostel." Try looking behind you occasionally. Surprising how many people cover 100 yards without turning round while a friend is tying a shoelace...

KEEPING IN TOUCH

1990s parents are nervous ones. When the 18th century scion of the family did his Grand Tour of Europe, mother had six other children to think about and did not expect more than a letter gracefully written from Rome. Parents seem to worry in inverse proportion to the number of children they have, so if you are unlucky enough to be an only child and a girl, they can be quite neurotic: phone or write once a fortnight if you don't want them to turn grey before you get back. Aerogrammes are a cheap way of writing from most countries. Registering letters usually costs only a few pence (or equivalent) from third world countries, and

236

---

is definitely worthwhile. On the receiving end; if an exact
address is not known, then the local *Poste Restante*, often at a
main post office, is a reliable place to send letters to be collected.
Also, remember that getting letters can be a great pick-me-up, so
distribute your address widely to friends and family before you
go in order to ensure a steady supply of mail. Parcels do usually
get through, but don't send anything valuable. Parents: if you
write the surname first, a letter is less likely to be filed under the
first name and lead to a long search the other end.

PHONE, E-MAIL, SNAIL MAIL

If you are on an organised voluntary work project or summer
camp, parents may not worry as much as if you are travelling
under your own steam. Wherever you are, however, do try to
phone home at least once every two weeks, even if it is only to
leave a few words on an answerphone. Dialling the UK usually
means: (access code)+ 44 (UK) + 171 (local code, central London)
+ number. BT produces a tiny leaflet giving most codes: *How to
call the UK from abroad*.

Use a credit card if you can. If you walk into any international
hotel you should be able to use a Visa or Mastercard to pay for
an international phone call (watch out for overcharging). Or you
can make a collect call: most parents would rather pay than not
hear from you. Or take one of British Telecom's chargecards with
you: the *International Chargecard* works in over 100 countries as
does the *Single Number Contact Card*, which is designed to call

TRAVEL

only one number, usually home. Both of these cards are free.

A new product is the *BT Globalcard*, obtainable from Thomson Tour operators and selected AA and Speedlink outlets. These cards are pre-paid in units of £10 to £20, recorded on an account; you don't need to find a phone with a card reader, just to get in touch with the operator. However all BT cards are part of the 'Quick Call' system and will not work in every country: you can use the cards to phone direct from the USA, but calls from Bermuda, for example, have to go through the operator. For further details on BT chargecards phone: Freephone 0800 345 144. If you can't get to a cybercafé to send an E-mail (see box above) or telephone, you can keep your parents quiet by sending post cards regularly, preferably once a week with just a sentence or two about where you are and where you might be heading next. That way, at least they will know you are alive.

AILMENTS

Take a roll of lavatory paper if you leave town, and expect to be ill when you travel. It's usually just food poisoning, but if vomiting and/or diarrhoea goes on for more than a few days, or you run a fever, have convulsions or breathing difficulties (or any unusual symptoms) get someone to call a doctor straight away. Don't be paranoid about foreign doctors — they do go to medical school

If the doctor advises being sent home for treatment and you have an insurance policy with a repatriation arrangement, get someone to call the insurance company's headquarters or office in the relevant country for help as soon as possible. If the illness is less urgent a British Embassy or British company operating in that country will usually be able to recommend a good local doctor. If your treatment is not free you should be able to pay by credit card. Make sure the details are written out on a receipt and keep all bills or receipts so you can claim on your insurance policy when you get home.

Travelling code

Simple really, but make sure your relaxed attitude doesn't upset others. Enjoying a trip should not involve being inconsiderate of other people's arrangements or feelings. For example:

RELIGIOUS CUSTOM

Women wear long sleeves and cover their legs in Muslim countries: don't wear a bikini top and shorts in city streets. Uncovered flesh, especially female, offends Islam. Similarly in Buddhist countries the head is sacred and so it is unconventional to touch it. Each culture or religion has its own holy 'laws', and casual Anglo-Saxon habits can offend.

BEING A GUEST

If contacts are expecting you to call as you pass through a country, whether just to pick up mail or for an emergency stay, let them know if and when you are coming before you get there. Don't automatically assume they will ask you to stay. If they do, don't sponge: check how long it will be OK to stay and ask first if you want to invite fellow travellers to visit you.

NASTIES

You wanna buy? No thanks. If people persist, you can usually crack a joke and move on. If you are offered strange drinks, unknown powders or pills, no way. Likewise unwanted advances from the sex-hungry. If pestering persists after you have said no, get to somewhere where there are other people within earshot and tell him/her loudly what they can do with

TRAVEL

[puny organs or worse]. If it gets really alarming, you just have to think quickly and remember your self-defence tactics. But only use violence as a last resort — it 's not worth fighting back against violent muggers. Let them have the money. Stick close to other people while you get back to base.

THEFT

If you have money, a camera or a passport stolen abroad (the chances are high), report the theft immediately to the nearest police station and make sure you have some written record from them giving the date that you did so (some insurance policies will not pay out if you allow more than 24 hours to elapse), with all relevant details. Dress smartly and expect an uphill battle; police in popular budget destinations may have had to deal with hundreds of insurance scams in the past and may not be sympathetic. It is very unlikely anyone will catch the thief or get your stuff back, but you may need a record for your insurance claim. Ask your parents to notify insurers and post a copy of the police notification home. Many insurers will not pay up for loss or theft unless police are notified. Likewise if you are involved in any accident likely to involve an insurance claim.

SAFETY: BORING BUT IMPORTANT

•**Travel in pairs if you can** •**Never hitch-hike or accept lifts from strangers** •**Avoid badly-lit streets after dark** •**Never discuss your own or your family's financial situation with strangers** •**Never try unknown substances or carry unopened parcels for people, especially when you fly** •**Don't swim in strong currents or heavy waves: several gap-year students have drowned this way** •**Avoid drinking soft drinks or mineral water from unsealed bottles and eating unwashed salad and fruit** •**Shake out clothes and shoes before you put them on: snakes, scorpions or allergy-causing plants may have got inside.**

WHO NEEDS ADVICE?

Only those who want it. If you take a tenth of the advice in this book you'll probably get described as anally retentive. Can't win, can you.

Letters home

Just to give you a taste, here are reports from returning gap-year travellers. Most of them had a good time, but no single report is typical. Some people revel in India, for example, while others find the poverty harrowing. Factual information contained in these travellers' tales may need to be updated because political, economic and legal circumstances are constantly changing.

Afghanistan... Albania... Algeria... Andorra... Angola...

Antigua
LOOP THE SLOOP

"I worked as the first mate of a yacht for four months in the Caribbean. I got the job through a friend who came with me, and we chartered a 50 foot yacht out for two weeks at a time. We didn't get paid but the guests on the boat were mainly from big businesses and spent lots of money on us, so we never had to pay for anything. We did a loop of the islands, taking the guests to the right bars and beaches, maybe teaching them how to scuba dive, and they paid for $1,000 meals in the evenings. It was brilliant fun but also involved a lot of hard work. We sailed them wherever they wanted to go and had to clean the boat every day which took anything from one to three hours. On Sundays the guests left at lunchtime and the new ones arrived in the evening, so we bust a gut cleaning the entire boat. I was lucky to get the job through a friend, but you can get a job on a boat through a crewing agency. They look for competent sailors for crewing, engineers for maintenance and hostesses to serve food and clean the cabins. Once you're out there you get loads

TRAVEL REPORTS

of job offers. One guy wanted me to sail his yacht from Antigua, through New York and on to Hawaii. The whole experience was amazing, and the worst bit was having to come home."

Will Dutton, Economics & Politics at Exeter University, 1998

Antigua... Argentina... Armenia... Austria... Azerbaijan... Bahamas... Bahrain... Bangladesh... Barbados... Belarus... Belgium... Belize... Benin... Bhutan... Bolivia... Bosnia... Botswana... Brazil... Brunei... Bulgaria... Burkina... Burma (Myanmar)... Burundi... Cambodia... Cameroon... Canada... Cape Verde... Central African Republic... Chad...

China   *SHANGHAI'D*

"I spent most of my gap year teaching English to primary school children with a fellow student, Jessica, in a village called Huzhou in China. Full of the optimism and foolishness of youth Jessica and I decided to go to Shanghai, despite the fact that we had nowhere to stay, no-one to meet us and the only Chinese either of us spoke came from a battered old phrase book. Once there we phoned every hotel for miles around and eventually we were offered a double room in a hotel on the outskirts of town for 180 yuan (roughly £18). Two buses and four hours later, having been directed to a place called Hi Ni Lu instead of the desired Hi Min Lu and with throbbing feet we arrived at an oasis of western comfort; two beds, hot water, even little bottles of shampoo.

At that moment, after living with the local people, it was a dramatic change. We completed this orgy of western indulgence with a burger and chips for dinner. The next evening we watched a huge firework display. It was awe-inspiring. With our eyes tied to the sky we followed the crowd and stumbled on a tiny restaurant. It was run by a particularly inquisitive and hospitable family who did their best to communicate, and at some point during the meal we became their guests rather than customers. The room began to heave, with the whole family fascinated by two western girls trying to talk Chinese and failing. After fabulous food we were taken by the hands and led by two of the children to a dance. After dancing the night away the father invited us to visit the family the next day, which we did. Everyone was so hospitable that it made all the travelling difficulties worthwhile. I cannot imagine an English family inviting strangers in to their home in such a trusting way, It was a unique experience, as China itself was. I can't wait to go back next year."

Claire Davies, Bristol University, 1995

TRAVEL REPORTS

"I went to China for a month, which was quite difficult at first. It was the worst culture shock of all the places I went to because the country is so ordered and regulated. They don't speak English and taxis are a nightmare because they've no idea where you want to go. As soon as we arrived at the airport we got into a taxi that took us 50 miles out of Beijing because the guy had no idea where we wanted to go. We were really tired and hung over and we spent hours in this taxi, completely lost. It was awful. Once we found our way back there was only one cheap hotel in Beijing that we could afford, and over the course of a month the hotel we stayed in changed into a really posh business hotel. I think China is changing extremely rapidly and beginning to adapt tourism. We quite often found that we were charged to see monuments that didn't exist. In Xiang, for example, we paid to see a tomb and walked up a huge hill only to find the tomb didn't exist."

Emma Ahlas, Archaeology at Manchester University, 1998

Colombia... Comoros... Congo... Costa Rica... Côte d'Ivoire... Croatia... Cuba... Cyprus... Czech Republic... Denmark... Djibouti... Dominica... Ecuador...

Egypt
CAMEL STABLES

"What made me decide to go to Egypt? I sorted out that I was going to travel for a month with my friend Rory, so that was settled. He wanted to go to Egypt whereas I wanted to go to India, so we did some research and it transpired that it was the rainy season in India at that time, so Egypt it was. Your attitude is important when you take a gap year — I hadn't planned to travel because I didn't imagine that I could, but then everyone around me was just taking off, so I found out about it and it didn't seem so terrible after all. I guess I was just having problems with the concept of my own independence.

We flew into Cairo, reading our guidebooks on the way. I would definitely advise the *Lonely Planet* guide, as it not only describes what you can do but gives detailed information about each site, hotel or whatever. The hotels cost about £5 a night (not usually including food as well), but you have to bargain for absolutely everything. In Egypt, as tourism is the mainstay of the economy, ability to speak English equals income, so we weren't at all worried about the language barrier. We ate in little food stalls, which are everywhere and serve astoundingly good *falafel* —

243

TRAVEL REPORTS

basically chickpeas mushed up with spices and then deep fried. I've never had such good *falafel* anywhere else, presumably because anywhere that meets health and safety guidelines will be leave something essential out of the recipe.

The Egyptians regard you as wallets with legs. Taxi scams are quite comon in Cairo: at the train station someone will come up to you and offer to take you to a hotel for £2 (rather than £10 or £15). On arrival at the hotel you will be greeted with a room charge of £35 a night, with the taxi driver getting plenty of commission to make up for his previous undercharging.

We had a bad Pyramid experience. We went for a drink and a game of backgammon with a friend or cousin of our friend from Abu Sir, who offered to take us to a 'government approved camel stables'. We went along with him to an extremely shady place where the animals were being treated atrociously, and were charged about £15 each to take a tour to the Pyramids, a price which was supposed to have included the entry fee. However when we got there they took us round the back somewhere, not at all close, and pointed out the Pyramids. When we realised that this was the extent of our grand tour we started making a fuss, and in the end another friend of Taha's who happened to come along took us round (illegally). We did get to see an amazing sunken village where the sand had almost completely swallowed the houses, but without filling them up, so you could look in through their skylights and see entire buried rooms, as if they were inside a normal house. We also saw some temples with mummified crocodiles in them.

When we went to stay with our friend the papyrus seller in Abu Sir we stayed up talking and drinking cup after cup of tea. Each cup is tiny, very strong, and has about four spoons of sugar in it. My friend who I was travelling with got really high and seriously needed to have a drink of water. Rather stupidly, he drank the water from their well, and was then laid low for several days with a stomach bug.

From Cairo we worked our way east to Suez and then on to Katerina, a definite must-go for anyone travelling to Egypt. It's where Mount Sinai is. We climbed the mountain before dawn and then stood where Moses stood to watch the sunrise. On the mountain we met a mad hippie, Bob, who was going to publish a book of his own poetry. He was travelling the world putting his poems up at 'sites of power'. He had tacked his poems up all over India, on the Wailing Wall, and now on top of Mount Sinai. When we left him he told us "I'll see you again soon, because we all meet again sometime."

Alex Thomson, Medicine at Queen's College, Cambridge University, 1997

TRAVEL REPORTS

Equatorial Guinea... Estonia...

Ethiopia   *KALASHNIKOVS*

"We travelled through Ethiopia which was astounding. The civil war had just ended and the public transport system was still chaotic, so we joined an overland group to be safe, with 10 of us travelling in a big truck. There were amputees everywhere. We had one nasty experience: we drove across about a month or two after the land borders reopened. On the first night we drove about five miles out of a small town to our camp site, and just as we were pitching camp a policeman arrived wielding a Kalashnikov and told us that our having a foreign vehicle was illegal. He had obviously not been told of the change in the law, or that the border had been opened. The guy who drove the truck, Doug, dealt with it superbly. He just stayed lying down on his mattress (he always slept out in the open) with a glass of beer in his hand and repeated to the policeman that he wasn't in the wrong and that he wasn't going to move. In the end, after a lot of brash gun-wielding and flicking on and off of the safety-catch the policeman left to check the facts. He never came back, so I assume that he realised we were legal.

It's interesting to come up against the different attitudes in other cultures, even when they take the form of discrimination. In Ethiopia for instance the Coptic tradition, which bears a great deal of Islamic influence, requires women to wear headscarves, and you get a lot of hassle if you don't make the effort to conform, especially if you are a white woman. To the Ethiopians all white women are 'loose', perhaps because the only images they ever see of white women come through porn."

Polly Someone, Cambridge University, 1997

Fiji... Finland... France... Gabon... Gambia... Georgia... Germany... Ghana... Greece... Grenada...   Guatemala... Guinea... Guinea-Bissau... Guyana... Haiti... Honduras... Hungary... Iceland...

India   *DELHI RICH KIDS*

"One unusual thing I did was staying with an Indian friend who had gone to my school in London. We'd just about stayed in touch, and I was keen to see him. We arrived at his home in Delhi six hours late after 40 hours on the train and found ourselves in a large, plush house in the fashionable part of Delhi. Amit took us in, fed us and let us borrow his clothes for a party we went to with him — our traveller's attire of sandals and baggy trousers not quite fitting in among all the Calvin Klein suits. We hung out with the Delhi rich kids (including a crazy Russian guy called Roman who assured me that his uncle owned the Guinness brewery). The next night was even more surreal. Amit took us to the pre-wedding party of one of his parents' friends, telling us it was 'just a small thing'. As the chauffeur-driven car pulled up outside the five-star hotel and the uniformed doorman held open the plate glass door to reveal an opulent interior dripping with chandeliers, I began to have serious doubts about my old mate's judgement, an impression strengthened by the hordes of well-heeled Indian people inside. There were at least 500 people there (we never got to meet the bridal couple), all dressed in DJs or gold-embroidered saris, as well as a band fronted by an Indian pop star. Waiters floated around dispensing free drinks to all, and the food was the best I've ever tasted anywhere. There was even a chap in the toilet giving out handtowels. A night to remember."

David Allan, English at Cambridge University, 1998

. . . AND POOR ONES

"We turned up in Calcutta after a nightmare four-day bus journey from Kathmandu. We dumped our stuff in the Salvation Army Guesthouse, where Mother Theresa's nuns are rumoured to hang out, and decided to go to the cinema that evening. It was the strangest experience of our six months: when we were watching the film we felt like we were in any English cinema, but when we emerged we were surrounded by lepers, begging streetkids, rickshaws and mangy dogs. It felt as if we'd been plopped straight from England into the very worst part of India."

Hermione Love, Music at Manchester University, 1998

Iran... Iraq... Ireland... Israel... Italy... Jamaica...

Japan   *TWITCHING TENTACLES*

"I travelled back to Bangkok and then flew to Tokyo via Taipei to stay with the grandparents of a Japanese schoolfriend in Minato-ku. I didn't meet up with many young people; I had discovered the Tokyo branch of the company I worked for in London and so I hung out with the expat community.

I needed work and I managed to do a couple of weeks at the company, which helped a lot. I would advise anyone planning to go to Japan to buy a Japan Rail Pass from the Japan Centre in Piccadilly before going out there as without this travel is impossibly expensive. I travelled all round Japan with my schoolfriend, to Kyoto, Nagasaki and through

TRAVEL REPORTS

Kyushu to Beppu, where there are hot springs. Our youth hostel had them within the building. First you have a wash in a shower, sitting on a small stool, then go through to the communal bath which is about the size of a small swimming pool. You sit in the steaming hot water, which is about mouth-level when you're sitting down, and practically fall asleep; it's wonderful. All round the town there are hot springs bubbling up out of the ground: in some places the water is bright, bright turquoise and the mud is bright red.

One meal I had in Nagasaki sticks in my memory particularly. The restaurant looked out over the sea. We were shown into a room with tatami matting and a low table which we knelt around (getting up after the meal was like having red hot spikes driven into my thighs) and we were served by waitresses in full kimono: Course 1: a soup tureen of sea water was brought in which had little fish swimming in it. The waitresses lifted them out with a sort of tea-strainer and put them in your tea-cup sized bowl, then you had to lift them ut with hashi (chopsticks) and somehow flip them into your mouth. They were sucker fish, so you had to crunch them them off your tongue, which was quite bizarre. Course 2: tempura. Course 3: a huge whole squid was brought in, ornately cut up into little chunks. You lifted the chunks out with hashi — which made the tentacles twitch. The same was done with a fish, which flipped about when you lifted bits out — both had been cut up literally seconds before and hadn't really had time to die properly. Course 4: rice and seaweed soup, pickles, mikan (tangerines) and of course Japanese tea. We finished up with some hot sake and a few more beers."

Justin Atkinson, Cambridge University, 1997

Kazakhstan..Kenya... Kiribati... Kirghizia... Korea (North)... Korea (South)... Kuwait... Laos... Latvia... Lebanon... Lesotho... Liberia... Libya... Liechtenstein... Lithuania... Madagascar...

Malawi
PHEW!

"My friend and I were smoking some gear through a big pipe at two in the morning on a beach in Malawi. We saw two policemen walking towards us so we buried the pipe in the sand and hid the rest of the gear. They found both and insisted on us coming to the police station, in spite of our attempted bribe of about £100. We stayed the rest of the night in a cell with two drunk guys and in the morning we gave statements and had our passports confiscated.

TRAVEL REPORTS

The next day we had to have our fingerprints taken and the gear was sent off to be analysed. The next time we went back to the station we found the police officer in the local beer house. He hadn't sent the gear or checked our fingerprints and said our court case would have to wait for another week. I couldn't wait that long, so we managed to bribe him £2 to fake the results.

Our court case was the next day. The courtroom was made of corrugated iron and the judge was sitting behind a school desk. We had to swear on the Bible, but we looked a bit silly. Because we didn't have anything else to wear, we turned up in swimming trunks and T-shirts.

The judge said "Do you agree you have to be punished?" We agreed. He then said, "You have to do six months in prison," and left a huge dramatic pause before continuing. "However, if you have a good enough reason, you can pay a fine..." We pleaded that we were students and had to get home to go to university, and they let us off with a fine of £3.20 each. We were extremely lucky, but I've heard of others who weren't. I certainly don't recommend the experience."

'Pete' (doing time at Edinburgh University), 1998

Malaysia... Maldives... Mali... Malta... Mauritania... Mauritius...

Mexico   *GRINDING HIPS*

"I was in Mexico for six weeks with a couple of friends. There is a really well-travelled route through Mexico which we took. Between Mexico City and Cancun there is a town called Merida which is famous for hammocks. The local men were hysterical — they were all called Carlos or Juan, and they spent the time in clubs grinding their hips and squatting. Plus they really don't believe in women dancing on their own. Valladolid was a nice little town near Chechenitza where there are really touristy pyramids. Don't go to Cancun which is a cheap package deal kind of place. But we went to Isla Mujeres, an amazing Caribbean island where you can get into a youth hostel for £2 a night. The island is one big beach, backpacker territory. We went on from there to Talun in the east, where there were gorgeous old ruins on the edge of a cliff. Instead of paying, we climbed along the cliff edge to get to it, and almost died. We stayed in little 'cabanas' and literally rolled on to the beach. Next stop was Chetumal on the border to Belize. You can get a coach straight through to Guatemala, but it's worth stopping in Belize for the amazing culture. No nightlife in Mexico is trendy — just a laugh, with lots of free tequilas for women.

248

In Mexico all the buses are little American school buses, but the slight difference is that American schoolkids aren't surrounded by loose squawking chickens and men wielding huge machetes. We travelled around Mexico City by underground, which I certainly don't recommend in the rush hour. My friend and I were surrounded by a whole gang of men who tried to grab our bags and grope us. We got separated and although my friend got away, I only managed to escape by screaming at the top of my voice until they let me go. It was the scariest moment of my travels."

Tiff Garside, Birmingham University, 1998

Moldova... Monaco... Mongolia... Morocco... Mozambique... Nauru...

Nepal   *WRAPAROUND*

"We had a bit of a nightmare while trekking in Nepal. My girlfriend Cat (who had turned up to work in a rural village wearing massive flares, a Michelin-man red Puffa and wraparound goggles that made her look like a huge fly) and I were trying to hitch a lift to get to the nearest town, Baglung, because it was almost nightfall. But there had been a landslide, so no large vehicles could get along the road. My girlfriend had a temperature of 104 degrees and could barely walk, so she got a lift on the back of a motorbike. As soon as they disappeared round the corner I realised what a crazy idea this was (I found out afterwards that the biker was an evil groper).

I was soon cheered up: the women in the village asked me where my 'wife' was, so I told them in Nepalese that she had eloped with a Nepalese man. They must have felt very sorry for me because they consoled me with vast amounts of food and drink. When they'd cleared the road I got a lift with a maniac driver. As he careered round the mountain roads, he switched his lights on at full beam at oncoming HGVs and lunged into their lane so that he could play chicken with them. In the truck with me was a toothless Nepalese guy who couldn't have been taller than four feet. He couldn't reach the sides to hold on and was being flung all over the place, so I told him to cling on to my waist and together we braced the nightmare journey.

I staggered back to the hotel after the most gruelling day of my life, with the thought of a hot shower keeping me going, only to find my girlfriend had lost control of her bowels all over the bathroom floor."

John Francis, Edinburgh University, 1998

TRAVEL REPORTS

**Netherlands... New Zealand... Nicaragua... Niger... Nigeria...
Norway... Oman... Pakistan... Panama... Papua New
Guinea... Paraguay... Peru... Philippines... Poland...
Portugal... Qatar... Romania...**

Russia   *MOSCOW NIGHTS*

"I chose to study Russian at A-level for two main reasons: I wanted to
go there and I'd seen A Fish Called Wanda. For four months I earned
money working as a school assistant in London asking everyone I knew
(and lots of people I didn't) if they had any friends or relatives working
in the CIS. In October a parent at the school offered to introduce me to a
friend of his. The friend was a partner in an Eastern European shipping
brokers, with a main office in Moscow. He arranged an interview and in
November offered me a positon as an intern, for three months, on a basic
salary.

One night the following April found me in the bowels of the Kremlin,
long after the tourists had gone, chatting to [the singer] Joe Cocker's
stage crew. A shipping broker arranges transport and customs for its
clients, and Joe Cocker's manager had employed us to get all 20 tons of
the band's gear into Moscow, then on to Belgium, in two days.
Unfortunately there was a small problem. The Russian promoters wanted to arrange for the truck to go to the airport after the show, or they
wouldn't let the show go on. Fine, but the truck didn't arrive, as
arranged, at 10.30. At 11.30 the crew opened a bottle of Absolut and told
me it couldn't be worse than Brazil (the stage collapsed and three trucks
broke down). By 12.30 they were quietly calculating how much it would
cost to hire equipment in Belgium. Eventually the truck arrived and by
8.00 a.m. all the gear was loaded up and with any luck would be in
Belgium in time for the show at 7.00 that night. At this point I decided
to part company with my jovially optimistic friends and go to the
American Bar which serves the best breakfast in Russia. The crew told
me not to worry and gave me the remaining bottle of vodka. Like everything else in Russia, events unfold with a peculiar inevitability. I later
found out that the show in Belgium did go on — a couple of hours late
— but Joe had a sore throat and had to stop after only an hour. Such is
the world of show business."

Alexander Wrottesley, King's College London, 1996

**Rwanda... El Salvador... San Marino... Saudi Arabia...
Senegal... Serbia... Somalia... South Africa... Spain...
St Christopher and Nevis... Saint Lucia... Saint Vincent and
the Grenadines... Seychelles... Sierra Leone... Slovakia...
Singapore... Solomon Islands... Sri Lanka... Sudan...
Suriname... Swaziland... Sweden... Switzerland... Syria...
Tadjikistan... Tanzania...**

Tanzania   *TO SEA ON A MURRAYMINT*

"On the coast of Tanzania we commandeered a dhow which was supposed to sail at midnight to an island called Pemba, north of Zanzibar.
The tide was out, so we sat there, five of us, and the three crew members
went to sleep. After five hours the tide came in and we set off. We were
getting quite hungry because all we had was a Murraymint each. It did-
n't make much difference because there was a storm and I was sick five
times. The crew were asleep again, the captain slumped over the tiller
and we had a plastic sheet about two feet square to shelter under. The
journey took 17 hours and when we finally set foot on Pemba we were
instantly arrested by the police for breaching immigration rules. They
also took our passports, tried to charge us a tourist tax and threw the
captain into prison. (This was odd as we thought Pemba was part of
Zanzibar and Zanzibar was a protectorate of Tanzania.) Luckily they let
us go after a few hours and we spent four glorious days camped on the
beach before moving on."

Jamie Campbell, University of Durham, 1996

**Taiwan... Thailand... Tibet... Togo... Tonga... Trinidad and
Tobago... Turkey... Turkmenistan... Tuvalu... Uganda...
UK... Ukraine... USSR United Arab Emirates... USA...
Uruguay... Uzbekistan... Vanuatu... Vatican City State...
Venezuela... Vietnam.. Western Samoa... Yemen (North)...
Yemen (South)... Zaire... Zambia... Zimbabwe...**

Back home

Around midsummer, gap-year students start to drift back home. Phones buzz with gossip, plans are laid for parties, and the rituals of family life begin again. Money runs out and restlessness sets in. What is left to do before October?

Term dates, money, work...

Those whose minds are thousands of miles away can check when the university term starts. Where there is a 'freshers' week' for new undergraduates, term may begin in September, not October, but if you go early you may have to pay extra rent for your room. What else? •**Your student loan**: is this sorted out? If not, it can wait (See CHAPTER 2) •**Work**: if there's time, before you go broke.

CHANGE

"Go with a completely open mind. Lose your preconceptions about where you are going, who you are going to meet, what it's going to be like and how people will talk to you. You can make your own preconceptions come true just by hanging on to them, so lose them. Go and look. A gap year is definitely not a good thing for everyone. I am incredibly glad I did one."

John Rodgers, Natural Sciences at Cambridge University, 1997

BACK HOME

PLODDING ON

"I had always been fairly independent due to being at boarding school since the age of nine, and I lived abroad anyway. What did strike me when I got back from my gap year was how little everything had changed and how life had just plodded on while I had been away. I had somehow expected a change. I would say take a gap year, but think carefully about it and plan it well, because it won't just happen. What did I gain? Well, travelling made me question a lot of things which I had utterly taken for granted while I was growing up. I didn't come away with any great realisations or single discoveries — just loads of good experiences and photos."
Justin Atkinson, Japanese at Cambridge University, 1997

THIS GREEN AND PLEASANT LAND

"I came home four weeks before I went to Uni and I wouldn't have wanted any less time. You're longing to be somewhere else, and you look at things really differently. I was looking at all the green rolling hills on the way back from Gatwick and even though I was on a motorway I just fell in love with England.
Home's great to come back to, but generally I'm a lot more independent and spontaneous and it helps that my parents now recognise that. It's still hard to explain to them that you just want to dash off and do something just for the hell of it!
My dad thought I got along better with people when I came back, but I think that wears off. When travelling you'll have a chat to anyone but in England everything's a lot more staid. I made sure all my travelling friends were home when I came back, because I knew I wouldn't be able to handle the culture shock if I was alone.
The first term at university was hard, but I think you should expect it. I look back constantly and think about my gap year. It makes it doubly hard to stick it out at Uni, but it really helps if you have someone to talk to who's feeling exactly the same. Luckily a load of my friends did the same stuff, so we reminisce the whole time. You get this rush when you start talking about it and you're off down Memory Lane."
Hermione Love, Music at Manchester University, 1998

BACK HOME

"Genius develops in quiet places, character in the full current of human life."
Goethe

"Though we travel the world over to find the beautiful, we must carry it with us or we find it not."
Ralph Waldo Emerson

All you need to know about the Internet

For anyone who's used a computer for more than a week

THE INTERNET GUIDEBOOK

What is the Internet? Using the Net
Only connect...The commercial players
E-mail... Pull: finding information
Push: creating Websites
Dirty tricks and protection
Education on the Net
Business on the Net
The framework... The future
Definitions

PAPERBACK (1997) 192 PP   ISBN 0 9527572 1 4

ORDER FORM

THE INTERNET GUIDEBOOK 1997/8

Credit card orders:

Tel: 0171-221 7404

Web: *www.peridot.co.uk*

Schools: please quote your order number.

SPECIAL OFFER!
A few unsold copies of this edition at:
£4
plus £1 post & packing

►Please send [   ] copies of this book to:

NAME...

SCHOOL...

ADDRESS..

....

POSTCODE..

—THE VISITING SPEAKERS DIRECTORY—